STOPOUT! WORKING WAYS TO LEARN

by Joyce Slayton Mitchell

Other Books by Joyce Slayton Mitchell

The Guide to College Life

The Guide to Canadian Universities

Other Choices for Becoming a Woman

Free to Choose: Decision Making for Young Men

I Can Be Anything: Careers and Colleges for Young Women

Work Out: Careers for Young Men, in press

The Workbook: A Guide to Skilled Jobs

ISBN 0-92048-18-9
LC 78-59186
Copyright (c) 1978 by Joyce Slayton Mitchell

Garrett Park Press
Garrett Park, Maryland 20766

TABLE OF CONTENTS

5   SOURCES AND ACKNOWLEDGEMENTS

7   AN INTRODUCTION TO STOPPING OUT

13   HOW TO USE THIS BOOK

17   THE ARTS CLUSTER

18   Appalshop
19   Boston Film/Video Foundation
20   Boston Museum of Science
21   Boston Visual Artists Union
23   Decordova Museum
24   International Program for Human Resource Development
25   Minneapolis Institute of Arts
26   Museum of African Art
29   New Jersey Shakespeare Festival

31   THE COMMUNICATIONS CLUSTER

32   Colonial Cablevision
33   Connecticut Public Television
33   Port Jefferson Record Newspapers
34   Radio Station WKCM
35   Washington Monthly
36   WFRV-TV News Intern

37   THE EDUCATION CLUSTER (including Special Education, Recreation, Student Lobby, and Advocacy Agencies)

38   Alternatives Unlimited
39   American Enterprise Institute for Public Policy Research
40   Association for World Education
41   Blue Grass Association for Mental Retardation
42   Boston Community Schools Program
44   Cambridge YWCA
45   Cheff Center for the Handicapped
46   Coalition of Independent College and University Students
47   College Republican National Committee
48   Community Services Program
49   Council for Retarded Citizens
50   Dayton Board of Education
51   French Library
52   Girls Club of Lynn
53   Institute for Responsive Education
54   J. U. Kevil Mental Retardation-Mental Health Center
56   Kentucky Community Educating Office
57   Kentucky School for the Deaf
58   Louisville YWCA
59   Muhlenberg County Opportunity Center

- 2 -

```
60    National Student Lobby
62    North American Student Cooperative Organization
63    Northwest College and University Association for Science
64    St. Paul's School
66    Political Discovery
67    United States National Student Association

69    THE ENVIRONMENTAL CLUSTER

70    Chesapeake Bay Center for Environmental Studies
72    Defenders of Wildlife
73    Environmental Action Foundation
76    Environmental Learning Center
77    Friends of the Earth
78    National Parks and Conservation Association
79    National Wildlife Federation
82    National Wildlife Federation Raptor Information Center
83    Nature Conservancy
84    Rachel Carson Trust for the Living Environment
85    Student Conservation Program

87    THE GOVERNMENT-SPONSORED AGENCIES CLUSTER (including city, state and
                                                          Federal agencies)

88    ACTION: Volunteers in Service to America
90    Alaska Bureau of Land Management
91    Atlanta Urban Corps
93    Boston City Council
94    California Coastal Commission
95    California Department of Alcoholic Beverage Control
96    California Department of Corrections
97    California Department of Education
98    California Department of Finance
99    California Department of Fish and Game
101   California Department of Food and Agriculture
102   California Department of Forestry
103   California Department of Health
104   California Department of Housing and Community Development
105   California Department of Motor Vehicles
106   California Department of Parks and Recreation
107   California Department of the Youth Authority
109   California Employment Development Department
110   California Highway Patrol
111   California Postsecondary Education Commission
112   California Public Utilities Commission
113   California State Library
114   California State Office of Substance Abuse
115   California State Water Resources Control Board
116   Connecticut General Assembly Legislative Intern Program
117   Kentucky Bureau of Corrections
118   Kentucky Office of Public Defender
120   Los Angeles City Volunteer Corps
121   Massachusetts Department of Corrections
```

```
123     Massachusetts Department of Food and Agriculture
124     Massachusetts Department of Mental Health Neighborhood Day School
125     Massachusetts House of Representatives - Representative James E. Smith
126     Metropolitan Washington Council of Governments
128     New York City Urban Corps
130     Rhode Island Intern Consortium
131     White House Fellowships

133  THE HEALTH CLUSTER

134     American Cancer Society, Massachusetts Division
135     Andrew W. Johnson Alcohol Detoxification Center
136     Appalachian Regional Hospitals
137     Boston Coordinating Council on Drug Abuse
140     Central Kentucky Community Action Council
141     Coalition of Concerned Medical Professionals
142     Direct Relief Foundation
144     Health/PAC
145     Occupational Health Project

147  THE PUBLIC INTEREST AND CONSUMER PROTECTION CLUSTER

148     Association of Community Organizations for Reform NOW
149     Bureau of Rehabilitation
151     Center for Defense Information
152     Center for National Security Studies
154     Citizens for Participation in Political Action
155     Citizens Organization for a Sane World
156     Common Cause
159     Community for Creative Nonviolence
160     Consumer Federation of America
161     Institute for Local Self-Reliance
163     National Abortion Rights Action League
164     National Committee Against Repressive Legislation
165     National Labor Federation
167     National Organization for the Reform of Marijuana Laws
169     National Self-Help Resource Center
170     National Taxpayers Union
171     Oxfam-America
172     Public Citizen
175     Zero Population Growth

177  THE RELIGIOUS-SPONSORED AGENCIES CLUSTER

178     Christian Service Corps
179     Church of the Brethren
181     Friends Committee on National Legislation
182     LAOS, Inc.
184     Lutheran World Ministries
185     Mennonite Voluntary Service
187     Neighborhood Ecumenical Witness and Service
188     United Church of Christ
189     United Presbyterian Church USA Voluntary Service
190     Volunteer Corps - The Episcopal Church
```

191   THE WOMEN AND MINORITIES CLUSTER

192   Aswalos House YWCA
193   Black Women's Community Development Foundation
194   Joint Center for Political Studies
196   Kentucky Neighborly Organization of Women
197   Lutheran Church and Indian People of South Dakota
199   National Organization for Women
200   National Women's Education Fund
201   National Women's Political Caucus
203   National Youth Alternatives Project
204   Women's History Research Center
205   Women's International League for Peace and Freedom

207   STOPOUT FOR MONEY

209   ALPHABETICAL INDEX

212   GEOGRAPHICAL INDEX

SOURCES AND ACKNOWLEDGMENTS

The primary source of information for Stopout! Working Ways to Learn is a questionnaire completed in March, 1978, by each listed agency.

The particular agencies were selected if their programs met the following criteria:
- --Are open to all students, not just from a single educational institution
- --Do not require a college degree; open to undergraduates
- --Do not charge tuition or other fees
- --Have at least a one academic-term program, not just a summer program
- --Operate within the United States
- --An individual must be able to get in on her or his own; interns do not have to be elected or recommended by a college or school or special group.

An initial working list of agencies came from several internship publications including:

Jobs in Social Change: Student Guide to Internships in Washington DC (SERF, 1975)

Options for Learning: A Catalogue of Off-Campus Learning Opportunities in Kentucky (University of Kentucky, 1974)

Reach Out and Grow (Massachusetts Internship Office, 1977)

Where to Look: A Sourcebook on Undergraduate Internships (American Association for Higher Education, 1975)

The introductory information is from two sources, the Carnegie Commission on Higher Education, 1971, and The Ford Foundation's Task Force on Higher Education, also called the Newman Commission, 1971 and 1974.

My first thanks go to each person who so thoughtfully and accurately described their agency's internship or volunteer program on a detailed questionnaire, resulting in the most up-to-date materials possible for Stopout.

To Karen Gottschalk, educational specialist at the Massachusetts Internship Office in Boston, I owe my gratitude for teaching me about internships in general as well as about specific programs and interns in action.

I am grateful to Linda Magoon who typed the manuscript with care and precision and to Anne Sansbury who prepared the final copy.

I owe my thanks to Sue Coil and Jean Feiwel at Avon Books for their encouragement and affirmation of this book for stopouts.

And to The Garrett Park Press, I owe a special thanks for initiating the idea that a book is needed for all the high school and college students who want to take a year off to use their classroom experiences in a life-experience situation.

Joyce Slayton Mitchell

Wolcott, Vermont

June 1978

AN INTRODUCTION TO STOPPING OUT

Half of all undergraduate college students leave school. Eighty-five percent of these students go back again. These are the stopouts. Stopouts are students who leave school to work, travel, study, goof-off, volunteer, or explore in a great variety of ways.

Educators have collected all kinds of academic and social information about stopouts and they have found that compared to traditional four-year students, stopouts:
- --Have the same high school marks
- --Score the same on college entrance tests
- --Maintain grades and attendance records as good or better
- --Usually have more money for college
- --Go on to graduate school as frequently
- --Appear to be more stubborn, assertive, skeptical, and independent
- --Tend to be more analytical and theoretical in their thinking
- --Support social change
- --Challenge the system
- --Earn better grades after their return to college

WHY GET OUT?

Many people have two reasons for doing things. The one they talk about and the other one . . . the real reason. The one they talk about most often is money. Money is seldom questioned as a motive for action and it is one of the most acceptable reasons for behavior there is. For example, women say they go back to work after having children--for the money; workers say they change jobs--for the money; people say they don't ski or travel because of a lack of money; and students say they leave school because of the money. Real reasons more often have to do with personal involvement in what they are doing. Mothers at home all day after their kids are in school; students in a college major they aren't committed to; people with no personal need for sports or adventure; or workers stuck in a job that doesn't turn them on. It's easy to see that it's much simpler to use money to explain our actions than the real reason!

Many students leave college not because, as they say, they can't afford it (a money reason), but more often the real reason is that <u>they want to do nonschool things</u>. They want to check out their own reasons for being in school and their own goals in life. A lot of you have been pushed through school to do your best and hardest work and have gone along without questioning your life style. You have used your parents' and peer values for working hard and staying in school. Now you want out. You want to work and test some of the things you've learned, or you are just sick of school and want to do anything else except school. Anything else except listening to more talk about it. Or you want to ski bum or beach bum for a year to clear your head and make decisions about which direction you can go next.

Questioning where you are now--and where you want to go--is a major reason for stopping out. For some, this time will be an escape from making decisions or from accepting college life as it is rather than as you had hoped it would be. For most of you, stopping out can be and will be an enriching experience where you will get a chance to extend your learning from the classroom to the rest of the world.

WHEN SHOULD YOU GET OUT?

It used to be that after the sophomore year, more college students transferred or left college than at any other time. And this is a natural time for you to stopout. Before you select your major. If you are a community or other 2-year college student, you may want to stopout before you transfer to a 4-year college. But as natural a time as this is, more stopouts are now coming straight from high school or after the first year of college. The advantages of going to college for a year first are that you learn what to expect from college and you learn what kinds of experiences and resources are there to help you to learn. You learn also what is not there. For many of you, the first year in college is the first year away from home. If you have already been away from home a year, you will know what it's like to be responsible for getting your meals, money, and clean laundry. A year away from home can prepare you in skills that will be necessary when you're on your own in an internship.

GETTING OUT

Stopping out of college started with students. Parents and educators are usually mortified when this privilege of going to college is being questioned by their kids and students. Their first reaction is to say-- absolutely NOT! And their second reaction is to say, "If you don't go now, we're not paying for it!" But hang in there for the third reaction, which is often to listen to you. Get your parents in on the planning and together find a program that is reasonable for you. A program that works for you and makes sense to your family as you stopout to learn.

College administrators have reacted in the same way. They were shocked that going to college was no longer top priority for many high school students. As the job market for college graduates crashed, as the non-draft no longer assured colleges that young men must be in college or the military, and as kids started thinking of things to do besides college, college applications zoomed down. Now colleges are eager to come up with plans to get applications back up. Plans that fit the times and the life style of the students. College admission officers have demonstrated their acceptance of stopouts by the instigation of several plans that include time away from the traditional 4-year college program. These programs include deferred admission, deferred transfers, leave of absence, and college credit for work experience and life learning. Taking one at a time:

1. Deferred admission. You are a high school senior and have been accepted at college. You defer or put off enrollment for a determined amount of time, usually a year.
2. Deferred transfer. You are a college student who is accepted for admission into another college. You defer or put off enrollment at the other college for a particular amount of time. Usually a year.
3. Leave of absence. You are a college student and you officially withdraw from college for a specified length of time. It used to be that the only acceptable reasons for a leave of absence were academic, financial, or medical. The recent trend is to accept almost any reason you want to leave--work and travel being the most common requests for a leave.

4. College credit for off-campus experience or "life long learning." You are a college student and you decide to stopout. You can receive academic credit for what you are going to do--a learning experience outside the classroom.

These four programs are often stated in the college catalog. But in some colleges they aren't and you must initiate the process yourself. As long as you have a reasonable plan for a semester or year's work, and you arrange the required supervision and evaluation for your off-campus work or experience, the college will generally cooperate and award you college credit. Many schools have already awarded college credit for life experience or life learning for mature students. It was first established for older women who had taken off years to raise a family or for older men who had gone into business but who now wanted a college education. Some colleges are applying the same evaluation system to stopouts who are getting off-campus learning experiences.

If you are already in college, check out the school's rules on leaving and getting back in--<u>before</u> you leave. Even if you think you will never go back--remember that 85% do. And it's much easier for you to get back in by officially checking out before you leave. Besides that, your parents, and your internship employer, will find it easier to accept your idea for being out if you are "officially" out of college. Try for a qualified leave, and talk about a program for leaving.

How long should you stay? Research in education has indicated that for most of you, one year out is the best experience. For a number of reasons, one semester or quarter isn't long enough. The time is too short to really get into another way of life, a non-student life. Your off-campus experience doesn't give you enough time to learn a new way of seeing things and when stopouts return to college in less than a year they usually have the same questions they had when they left. More than a year away appears too long for most students. Going away for over a year makes it hard for stopouts to feel a part of student life again when they return. If you want to consider reactions of other students, who have tried different lengths of time out, and all other things being equal, opt for the one year stopout.

WHAT WILL YOU DO WHEN YOU'RE OUT?

Most students work or travel. Work includes both paid and unpaid work. Many students get credit while they work or travel and some students use this time to study somewhere else. They choose a professional music or art school, or a different part of the country, or they go abroad and take courses just for the change and a new experience. Others sit around deciding what to do the whole time they are out and never get around to do anything. Still others ski bum, beach bum, play sports, play music, make crafts, and live a combination life of part-time volunteer or paid work, seasonal work or play, and travel in between. This book is designed for those of you who decide to work. <u>STOPOUT! Working Ways to Learn</u> describes internship and volunteer programs, which are working programs. With few exceptions they are full-time and last for at least a semester, many for a year. Read "How to Use This Book" for the next steps toward your plan to stopout.

GETTING BACK IN

If you like being out and working more than being in, you may seriously want to consider staying out. Especially if you've found a job that leads you in the directions you want to go. But if you find that you are goal directed toward a college degree, or more learning, or turning your learning around from where you started, you will want to go back to college.

If you left on a leave of absence, it can be as easy as registration to start the next term or year. If you go in on a deferred enrollment or transfer plan, it will be simple to get back in because you settled all that before you left. If you withdrew from school without notice--either from high school or college--then you must start from the beginning in terms of college admissions, just as if you were a high school senior or a college transfer.

College admissions officers are usually very positive toward stopouts because they know from research that stopouts are more mature and therefore will have better grades when they return. Admissions people will consider you the same as any new or transfer student in the admissions procedure. But in most cases you will have a plus for your experiences, and independence, and the things you learned outside the classroom. Because they have to, college officials are agreeing with students that education is a part of life, not just a part of school. The widespread acceptance of this concept will be a help to you as you stopout. And then stopin.

MORE TO READ

General

Behrens, David. "Students on Sabbatical." In Newsday, November 22, 1974.

Brewster, Kingman, Jr. "Colleges Encouraging a Year's Dropout." In New York Times, August 11, 1974, LV, 9.

Bird, Caroline. The Case Against College. New York: Bantam, 1975.

Directory of Cooperative Education, Cooperative Education Association, c/o Drexel University, 32nd and Chestnut Streets, Philadelphia, Pennsylvania, 19104 (revised every two years).

Haagen, C. H. Venturing Beyond the Campus: Students Who Leave College. Middletown, Connecticut: Wesleyan University Press, 1978.

Mitchell, Joyce Slayton. Free to Choose: Decision Making for Young Men. New York: Dell, 1977.

_____. I Can Be Anything: Careers and Colleges for Young Women. New York: College Entrance Examination Board, 1978.

_____. Other Choices for Becoming a Woman. New York: Dell, 1975.

_____. Workout: Careers for Young Men. New York: Bantam, 1978.

"When In Doubt, Stop Out," Time, May 22, 1978.

Internships - Summer

Bryn Mawr and Haverford Colleges Placement Offices. <u>National Directory of Summer Internships for Undergraduate Students</u>. Haverford, Pennsylvania, biannual publication.

Internships - Washington

<u>Directory of Washington Internships</u>. National Center for Public Service Internship Programs, 1735 Eye Street, N.W., Suite 601, Washington, DC 20006, $6.00 (revised periodically).

Internships - International

Calvert, Robert, Jr. <u>Your Future in International Service</u>. New York: Richard Rosen Press, 1969.

Garraty, John A., Lily von Klemperer, and Cyril J. H. Taylor. <u>The New Guide to Study Abroad</u>. New York: Harper & Row, 1976, $4.95.

<u>International Directory for Youth Internships</u>. Revised often. UN Headquarters NGO Youth Caucus, c/o Social Development Division, Room DC-977, United Nations, New York, NY 10017, $2.00.

<u>Work Camp Programme Directory</u>. Send postage to The Coordinating Committee for International Voluntary Service, UNESCO, 1 Rue Miollis, 75015 Paris, France.

Study

<u>A Handbook for Students: Guide to Study in Europe</u>. European Community Information Service, 2100 M Street, N.W., Washington, DC 20037, $4.40. (Book comes in English, French, German, Italian, Dutch, and Danish, so specify language desired.)

<u>Guide to Alternative Colleges and Universities</u>. By Blaze, Hertsberg, Kranz, and Lehrke. Boston: Beacon Press, 1974.

Mathies, Lorraine and W. Thomas. <u>Overseas Opportunities for American Teachers and Students</u>. New York: Macmillan Information. Ask for most recent edition.

<u>Study Abroad</u>. UNESCO, Place de Fonenoy, 75700 Paris, France, $6.00.

<u>Ten O'Clock Scholar: Alternative Ways to Earn College Credit</u>. Washington: U. S. Department of Labor, 1977.

Travel

<u>Research and Training Opportunities Abroad and Foreign Curriculum Consultants in the United States</u>. Washington: U. S. Office of Education. Order from U. S. Government Printing Office, Washington, DC 20402. (Stock number 017-080-01425-4) $0.55.

The Whole World Handbook. Published annually by the Council on International Educational Exchange, distributed by Simon and Schuster, 630 Fifth Avenue, New York, NY 10011. Also available from the Council at 777 United Nations Plaza, New York, NY 10017. $3.50. A student guide to work, study, and travel abroad.

Volunteerism

"Focus on Volunteering," Seventeen, February, 1976, pp. 28-29.

Invest Yourself. Commission on Voluntary Service and Action, 475 Riverside Drive, Room 1700A, New York, NY 10027. $2.00. Very complete.

Koslow, S. P. and C. Calvert. "Student Volunteers," Mademoiselle, December, 1975, pp. 27-28 plus options for volunteering during the summer break.

Loeser, Herta. Women, Work, and Volunteering. Boston: Beacon Press, 1975, $4.45.

Steinem, Gloria. "Volunteerism: Your Money or Your Life?" Ms, February, 1975, pp. 70-75 plus.

HOW TO USE THIS BOOK

The internship descriptions are arranged in clusters by work topics or by the type of sponsoring agency. Read through several descriptions that sound good to you. Notice the variations in requirements to get in, and the specifics of what the agency does--its current projects and activities. If you are interested in a legislative internship, read the Public Interest and Consumer Protection Cluster; if service is your top priority and church work is where you want to be, look first at the Religious-Sponsored Agencies Cluster.

Within each entry, information is organized in a standard format. The agencies completed a questionnaire on which the format is arranged. Every format begins with the

<u>Name, city, and state</u> of the agency or organization.
Then come these sections.

WHAT'S IT DO?
<u>Purpose and goals</u> which describe the sponsoring agency.
<u>Current projects and activities</u> which cite the specific work being carried on by the agency.
<u>Number of permanent staff</u> tells you the number of people working in the headquarters office of the organization where the intern will be working.
<u>Annual budget</u> gives you the total funds being spent on agency projects.
<u>Publications</u> indicate the kind of information that gets out from the agency to the rest of the world.

WHAT CAN I DO?
<u>Internship descriptions</u> cite the specific jobs available for the internship or volunteer position.

CAN I GET IN?
<u>Academic requirements</u> designate the lowest school level necessary for the job.
<u>Age</u> notes the lowest age required for the internship.
<u>Experience and special</u> describe unusual requirements for the job, other than academic.
<u>Length of commitment to internship</u> indicates the usual time interns stay on the job--in many cases you can negotiate the time commitment.
<u>Number of 1978 interns</u> gives you an idea of the competition for internships and also the size of the group you'll be working with.

DO I GET PAID, EXPENSES, OR CREDIT?
<u>Pay and expenses</u> are usually a stipend or necessary spending expenses. In other words, not much money. Internships and volunteer programs are designed for students who have enough money to live on.
<u>College credit</u> is usually followed by, "can be arranged." That means that you have to arrange your own college credit with your college or university. The agencies state clearly that they are not in the awarding credit business. They do, however, agree to evaluate and supervise students in necessary ways as prescribed by the college so that you can get college credit. But, once again, it's up to you to

arrange it. Some of you will not want to leave college without an arrangement for credit, while others of you will not want to bother right now because you are tired of the whole credit concept.

HOW DO I GET IN?
Closing date for application is usually flexible. Most are "on-going" dates which means that you can apply any time of year. Don't get discouraged when you can't obtain precise information on closing dates and other application procedures or when you will know the outcome of your application. The "on-going" or the "no formal plan or date" entry simply means the dates are open and negotiable. Take advantage of the non-structure in internships and plan these things the way it would best fit you--your schedule and time, your abilities and interests.

WHERE CAN I GET MORE INFORMATION?
Includes a person, phone number, or publication for you to write, phone, or read.

Even though there are 137 internship programs described here, this number represents only the tip of the iceburg of working possibilities for you. You can use this guide to find a specific program for you. You can use this guide also to get an idea of the range of experiences there are-- with a view beyond these particular listings. You can assume that there are many more agencies in all parts of the country with similar needs for interns and volunteers, even if they don't have it in writing, or in practice yet. For example, in STOPOUT! there is an entry for Massachusetts House of Representatives--Representative James E. Smith. You should know that almost every Representative and Senator on a state or Federal level needs and uses interns and volunteers. Even though they may not have a formal internship program established, they would be open for that suggestion from you. Read the description of Representative Smith on page 125 to get an idea of the specific activities in the job that all politicians need help with. Then if government and politics is what you want to do, check with your own state representative for the same kind of internship that you read about in STOPOUT!

The American Cancer Society, Massachusetts Division (page 134) in Boston is part of a much larger network of similar services in other cities. It just happens that this is the one that has been written about in this book. If you live in Los Angeles, or Houston, or Wichita, and it sounds like an interesting program, check with the American Cancer Society for the same thing--where you want to do it. The same point can be made for the Cambridge YWCA, or the Girl's Club of Lynn. There are youth clubs for both girls and boys anywhere you want to be in the country.

The California internships are highly developed but as you read about its internship programs you should know that your own state government in New Mexico or Pennsylvania or Illinois must have the same need. Check with Personnel at your state capitol for the programs that interest you after reading about the California programs. Do the same with the Urban Corps of Atlanta. Most major cities have an urban corps. If you want to be in Detroit, Cincinnati, or Minneapolis, look into their urban corps after reading the Atlanta Urban Corps description on page 91 in STOPOUT! While you are looking at the Atlanta description under "What Can I Do?" read their definition of an internship. Many people will be asking you, "Just what is an internship anyway? I thought it was only for medical school!" The Atlanta group summarizes an internship as a balanced "service-learning" experience. More about an internship is cited in the "What Can I Do" section in the Metropolitan Washington Council of Governments entry, page 126. Suggest that your parents read this section about the opportunities and benefits an internship can provide for you.

If you want to know what kinds of work activities and duties are needed in a museum because you want to apply for an internship in a museum not included in STOPOUT! read the entry for The Museum of African Art, page 26, for a department by department account of its activities.

Look at the Port Jefferson Record Newspapers (page 33) for an example of a newspaper internship that you could describe to any newspaper you want to be with.

And again, if you are looking for a clearinghouse, read the entries of the Rhode Island Intern Consortium Division of Youth Development, page 130; the New York City Urban Corps, page 128; and the United Church of Christ, page 188, for illustrations of clearinghouses that place hundreds of interns. These agencies are internship or volunteer placement agencies.

In other words, use these internship descriptions for learning about the programs they represent . . . and more. Use them also as examples of other programs not even mentioned. Use them as case studies from which you can learn what internship programs are like, what the work activities involve, and as ideas for you to try here--or somewhere else.

If there is anything that is consistent about internship and volunteer positions, it is that they expect the student to take the initiative. For example, look at the entry for Women's History Research Center, page 204. It states that the interns must plan ahead to be responsible for their own financial and emotional support. Or read the Radio Station WKCM entry, page 34. This organization does not want to get you there with a promise of fulfilling your needs for a city life, or night life, or social life. They want you to be as knowledgeable as you can be--so that even though your expectations are high, the high won't lead you into a disappointing experience. Its lifestyle is different from other nonschool places. And that style varies again from work situation to work situation. Some agencies are very specific about their lifestyle and the expectations of where the intern will live. Read "Personal and Unit Life," page 185, under the Mennonite Voluntary Service entry for an example of a specific lifestyle designed as part of the learning experience.

Crucial in the steps to take to get what you want is the application procedure including the resume and cover letter to the agencies. Most agencies have no formal application form or procedure and that makes your approach even more important. Read the application procedure in the entry for the Center for National Security Studies, page 152, to see where to begin. Some help on the resume can be found in the Lutheran World Ministries entry; look on page 184 and use it for a good illustration for any resume. Also, on page 62 read the North American Student Cooperative Organization description as an example of an open internship to be worked out between the applicant and the agency. Although each agency doesn't say it, most are organized in a similar way.

STOPOUT! is written for undergraduates who go after their own program. You don't have to be selected by your college, or department, or high school, or be affiliated with a special group or program in order to get an internship. You are on your own. Use these descriptions as case studies to learn all your options for a year of work. Because you are doing it on your own, you have to take the initiative and responsibility for getting what you are going after. And with an internship or volunteer program you are going after: a working way to learn.

THE ARTS CLUSTER

Appalshop
Boston Film/Video Foundation
Boston Museum of Science
Boston Visual Artists Union
Decordova Museum
International Program for Human Resource Development
Minneapolis Institute of Arts
Museum of African Art
New Jersey Shakespeare Festival

APPALSHOP

Whitesburg, Kentucky

WHAT'S IT DO?
  Purpose and goals:
    To preserve mountain drama, film, and music. Also to provide the
    opportunity for the people of the Appalachian Mountains to express
    themselves through the arts.
  Current projects and activities:
    Appalachian film workshop (16 mm film), June Appal recordings; Roadside
    Theatre, mountain photography workshop, and publication of a journal.
  Number of permanent staff: 20 to 25
  Annual budget: $250,000
  Publications: Mountain Review, a quarterly journal; brochures, films,
  records, magazines, and photography books.

WHAT CAN I DO?
  Internship descriptions:
    Interns train in the various media and projects as listed above. They
    also work in clerical jobs and in marketing and distributing the products.

CAN I GET IN?
  Academic requirements: None
  Age: Open
  Special: Preference is given to students from the Appalachian region
  Length of commitment to internship: At least 6 months
  Number of 1978 interns: 4
  Number planned for the future: Open

DO I GET PAID, EXPENSES, OR CREDIT?
  College credit: Can be arranged

HOW DO I GET IN?
  Closing date: On-going
  Interview required: Yes
  When will I know: Soon after interview

WHERE CAN I GET MORE INFORMATION?
  Write: Linda Davis, Coordinator, Appalshop, P.O. Box 743, Whitesburg,
    KY 41858
  Phone: (606) 633-5708
  Read: "Appalshop," by P. Primack, Appalachia, Vol. II, #1, August 1977.

BOSTON FILM/VIDEO FOUNDATION

Allston, Massachusetts

WHAT'S IT DO?
  Purpose and goals:
    The Boston Film/Video Foundation, which has recently merged with the
    WGBH New Television Workshop, is an organization of independent artists
    who have come together to share skills, ideas, and cooperatively owned
    equipment and studio space.
  Current projects and activities:
    Members use BF/VF as a meeting place, an information bank, a screening
    facility, an editing facility in both video and 16 mm, a source of low-
    cost equipment use, and a production studio. It is open from 12 noon to
    9 weekdays and, when possible, weekends. Activities change daily--
    anything related to the above.
  Number of permanent staff: 3
  Annual budget: $45,000
  Publications: Visions (monthly)

WHAT CAN I DO?
  Internship descriptions:
    Media access assistant. This job will involve facilitating equipment
      access, helping to run the office, typing, assisting with renovations,
      assisting on productions, helping with scheduled screenings and events.
        Relevant administrative or technical skills and experience is
      desirable but not necessary.
    Financial affairs assistant. This job will involve helping with
      financial records, control of petty cash, payment of bills, typing,
      grant proposals, and other associated office tasks and administrative
      backup. When useful, assistance in facilitating media access,
      renovating studio space, working on film or video productions may be
      required. Business skills are highly desirable as is an interest in
      film and video.
        General assistance with all phases of production including office
      work.

CAN I GET IN?
  Academic requirement: High school graduate
  Age: 19
  Experience: Film or video
  Length of possible commitment to internship: Semester
  Number of 1978 interns: 2
  Number planned for the future: 4

DO I GET PAID, EXPENSES, OR CREDIT?
  College credit: Can be arranged

HOW DO I GET IN?
  Closing date for application: On-going
  Interview required: Yes

WHERE CAN I GET MORE INFORMATION?
 Write: Stuart Fordyce, Boston Film/Video Foundation, 39 Brighton Avenue, Allston, MA 02134
 Phone: (617) 254-1616
 Read: Visions

BOSTON MUSEUM OF SCIENCE

Boston, Massachusetts

WHAT'S IT DO?
 Purpose and goals:
   Boston's Museum of Science is a non-profit organization, envisioned as a popular teaching institution embracing all the sciences. Through the years the Museum has pioneered in innovative teaching methods while orienting its education and exhibit programs to the modern space-age world. In addition to the exhibits themselves as educational resources, the Museum offers special programs and courses catered to all age groups and a variety of interest groups.
 Current projects and activities:
   Visitory guide program, Project Eye-Opener (tours for inner city children ages 4 to 10), gift shop, library, animal care, exhibit maintenance, fund raising, and special events.
 Number of permanent staff: 110

WHAT CAN I DO?
 Internship descriptions:
   Visitor Guide internships. Visitor guides are a part of the Museum's education department, the program designed to help visitors reap more from the exhibit areas. Participants in the program are all ages (14 and above) and both sexes. They ask and answer questions of visitors, interpret exhibits, provide supplemental information, and suggest sources for further study. The guides relate to visitors on a one-to-one basis; they do not give group tours. Rather, they take the initiative to approach puzzled, interested, or distressed individuals, offering information or assistance as required. Most guides work as floaters in the exhibit halls. Those who qualify may become specialists in particular exhibit areas, ready to answer questions about the subject of their particular interest as well as about the Museum and its exhibits in general. Guides sometimes use small pocket props to supplement material presented in an exhibit or to help illustrate an explanation.
   Project Eye-Opener internship. Project Eye-Opener is a program designed for inner-city children from Title I schools, predominantly second graders. The objective of the program is to provide a unique, educational experience for "culturally" deprived youth.
   In addition there are volunteer opportunities in the gift shop, in the library, in clerical and office work, maintaining the animals, and exhibits maintenance.

- 21 -

CAN I GET IN?
  Academic requirements: High school students   Age: 14
  Special: Strong interest in sciences desirable
  Length of commitment to internship: Semester or longer

DO I GET PAID, EXPENSES, OR CREDIT?
  College credit: Can be arranged

HOW DO I GET IN?
  Closing date for application: On-going
  Interview required: Yes
  When will I know about application: During interview or shortly after

WHERE CAN I GET MORE INFORMATION?
  Write: Christine Broderick, Volunteer Office, Boston Museum of Science,
    Boston, MA 02114
  Phone: (617) 723-2500, ext. 258
  Read: <u>Volunteer Handbook</u>, Boston Museum of Science

BOSTON VISUAL ARTISTS UNION

Boston, Massachusetts

WHAT'S IT DO?
  Purpose and goals:
    The Boston Visual Artists Union was incorporated in 1972 and is a non-
    profit, tax-exempt cultural institution. It is an organization of more
    than 1,000 Boston and New England area artists and art related individuals
    whose common goals include:
      The coming together of visual artists working in various services.
      Support of artists through exhibitions and varied services.
      Exchange of information (communication) essential to artists.
      Improved community and cultural recognition of the contemporary artist.
      Better public understanding of and access to continuing activities in
    the visual arts.
      Greater Boston as a center of the arts with a community of artists
    interacting with an interested, supportive public.
  Current projects and activities:
    In addition to the regular committees of the Union, the Union has been
    working on such problems as the question of copyright and the visual
    artist; the establishment of a national artists organization; and a
    larger, broader working slide registry that becomes increasingly more
    informative to the artist as well as the general public.
  Number of permanent staff: 2
  Annual budget: Union - $33,190; Gallery - $32,800

WHAT CAN I DO?
  Internship descriptions:
    Union committee internship. The work might involve helping one of the
      committee chairpersons with such things as legislative problems, housing,
      jobs, newsletter, slide registry, and credit union. These would be
      primarily administrative tasks such as filing, typing, and the general

organization of written material and publications. It may involve telephone work, and some writing depending on the committee. In the past, interns have worked on the slide registry, helping to coordinate and inform the general public of its potential resource information, and on the outside exhibitions committee, helping to locate new spaces for upcoming exhibitions throughout the New England area (this sometimes includes some leg work, and intensive work directly with the curator of a show).

Union coordinator internship. The work will consist primarily of administrative tasks, such as filing, typing, and the general organization of written materials and publications. Occasionally, there will be a need to help with hanging shows or working with the members on specific organizational tasks of maintenance, such as painting and general cleaning. In the past, interns have worked on such things as insurance policies, and locating and gathering information on new and efficient mailing systems, and fund raising activities.

CAN I GET IN?
  Academic requirements: College student   Age: 18
  Length of commitment to internship: Open
  Number of 1978 interns: 7
  Number planned for the future: 4; more if needed

DO I GET PAID, EXPENSES, OR CREDIT?
  College credit: Can be arranged

HOW DO I GET IN?
  Closing date for application: On-going   Interview required: Yes
  When will I know about application: Within a week after interview

WHERE CAN I GET MORE INFORMATION?
  Write: Ellen Ganter, Union Coordinator, Boston Visual Artists Union, 77 North Washington Street, Boston, MA 02114
  Phone: (617) 227-3076
  Read: "The BVAU: Why Artists Need a Union," Nightfall: November, 1977.

DECORDOVA MUSEUM

Lincoln, Massachusetts

WHAT'S IT DO?
  Purpose and goals:
    To involve as many people as possible in a participatory art appreciation and to exhibit contemporary New England artists. The DeCordova Museum is an art museum and school complex serving a large membership drawn primarily from a 50 mile radius.
  Current projects and activities:
    Art school with three terms offering over 100 art classes per term with 1,000 students per term. Summer concert services. Changing exhibits of contemporary New England artists--about five or six a year.
  Number of permanent staff: 13   Annual budget: $800,000
  Publications: Membership newsletter, exhibit catalogs

WHAT CAN I DO?
  Internship descriptions:
    Publicity internship. Develop file of New England media including publications, radio, and television. Assist in special public relations projects. Handle publicity for associate council, a volunteer organization of the museum.
    Membership internship. Assist development director with annual appeal. Research membership renewal patterns. Compile membership statistics.

CAN I GET IN?
  Academic requirements: Good writing skills   Age: 18
  Length of commitment to internship: Semester or more
  Number of 1978 interns: 6   Number planned for future: 8

DO I GET PAID, EXPENSES, OR CREDIT?
  College credit: Sometimes is arranged

HOW DO I GET IN?
  Closing date for application: On-going
  Interview required: Yes
  When will I know about application: Within two weeks after application is in

WHERE CAN I GET MORE INFORMATION?
  Write: Julie Horner, DeCordova Museum, Sandy Pond Road, Lincoln, MA 01773
  Phone: (617) 259-8355
  Read: Membership newsletter

INTERNATIONAL PROGRAM FOR HUMAN RESOURCE DEVELOPMENT

Bethesda, Maryland

WHAT'S IT DO?
  Purpose and goals:
    IPHRD is a small non-profit international corporation dedicated to the promotion of educational and employment opportunities in developing countries. A primary project of IPHRD is the marketing of handicrafts from over 40 developing countries through a retail and wholesale outlet located in Bethesda, Maryland.
    The primary goal of the organization is to explore ways and means of generating job and training opportunities for the poor and socially-disadvantaged in low-income areas of the world, including parts of the United States. Its emphasis is on an integrated, area-based development centering around employment. The way the organization attempts to achieve this goal is by providing technical assistance and seed money, and developing a U.S. market for handicrafts.
  Current projects and activities:
    The World of Crafts Project. The World of Crafts is the international handicraft center established and maintained by IPHRD as its main retail outlet. Located in Bethesda, it displays and sells a wide variety of arts and crafts representing the life and culture of peoples in developing countries.
    IPHRD has also developed the Aid and Trade Center International as its wholesale marketing entity. It imports handicrafts and sells them to other retail stores and marketing organizations.
    Peoples Together Project. IPHRD is setting up a textile project to import hand-woven, embroidered, printed, or decorated fabric from developing countries and use it in producing marketable clothes, pillows, tapestries, and the like, employing those presently unemployed in the Washington area. The new producers will be given training, organizational support, and marketing assistance to get them started. Subsequent plans include similar efforts in wood-related crafts and jewelry.
    Technical and Design Resource Center. The marketability of the crafts can often be enhanced by making adjustments in design, color, or size that do not significantly alter the items. It is important, however, that the basic integrity of the craftspeople and the traditional nature of the crafts not be compromised for the sake of marketability. A Technical and Design Resource Center (TDRC) is planned to respond to this need.
    Consulting Service. IPHRD has set up a consulting service to assist other interested voluntary organizations. IPHRD has expertise in local planning, rural development, handicraft marketing, institution building, and similar areas.

WHAT CAN I DO?
  Internship descriptions:
    Currently, the staff is small, with three internship positions--one in administration and two in marketing. The administrative position includes routine clerical duties such as typing, filing, and organization of office records. It also involves editing, aiding the president of the corporation with correspondence, and helping out in other areas such as the

retail store and crafts fairs. One marketing position involves store management and design, responsibility for retail sales, and attendance of crafts fairs. The other position in marketing includes responsibilities connected with attendance of crafts fairs. It also involves duties in wholesale marketing and shipping.

CAN I GET IN?
  Academic requirements: A willingness to work hard is more important than academic level.
  Length of commitment to internship: At least six months
  Number of 1978 interns: 3   Number planned for the future: Open

DO I GET PAID, EXPENSES, OR CREDIT?
  College credit: Can be arranged

HOW DO I GET IN?
  Closing date for application: On-going
  Interview required: No
  When will I know about application: No formal date

WHERE CAN I GET MORE INFORMATION?
  Write: Lisa Huff, Administrative Assistant, IPHRD, Connor Building, 7720 Wisconsin Avenue, Bethesda, MD 20014
  Phone: (301) 656-1200

MINNEAPOLIS INSTITUTE OF ARTS

Minneapolis, Minnesota

WHAT'S IT DO?
  Purpose and goals:
    The Minneapolis Institute of Arts is a large art museum with general collections ranging from pre-historic and ancient art through contemporary art in the following media: paintings, sculpture, decorative arts, photography, prints and drawings.
  Current projects and activities:
    Display of permanent collections and temporary exhibitions.
  Number of permanent staff: 40   Annual budget: $1.7 million
  Publications: Yearly bulletin of new acquisitions; exhibition catalogues, monthly calendar of events.

WHAT CAN I DO?
  Internship descriptions:
    Internships are available in any of the following areas:
      Curatorial. Paintings; prints and drawings; decorative arts and sculpture; photography; pre-Columbian, Oceanic, African, and Native American; Oriental; Minnesota artists gallery; registrar's office.
      Education. Adult programs; young people's programs; tours and interpretive services; teacher training and school programs; resource center; mobile exhibitions; audio-visual programs.
      Services. Library; publicity and public relations; design; administration; publications.

Each intern's program is individually designed after consultation with the intern coordinator and the intern's departmental supervisor.

CAN I GET IN?
  Academic requirements: College students with backgrounds or training in museology, art history, studio art, art education, arts administration, journalism, or related humanities.
  Age: 20
  Length of commitment to internship: Semester or year
  Number of 1978 interns: 10
  Number planned for the future: Same

DO I GET PAID, EXPENSES, OR CREDIT?
  College credit: Can be arranged

HOW DO I GET IN?
  Closing date for application: April 15
  Interview required: Preferred
  Other procedures:
    --Applications should include a complete resume, all academic transcripts, three letters of recommendation, and statement of purpose.
    --Applicants whose candidacy passes the preliminary screening may be required to come for personal interviews.
  When will I know about my application: May

WHERE CAN I GET MORE INFORMATION?
  Write: Maxine Gaiber, Intern Coordinator, Minneapolis Institute of Arts, 2400 Third Avenue South, Minneapolis, MN 55404
  Phone: (612) 870-3190
  Read: Museums USA, published by the National Endowment for the Arts; Minneapolis Institute of Arts Bulletin; and the Institute's Guide to the Collection.

MUSEUM OF AFRICAN ART

Washington, D.C.

WHAT'S IT DO?
  Purpose and goals:
    To exhibit African art, and artifacts of another culture in the United States.
  Current projects and activities:
    The interns learn the operation of the Museum by participating in the work of key departments to gain a general familiarity with museum policies and procedures. They will perform the routine tasks of the departments as well as complete a special project. Projects vary with each department. Students will have the opportunity to work with the following departments: curatorial, archives, education, conservation, library, and administration.
  Number of permanent staff: 32

Publications:

Audio-Visual Materials:

1) "Tribute to Africa: The Photography of Eliot Elisofon"
   13 minute color film made of 160 of Elisofon's best color slides of traditional and modern Africa.

   Winner of the Golden Eagle (the "Oscar" of non-theatrical films). Superb sound effects, music, and narration; makes Africa come alive. $168.00.

2) "The Creative Heritage of Africa"
   Multimedia slide kit, with 58 slides, each 35 mm and in color. Record lecture; 8 full color bulletin board display cards; teacher's guide prepared by the Museum and produced by Encyclopedia Britannica Educational Corporation. $75.00.

Exhibition Catalogues:

1) "The Sculptor's Eye: The African Art Collection of Chaim Gross" (1976) With 12-page introductory essay by Professor Arnold Rubin of UCLA, style maps, bibliography. 84 pages, 92 illustrations, with annotations. $8.75.

2) "The Language of African Art: A Bicentennial Exhibit from the Museum of African Art" (1976) Catalog of traveling exhibit to universities, featuring an essay on African art as language. 37 pages and 57 illustrations annotated. $5.50.

3) "Tribute to Africa: The Photography and Collection of Eliot Elisofon" (1974) A memorial exhibition to the late LIFE Photographer, with testimonial essay by Warren Robbins. Also includes four brief, unpublished essays by Elisofon. 48 pages and 53 illustrations. $6.00.

4) "African Art in Washington Collections" (1973)
   Introductory essay on the relevancy and meaning of African art by Warren Robbins. 24 pages and 37 annotated illustrations and map. $5.50.

5) "African Art: The DeHavenon Collection" (1971)
   Unique collection superbly illustrated with 287 photographs; four color plates plus cover in full color. 244 pages plus map and introductory essay. $15.00.

6) "The Language of African Art" (1970)
   Includes 4-page illustrated essay "African Art in America" by Museum Director, Warren Robbins. 24 pages and 37 illustrations. $1.00.

Essay:

"How to Approach Traditional African Sculpture" September 1972 issue of Smithsonian Magazine containing an 8-page article with color arrangements by Lee Bolton, written by Warren Robbins. $1.50.

Afro-American Art and History Catalogs:

1) "The Art of Henry Ossawa Tanner, 1859-1937"
   Exhibition catalog of America's foremost Afro-American painter.
   32 pages and 12 illustrations, plus bibliography and notes. $2.50.

2) "Afro-American Panorama" Contributions of 50 major Afro-American
   figures to U. S. development. 24 pages and 12 illustrations. $1.00.

WHAT CAN I DO?
  Internship descriptions:
    Curatorial internship. The interns will become familiar with registration
      of gifts and loans, matters pertaining to office procedures, security,
      and insurance. They will assist with the mounting and dismantling of
      exhibitions at the Museum and for extension exhibits at other locations.
      They will learn the correct procedures for handling works of art.
      Conducting research for information on sculpture, and assisting in the
      restoration and maintenance of sculpture, as well as maintenance of
      the Museum's galleries, will be among the interns' duties.
    Photographic Archives internship. Interns will learn the process of
      accessioning slides and photographic negatives and prints, and will
      become familiar with sale and loan procedures. Other duties will
      include the preparation of slide shows and photo exhibition materials.
      Procedures of cataloguing, indexing, and storing the slides and photos
      will be covered.
    Education internship. Interns with special interests in education will
      have the opportunity to observe the lectures given to various age and
      educational levels, and learn the techniques of tour-guiding. In
      addition, they may participate in certain docent activities, and work
      in department of higher education projects.
    Library internship. Interns will be instructed in acquisition policies
      and procedures for the classification of books. Reference books and
      reference services, serials, and preparation of finding aids will be
      covered in the instruction program.
    Administration internship. Interns will become familiar with public
      relations with the press, radio, television and other media for
      publicity for museum functions. Membership, grantsmanship, and accounts
      receivable and payable can also be covered for those with special
      interests in administration.
    In addition to the above, a portion of the internship will be designed
    to give the interns experience with telephone and reception duty at the
    front desk, and with the operation of the museum shop, Boutique Africa.

CAN I GET IN?
  Academic requirements: College student
  Special: The internship program is designed for art history, anthropology,
    and African studies majors.
  Length of commitment to internship: Semester or year
  Number of 1978 interns: 6   Number planned for future: 6

DO I GET PAID, EXPENSES, OR CREDIT?
  College credit: Can be arranged

HOW DO I GET IN?
  Closing date for application: 6 weeks before the semester begins
  Interview required: Yes
  When will I know about application: Soon after the interview

WHERE CAN I GET MORE INFORMATION?
  Write: Nancy Nooter, Department of Higher Education, Internship Coordinator,
    Museum of African Art, 316-318 A Street, N.E., Washington, DC 20002
  Phone: (202) 547-7424
  Read: Publications listed above

NEW JERSEY SHAKESPEARE FESTIVAL

Madison, New Jersey

WHAT'S IT DO?
  Purpose and goals:
    The purpose of the New Jersey Shakespeare repertory company is to bring
    Shakespeare and other theatre to the area and to provide a training
    ground for the serious actor or technician intent upon a career in the
    professional theatre. Teamwork and the importance of the ensemble are
    stressed. Interns work and train in a variety of theatrical disciplines,
    and are encouraged to develop advanced skills in those areas in which
    they are most interested.
  Current projects and activities:
    The New Jersey Shakespeare Festival season begins rehearsal in late May
    and plays June through November. Six major productions were offered in a
    recent year, in nightly rotating repertory: "Hamlet," "Rosencrantz &
    Guildenstern are Dead," "Love's Labour's Lost," and three others.
  Number of permanent staff: 6   Annual budget: $260,000
  Publications: Seasonal brochures, newsletters and annual reports

WHAT CAN I DO?
  Internship descriptions:
    There are acting, technical, and administrative internships. The Festival
    is a professional (Actors' Equity) repertory theatre company.
    The Festival does not utilize "stars" but hires a professional (equity)
    resident company of actors with experience in on- and off-Broadway and
    major regional theatres. Designers' credits include experience with both
    professional and educational theatres across the country. Acting interns
    perform supporting roles in the major plays, understudy leading roles,
    and direct, design, and perform in workshop productions. All interns
    perform additional technical assignments throughout the course of the
    season. Classes are given (without charge) in voice and movement and
    weaponry. Additional classes are offered in a number of areas, and are
    scheduled as time permits.
    Interns have played roughly half of each season's roles, including, in
    addition to ensemble work, such important parts as Daisy in "Rhinoceros,"
    the Samurai in "Rashomon," Jo in "A Taste of Honey," Dromio of Syracuse
    in "A Comedy of Errors," and Rosa and Jack in "The Rose Tattoo." Each
    season interns will be given equally important casting consideration.

Interns who prove their value as actors or technicians are invited back for a second season and some are awarded full Equity contracts in the last two weeks of that season. It is not uncommon for the Festival's professional company to include former interns.

CAN I GET IN?
  Academic requirements: High school graduate
  Age: 18
  Experience: Theatre
  Special: Acting interns audition in New York
  Length of commitment to internship: Negotiable, depending on season
  Number of 1978 interns: 60
  Number planned for future: Same

DO I GET PAID, EXPENSES, OR CREDIT?
  Interns must meet their own living expenses.
  College credit: Optional credit available through Drew University

HOW DO I GET IN?
  Closing date for application: May 1 before season you wish to attend
  Interview required: Only for acting interns, when audition is required
  When will I know about application: 3 or 4 weeks after applying

WHERE CAN I GET MORE INFORMATION?
  Write: Paul Barry, Artistic Director, New Jersey Shakespeare Festival, Madison, NJ 07940
  Phone: (201) 377-5330   But they prefer letters!

THE COMMUNICATIONS CLUSTER

Colonial Cablevision
Connecticut Public Television
Port Jefferson Record Newspapers
Radio Station WKCM
Washington Monthly
WFRV-TV News Intern

COLONIAL CABLEVISION

Revere, Massachusetts

WHAT'S IT DO?
  Purpose and goals:
    Studio Six, (CATV-SIX) provides public service and general interest programming for cablecasting on Channel Six. Its goal is to become a local and regional advertising vehicle, using funds obtained to improve and expand television operations.
  Current projects and activities:
    News, sports, documentaries, telethons, theater, Italian language shows, public service, and political coverage.
  Number of permanent staff: 2 plus 2 volunteers
  Annual budget: $24,000

WHAT CAN I DO?
  Internship descriptions:
    Production internship. General production related work, including camera work, switching, set-up, and lighting for live and video taped shows. Students are encouraged to produce their own show ideas so as to get all-around exposure to the creative and technical process of production.
    Marketing internship. Assist advertising marketing efforts. Help formulate local advertising policy.
    Interns are provided with knowledge that cannot be obtained in college. Besides the basics they learn in college, Channel Six provides a technical insight in the process of creating a program. Cable TV is a growing industry and eventually will absorb a large percentage of TV production-oriented people. The interns learn theory of cable transmission and signal origination and have the opportunity to refine their visual language and expression. Understanding the equipment, its limitations and capabilities, the creative process of communicating effectively and working in direct contact with the public in a community-oriented station should provide the interns with a knowledge package that will help them penetrate the highly competitive media business. Interns are encouraged to express their own opinions and experiment with their own concepts.

CAN I GET IN?
  Academic requirements: College student
  Experience: Basic film or video or photography experience
  Length of commitment to internship: Semester or year
  Number of 1978 interns: 6   Number planned for future: 8

DO I GET PAID, EXPENSES, OR CREDIT?
  College credit: Can be arranged

HOW DO I GET IN?
  Closing date for application: On-going   Interview required: Yes
  When will I know about application: At the interview

WHERE CAN I GET MORE INFORMATION?
  Write: Andrei Campeanu, Station Manager, CATV-Six, 334 Broadway, Revere, MA 02161
  Phone: (617) 284-6833

CONNECTICUT PUBLIC TELEVISION

Hartford, Connecticut

WHAT'S IT DO?
  Purpose and goals: Public broadcasting in Connecticut
  Current projects and activities:
    Programming production for local, regional, and national distribution
  Number of permanent staff: 80   Annual budget: $2.3 million

WHAT CAN I DO?
  Internship descriptions: Production interns work in a variety of capacities
    including camera, audio, lighting, and set construction. Interns are
    responsible to the production manager.

CAN I GET IN?
  Academic requirements: Must be a Connecticut college student, or a
    Connecticut resident attending college out of state.
  Length of commitment: A semester or year. In addition, a full-time, 40
    hour week is required on the part of each intern, with the schedule
    varying depending upon production schedules for each week.
  Number of 1978 interns: 15   Number planned for the future: 15

DO I GET PAID, EXPENSES, OR CREDIT?
  College credit: Can be arranged

HOW DO I GET IN?
  Closing date for application: There is a six months waiting list.
  Interview required: No
  When will I know about application: Four weeks before starting date

WHERE CAN I GET MORE INFORMATION?
  Write: Ken Horseman, Production Manager, Connecticut Public Television,
    24 Summit Street, Hartford, CT 06101
  Phone: (203) 278-5310

PORT JEFFERSON RECORD NEWSPAPERS

Port Jefferson, New York

WHAT'S IT DO?
  Purpose and goals:
    The Record is a weekly tabloid newspaper, with a circulation of approximately 6,000 and an average size of 32 pages, located in the middle of
    Long Island's north shore. Despite having an editorial staff of only two
    full-time employees, it has garnered a large number of state prizes for
    its journalistic efforts (29 in the past three years) and has won national
    recognition by winning first place among weekly newspapers for its life-
    style section in the Penney-Missouri competition.

WHAT CAN I DO?
  The newspaper's internship program began a little more than two years ago,
  and has since served ten interns for periods ranging from one month to a
  full college semester. One of the interns did so well that a four-part
  series on learning disabilities, which she researched and wrote, won first

place in a competition sponsored by the Public Relations Society of America. This provided her with a springboard to a full-time position on a New York City weekly. The amount of work put in will depend on the intern and his or her interests. Students receiving credit for their work will be expected to put in the amount of time commensurate with the amount of credit received, and a written evaluation of their work will be given at the end of the internship. Interns who are not students, obviously, do not have these constraints and are free to work as little or as much as they wish. Most work will consist of re-writes, feature story writing, and, depending on the reliability and accuracy of the intern, news reporting. Instruction in lay-out and headline composition will be given as desired.

CAN I GET IN?
  Academic requirements: Quite flexible about the age, experience or academic background of intern applicants. Interns need a strong desire to do the work and a good command of the English language, as they work almost exclusively with the editorial staff. All applicants must take a writing test which measures writing ability as well as grammatical knowledge. The results are assessed before an invitation to join the program is extended.
  Special: Applicants are required to know how to type. Ownership and knowledge of how to use a 35-mm camera are helpful but not essential.
  Number of 1978 interns: 2   Number planned for future: About the same

DO I GET PAID, EXPENSES, OR CREDIT?
  College credit: Can be arranged

HOW DO I GET IN?
  Closing date for application: Since the length of internships is flexible, there is no deadline for applications, and applicants should clearly indicate when they would be able to join the program. The only constraint on when an intern will be accepted is an unwillingness to have more than two interns in service at the same time.

WHERE CAN I GET MORE INFORMATION?
  Write: Andy Zipser, Editor, Port Jefferson Record, Port Jefferson, NY 11777
  Phone: (516) 473-1370
  Read: The Port Jefferson Record

RADIO STATION WKCM

Hawesville, Kentucky

WHAT'S IT DO?
  Purpose and goals:
    WKCM broadcasts modern country music, is an ABC network affiliate, and was named by Associated Press as the #1 news station in Kentucky small markets. It also has won awards from the Indiana Associated Press. There are two stations: WPFR-FM (a 50,000 watt station) at Terre Haute, Indiana; and WKCM (a learn channel daytime station) near Tell City, Indiana (on the Kentucky side of the Ohio River at Hawesville).

WHAT CAN I DO?
  Internship descriptions:
    WKCM is a training ground. It wants interns who have had some broadcasting experience in college. They can learn just about anything as an intern in

broadcasting. Most interns do an on-the-air shift (about four hours a day) and sell commercial time and cover news the rest of their time. Hours tend to be long because learning about news coverage and commercial productions is involved. Many interns sell air time on commission.

CAN I GET IN?
  Academic requirements: Some broadcasting experience
  Special: Hawesville is a small community. Costs of living are low, but so is the excitement. This is a job only for committed and interested people. If you don't find excitement in your work, you won't find it in the community.
  Length of commitment to internship: One year to 18 months
  Number of 1978 interns: 2   Number planned for the future: 2

DO I GET PAID, EXPENSES, OR CREDIT?
  Pay: Interns earn minimum wage for the air-shift. They also earn from $450 to $1,000 a month on commissions from air time sales, depending on their time and performance.
  College credit: Can be arranged, although most don't get credit.

HOW DO I GET IN?
  Closing date for application: On-going   Interview required: Yes
  Other procedures: After 15 to 18 months, most of the interns move on to good positions. WKCM has been on the air five years and has had interns move directly to Washington, Indianapolis, Minneapolis, and Nashville. All of the people who were with WKCM the first two years are now in management positions in various parts of the country.

WHERE CAN I GET MORE INFORMATION?
  Write: J. Richard Warner, Manager, Radio Station WKCM, P.O. Box 1140, Hawesville, KY 42348
  Phone: (812) 547-8121

WASHINGTON MONTHLY

Washington, D.C.

WHAT'S IT DO?
  Purpose and goals: Publication of a monthly public affairs magazine emphasizing in-depth articles on politics and government.
  Number of permanent staff: 7   Publications: The Washington Monthly

WHAT CAN I DO?
  Internship descriptions:
    Practically everything that goes into publishing The Washington Monthly happens right in the magazine's office. The aim is to give interns as much experience as possible in all phases of magazine publishing--circulation, promotion, editorial, production, graphics. Because there is a full-time staff of only seven, supervisory time is limited. After some initial guidance, interns are usually very much on their own. Curiosity is welcomed; initiative is a must. Here are the activities in which interns participate: reading and commenting on manuscripts; doing research for writers; working on articles for possible publication in The Washington Monthly; preparing subscription orders for computer processing; stuffing and metering invoices, special mailings, magazines; checking newsstands; setting copy on phototypesetter; proofreading; assisting with graphics and pasteup.

CAN I GET IN?
  Academic requirements: Enthusiasm, interest, and initiative
  Length of commitment to internship: Semester or year
  Number of 1978 interns: 12, about 6 at one time
  Number planned for the future: About the same

DO I GET PAID, EXPENSES, OR CREDIT?
  College credit: Can be arranged

HOW DO I GET IN?
  Closing date for application: On-going
  Interview required: Preferred
  When will I know about application: Soon after application is completed

WHERE CAN I GET MORE INFORMATION?
  Write: Carol Trueblood, The Washington Monthly, 1028 Connecticut Avenue, N.W., Washington, DC 20036
  Phone: (202) 659-4866
  Read: The Washington Monthly

WFRV-TV NEWS INTERN

Green Bay, Wisconsin

WHAT'S IT DO?
  Purpose and goals:
    Trains potential TV journalists for a career in broadcast journalism.
  Current projects and activities:
    Training projects for reporter-photographer.
  Number of permanent staff: 25   Annual budget: $500,000

WHAT CAN I DO?
  A semester internship in all aspects of TV journalism

CAN I GET IN?
  Academic requirements: Junior in college
  Length of commitment to internship: Semester
  Number of 1978 interns: 6   Number planned for the future: 6

DO I GET PAID, EXPENSES, OR CREDIT?
  Pay: $120 a week
  College credit: Can be arranged

HOW DO I GET IN?
  Closing date for application: February 1
  Interview required: Yes
  When will I know about application: March 1

WHERE CAN I GET MORE INFORMATION?
  Write: Robert McMullen, News Director, WFRV-TV, P.O. Box 1128, Green Bay, WI 54305
  Phone: (414) 437-5411

THE EDUCATION CLUSTER

Including Special Education, Recreation,
Student Lobby, and Advocacy Agencies

Alternatives Unlimited
American Enterprise Institute for Public Policy Research
Association for World Education
Blue Grass Association for Mental Retardation
Boston Community Schools Program
Cambridge YWCA
Cheff Center for the Handicapped
Coalition of Independent College and University Students
College Republican National Committee
Community Services Program
Council for Retarded Citizens
Dayton Board of Education
French Library
Girls Club of Lynn
Institute for Responsive Education
J. U. Kevil Mental Retardation-Mental Health Center
Kentucky Community Educating Office
Kentucky School for the Deaf
Louisville YWCA
Muhlenberg County Opportunity Center
National Student Lobby
North American Student Cooperative Organization
Northwest College and University Association for Science
St. Paul's School
Political Discovery
United States National Student Association

ALTERNATIVES UNLIMITED

Uxbridge, Massachusetts

WHAT'S IT DO?
  Purpose and goals:
    Alternatives Unlimited is a private, non-profit organization which operates residential and vocational programs for developmentally and psychiatrically disabled individuals within the Blackstone Valley area of Massachusetts. These programs seek to enable clients to achieve a maximum level of development, to strengthen interpersonal relationships, and to assist them in leading normalized, productive lives in the community.
  Current projects and activities:
    Alternatives currently operates six community residences, a cooperative apartment program, a day activity center, and a sheltered workshop. These residential programs provide services to approximately 70 clients while the vocational programs have a capacity of approximately 175 clients.
  Number of permanent staff: 6

WHAT CAN I DO?
  Internship descriptions:
    Vocational Rehabilitation internship. Provides a comprehensive view of the various programs within both day activities and sheltered workshop settings. Ideally an intern should spend at least 30 hours a week in this program. After a two to three week orientation period, working directly as a floor supervisor with vocational instructors at the workshop, the student will move to specific program areas and become involved in program design and implementation with a small group of clients. Possible areas of involvement include daily living activities, gross motor activities, vocational skill training, community awareness, vocational counseling, exposure to sub-contract work and an introduction to rehabilitation counseling. This program is flexible enough to accommodate individual student interest but specific enough to assure that proper instruction and supervision are provided. Periodic evaluations will be made by the various supervisors.
    Community Resident Program internship. This area offers a first-hand, practical experience in the daily routine and group process of community residence programs. The community residences house both staff and disabled persons in a mutual growth milieu.
    The interns in this program will be required to become involved in the routine of life in various challenging mutual experiences with residents. Gradually, interns will come to assist the residents in a sensitive, yet challenging way, in meeting their treatment goals.
    Combined Workshop-Residence Program internship. This combined internship is designed to offer a participating role in the human service delivery system for disabled individuals in the community.

CAN I GET IN?
  Academic requirements: College students interested in psychology, counseling, rehabilitation, community service, or related subjects.
  Age: 18   Experience: Not necessary, but helpful
  Length of possible commitment to internship: From one semester to negotiable

Number of 1978 interns: Began in 1978
Number planned for the future: Open

DO I GET PAID, EXPENSES, OR CREDIT?
  Pay: Room and board in community residence programs
  College credit: Can be arranged

HOW DO I GET IN?
  Closing date for application: No formal date
  Interview required: Yes
  Other procedures: Intern must be accepted by residents and staff

WHERE CAN I GET MORE INFORMATION?
  Write: Frederick Misilo, Assistant Program Director, Alternatives Unlimited,
    62 North Main Street, Apt. 3, Uxbridge, MA 01569
  Phone: (617) 234-5767

AMERICAN ENTERPRISE INSTITUTE FOR PUBLIC POLICY RESEARCH

Washington, D.C.

WHAT'S IT DO?
  Purpose and goals:
    The American Enterprise Institute for Public Policy Research is an independent, non-profit, nonpartisan research and educational organization. The Institute studies national problems, fosters innovative research, identifies and presents varying points of view on issues, develops practical options and analyzes public policy proposals. Areas of concentration include government regulation, social security and retirement, health, law, economics, foreign policy, political and social processes, defense, energy and tax policy.
  Current projects and activities:
    AEI works to place scholarly studies on public issues into the mainstream of political debate. It pursues this objective by commissioning scholars to undertake original research and publishing their findings. Also by sponsoring conferences and debates, round tables, and other forums and making the proceedings available for wide public dissemination on television and radio, and in newspapers, periodicals and scholarly journals. This is designed to bring about broader understanding of issues and to increase the options available to those who make public policy.
  Number of permanent staff: AEI has a staff of about 100 people at its
    Washington headquarters. In addition, there are adjunct scholars and academic associates doing research and teaching in 68 universities around the country. AEI also has established Centers for Public Policy Research on 352 campuses.
  Publications: About 90 per year

WHAT CAN I DO?
  Internship description:
    Interns usually function as research assistants for a predetermined length of time, during which the Institute provides a stipend to cover living expenses while in the Washington area. Students work on public policy

research that is going on at the time of their internship. Some assist with conferences, others with research and publication, and still others with the media and getting the policy out to the public.

CAN I GET IN?
  Academic requirements: Interns must have strong academic skills and an interest in government.

DO I GET PAID, EXPENSES, OR CREDIT?
  Interns receive a stipend to cover living expenses in the Washington area.

HOW DO I GET IN?
  Closing date for application: The program is informal. Interested students should send their college transcripts and resume at the time they inquire about an internship.

WHERE CAN I GET MORE INFORMATION?
  Write: Gary L. Jones, Assistant to the President for Administration, AEI, 1150 Seventeenth Street, N.W., Washington, DC 20036
  Phone: (202) 296-5616
  Read: Send for New Titles, the free list of current publications by the AEI.

ASSOCIATION FOR WORLD EDUCATION

Huntington, New York; Storrs, Connecticut; New York, New York

WHAT'S IT DO?
  Purpose and goals:
    To promote intercommunication among colleges, universities, and postsecondary institutions or research centers which are working toward a global view in education. To enable world-minded persons to exchange knowledge and experience, thus creating an educational system from a world perspective. To assist members to a clearer understanding of the role of education in developing a creative and harmonious world community. To assist members with world educational resources. To promote research related to world education. To foster, through the concept of a world university, concern for the advancement of humanity.
  Current projects and activities:
    Regional and world conferences on world education topics
    Expansion of membership to various regions of the world
    Exploring a resource center for world education
  Number of permanent staff: 1 in each office
  Annual budget: $11,000
  Publications: Quarterly publication: Journal of World Education

WHAT CAN I DO?
  Internship descriptions:
    Interns get assignments according to their interests and abilities. They work on the Journal, on conference planning, or on membership campaigns. One intern in New York City developed a "Resource Guide in World Issues and Education."

CAN I GET IN?
  Academic requirements: High school graduate, some college experience is
    preferred
  Experience: Typing is an asset (male or female)
  Length of commitment to internship: Negotiable
  Number of 1978 interns: 2   Number planned for future: Open

DO I GET PAID, EXPENSES, OR CREDIT?
  College credit: Can be arranged

HOW DO I GET IN?
  Closing date for application: On-going   Interview required: Yes
  Other procedures: Letter of application stating interests is desirable
  When will I know about application: No formal procedure

WHERE CAN I GET MORE INFORMATION?
  Write: Leah R. Karpen, Associate Editor, Association for World Education,
      3 Harbor Hill Drive, Huntington, NY 11743
            Barbara Stone, Coordinator, Association for World Education,
      c/o Department of Education, University of Connecticut, Storrs, CT 06268
            Shirley Stewart, Editor, Journal of World Education, 530 86th Street,
    New York, NY 10028
  Phone: Huntington, NY (516) 427-0723
  Read: Journal of World Education

BLUE GRASS ASSOCIATION FOR MENTAL RETARDATION

Lexington, Kentucky

WHAT'S IT DO?
  Purpose and goals:
    To promote, secure and carry on adequate programs for mentally retarded
    children and adults.
  Current projects and activities:
    Four pre-school classes for retarded children, sheltered workshop for
    vocational training, social and academic training, residential services
    for adult retarded citizens.

WHAT CAN I DO?
  Internship description:
    Administrative aide to participate in the day-to-day management of agency
    affairs including budget preparation, audit, development of operating
    guidelines, and procedures; special projects are primarily program
    evaluation, survey, and research. In addition the Association may
    utilize interns in any of its programs depending on the objectives and
    the skills possessed by the intern.

CAN I GET IN?
  Academic requirements: A college student with a major in education, special
    education, educational administration, sociology, or business administra-
    tion
  Length of commitment to internship: Semester or year

DO I GET PAID, EXPENSES, OR CREDIT?
  Pay: Interns would be paid at least the minimum wage depending upon their qualifications.

HOW DO I GET IN?
  Closing date for application: On-going; indicate which service program you are applying for

WHERE CAN I GET MORE INFORMATION?
  Write: Carleton D. Scully, Executive Director, Blue Grass Association for Mental Retardation, 898 Georgetown Street, Lexington, KY 40505
  Phone: (606) 233-1483

BOSTON COMMUNITY SCHOOLS PROGRAM

Boston, Massachusetts

WHAT'S IT DO?
  Purpose and goals:
    The Boston Community Schools program represents a unique partnership between Boston's neighborhoods and the city. A total of 18 Community School facilities exist, in nearly every Boston neighborhood. Approximately 30,000 people a week use these facilities for a wide range of programs. The diversity of the programs and participants equals the diversity of Boston's residents. Irish history programs are taught in Charlestown and South Boston, while English as a Second Language courses are offered to Spanish-speaking residents of the South End and Dorchester and to Chinese residents in Chinatown and Brighton.
  Current projects and activities:
    The BCS program defines "community education" in its broadest terms and the resultant programs and services cover a wide range of activities for people of all ages. For pre-school children full-day and half-day child care centers are operated in addition to drop-in nursery programs. A wide range of recreational after-school programs are offered for elementary age children from sports of every kind to arts and crafts. The children can also supplement their regular school with tutorial programs and activities emphasizing learning games. Teens make heavy use of Community School recreational facilities. Several schools run drop-in teen centers, and when funds permit or resources can be developed, counseling and vocational training programs are operated. Adult courses range from "light" programs in cake decorating, ceramics, and belly dancing, through courses in home repair, consumer rights, and parent effectiveness, to educational courses in Spanish and history. Community Schools provide a variety of activities for senior citizens including hot lunch programs, bingo, field trips, recreational activities such as crafts, and even exercise.
  Number of permanent staff: 20   Annual budget: $1,400,000

WHAT CAN I DO?
  Internship descriptions:
    Child care internship. 1) Pre-School Aides - Six schools run pre-school programs for children 3 to 5. 2) After-School Aides - Eight schools run formal after-school day care programs; others run after-school

activities for children 5 to 8. Interns with skills in arts and crafts, music, drama, and tutoring are needed to work with this age group. Interns will get a valuable experience in working in structured child-care programs with good supervision. Bilingual child-care assistants, especially in Spanish and Chinese, are desperately needed.

Recreation internship. Recreation interns are needed in every Community School to help run programs for all age groups in modern gymnasiums and swimming pools. Gym interns only need aptitude and coordination to work with the children, teens or adults in a wide variety of gym programs, such as gymnastics, basketball, slimnastics, volleyball, and tennis. There is also an opportunity for students to work in any Boston neighborhood they wish. Physical education is preferred, but interest is more important than formal training.

Tutor/Counselor Internship. Interns are needed in most Community Schools to work primarily on a one-to-one basis in four main areas: 1) Young children; 2) Teen tutoring/counseling - Interns are needed to participate in vocational and personal counseling activities, also in some educational tutoring; 3) Literacy tutoring - There is a special need for English as a Second Language tutoring; 4) Learning disabilities - Spanish, psychology (counseling), or education majors are preferred, but commitment most important qualification.

CAN I GET IN?
  Academic requirements: None   Age: 18
  Experience: Interest most important
  Length of commitment to internship: Negotiable

DO I GET PAID, EXPENSES, OR CREDIT?
  College credit: Can be arranged

HOW DO I GET IN?
  Closing date for application: On-going
  Interview required: No
  When will I know about application: Immediately

WHERE CAN I GET MORE INFORMATION?
  Write: Diane Petereit, Boston Community Schools, 73 Hemenway Street,
    Boston, MA 02115
  Phone: (617) 266-9390

CAMBRIDGE YWCA

Cambridge, Massachusetts

WHAT'S IT DO?
  Purpose and goals:
    "The YWCA of the U.S.A., a movement rooted in the Christian faith as known in Jesus and nourished by the resources of that faith, seeks to respond to the barrier-breaking love of God in this day. The Association draws together into responsible membership women and girls of diverse experiences and faiths, so that their lives may be open to new understanding, deeper relationships and that together they may join in the struggle for peace and justice, freedom and dignity for all people."
  Current projects and activities:
    The YWCA in the Community. The Cambridge YWCA, located in historic buildings in Cambridge, Burlington, and Marshfield, serves members of diverse economic, racial and ethnic backgrounds from 50 Massachusetts cities and towns. There are 8,600 women members and men associates who choose to identify themselves with the YWCA. In support of its imperative on the elimination of racism, courses and public lectures are offered on various aspects of racism. The Y holds public forums on housing issues in Cambridge, and on women's roles in a changing society. It supported farm workers, legal abortion, bilingual and multicultural courses in public schools, and quality school desegregation. Major areas of activities include education and recreation, day care, day camp, trippers, and a residence center for 110 women.
  Number of permanent staff: 28   Annual budget: $650,000
  Publications: Annual Report, Winter Cambridge YWCA, and newsletters

WHAT CAN I DO?
  Internship descriptions:
    Art internship. Duties may include poster making, publicity distribution, designing bulletin boards, flyers, and art work for on-going public relations needs of the organization and other related work as assigned.
    Program internship. Duties may include program planning and evaluation, budgeting, working with volunteer committees, registering class participants, hiring and training staff, public relations, and basically learning about the programming and administrative aspects of the YWCA.
    Public Relations internship. Duties may include working on newsletter and catalog, establishing media contacts, writing news releases, helping design an annual report, and working with public relations committee, composed of staff and volunteers.
    Recreation Coordinator internship. Develop with residents' help a program of individual and team sports and exercise (volleyball, basketball, hiking, camping).
    Residence Counselor internship. Develop support groups for residents to share common needs and concerns, as women in transition. Work with individual residents on an on-going basis on personal, marital, and vocational goals.

CAN I GET IN?
  Academic requirements: None   Age: 18
  Length of possible commitment to internship: Negotiable
  Number of 1978 interns: 6   Number planned for future: 8

DO I GET PAID, EXPENSES, OR CREDIT?
  College credit: Can be arranged

HOW DO I GET IN?
  Closing date for application: On-going   Interview required: Yes
  When will I know about application: After interview

WHERE CAN I GET MORE INFORMATION?
  Write: Sandra Aylor Scott, Associate Director, Cambridge YWCA, 7 Temple
    Street, Cambridge, MA 02139
  Phone: (617) 491-6050
  Read: Annual Report, brochure, and newsletter

CHEFF CENTER FOR THE HANDICAPPED

Augusta, Michigan

WHAT'S IT DO?
  Purpose and goals:
    To teach therapeutic horseback riding to handicapped persons, and to
    train instructors to work as therapeutic horseback riding instructors.
  Current projects and activities:
    Working with over 200 handicapped persons weekly and training programs
    for instructors.
  Number of permanent staff: 6   Annual budget: $190,000
  Publications: It Is Ability That Counts (Olivet College Press, Michigan),
    Annual Report

WHAT CAN I DO?
  Internship descriptions:
    Physical therapy through horseback riding; training internships and
    volunteers for all phases of the program.

CAN I GET IN?
  Academic requirements: At least 2 years of college   Age: 21
  Experience: Work with children, such as camp counselor
  Special: 5 years riding experience necessary
  Length of commitment to internship: Semester
  Number of 1978 interns: 2   Number planned for the future: Open

DO I GET PAID, EXPENSES, OR CREDIT?
  Pay: $225 per month plus housing expenses
  College credit: Can be arranged

HOW DO I GET IN?
  Closing date for application: July   Interview required: Yes
  When will I know about application: August

WHERE CAN I GET MORE INFORMATION?
  Write: Lida L. McCowan, Director, Cheff Center for the Handicapped, R.R.1,
    Box 171, Augusta, MI 49012
  Phone: (616) 731-4471
  Read: It Is Ability That Counts by Lida L. McCowan; Quarter Horse Journal,
    March 1973

COALITION OF INDEPENDENT COLLEGE AND UNIVERSITY STUDENTS

Washington, D.C.

WHAT'S IT DO?
  Purpose and goals:
    COPUS is a new student lobby and research group located nationally in Washington, D.C. and locally on college campuses throughout the country. COPUS confronts the specific problems faced by students of these institutions, especially issues involving Federal and state financial aid and student assistance programs. COPUS is attempting to insure that, regardless of cost, students have the opportunity of attending the school best suited to their educational needs and desires.
  Current projects and activities:
    Federal appropriations for student financial aid and other legislative bills and issues are studied, such as tuition tax credits, energy and tax matters as they affect students and private colleges.
  Number of permanent staff: 2   Annual budget: $30,000
  Publications: Legislative Update, newsletter twice a month, annual report

WHAT CAN I DO?
  Internship description:
    Participants in volunteer and intern program serve as staff for the national office or, if they wish, COPUS will help make available to them public service internship opportunities in the metropolitan Washington area. Students working directly for COPUS carry out the various research and lobbying efforts it undertakes, as well as initiate and complete projects along the lines of their own personal interests.
    COPUS interns work in three basic areas:
      1) Communications and organizing
      2) Legislation research and advocacy
      3) Fundraising for special projects and the COPUS national organization
    Specific jobs might include preparing testimony on bills before Congress, researching the student assistance program structure of different Federal and state agencies, relating COPUS positions to the press and public at large, recruiting member schools, preparing and editing the COPUS newsletter, directing financial aid panel discussions at colleges throughout the country, and working with other groups on issues of joint concern. However, interns are encouraged to be innovative and are not limited in the realm of what they may accomplish.
    The public service internships range from those with Congressional and legislative staffs to service jobs in hospitals, day care centers, museums, and political interest groups. In this way, COPUS serves not only as a place of educational endeavor for its own interns, but also as a resource for placement opportunities to independent college and university students.

CAN I GET IN?
  Academic requirements: Must attend a private college
  Age: 18 to 23
  Experience: Should have basic knowledge of student financial aid
  Length of commitment to internship: Semester or year
  Number of 1978 interns: 4   Number planned for the future: Open

DO I GET PAID, EXPENSES, OR CREDIT?
　Pay:　Some internships are provided with a stipend, but most are not.
　College credit:　Can be arranged

HOW DO I GET IN?
　Closing date for application:　July 30 for fall semester and December 15
　　for the spring semester
　Interview required:　No, but helpful
　Other procedures:　A resume, a statement of interests in working for
　　COPUS, and recommendations should be sent with application.
　When will I know about application:　No formal date

WHERE CAN I GET MORE INFORMATION?
　Write:　William G. Litchfield, Executive Director, COPUS, 1730 Rhode Island
　　Avenue, N.W., Suite 500, Washington, DC 20036
　Phone:　(202) 659-1747
　Read:　Legislative Update

COLLEGE REPUBLICAN NATIONAL COMMITTEE

Washington, D.C.

WHAT'S IT DO?
　Purpose and goals:
　　To promote the Republican Party, its candidates and philosophy on
　　American college campuses; to lobby for student issues like passage of a
　　tuition tax credit bill, student right-to-work legislation, and the jobs
　　creation act.
　Current projects and activities:
　　Campaigns, Washington campus news service, women's task force, and
　　minority affairs task force.
　Number of permanent staff:　8
　Publications:　The College Republican, 13,000 readership

WHAT CAN I DO?
　Interns do office and clerical work; work as assistants to the Committee on
　the U.S. Youth Council; assist in research, the newsletter, and the campus
　media service.

CAN I GET IN?
　Academic requirements: College student　　　　Age:　17 to 22
　Special:　An interest in politics and a registered Republican or Independent
　Length of commitment to internship:　Semester or year
　Number of 1978 interns:　6　　　　Number planned for the future:　Same

DO I GET PAID, EXPENSES, OR CREDIT?
　Interns are reimbursed for expenses incurred while working.

HOW DO I GET IN?
　Closing date for application:　2 months before internship
　Interview required:　No
　Other procedures:　Clearance by state Republican officials from intern's
　　home state.

When will I know about application: One month before internship

WHERE CAN I GET MORE INFORMATION?
  Write: Jerry Lindsley, Executive Director, College Republican National
    Committee, 310 First Street, S.E., Washington, DC 20003
  Phone: (202) 484-6527
  Read: <u>The College Republican</u>, a newsletter

COMMUNITY SERVICES PROGRAM

Prestonsburg, Kentucky

WHAT'S IT DO?
  Purpose and goals:
    The Community Services Program offers non-credit classes to the general
    public. It makes continuing education activities available to the adults
    in the community.
  Current projects and activities:
    Family life activities, senior citizens consumer education, health and
    safety, consumer education in five counties, potters' guild, art guild,
    and consumer education for ex-offenders.
  Number of permanent staff: 2
  Annual budget: $22,000 (not including staff)
  Publications: Prestonsburg Community College Community Service program
    schedules, annual book reviews

WHAT CAN I DO?
  Internship descriptions:
    In cooperation with the University of Kentucky, an internship is offered
    in gerontology through the School of Social Professions. This person
    will work directly with the senior citizens centers in the area. Other
    possible volunteer positions include: prepared childbirth instructor/
    trainees; coordinator of CPR program; potter instructor; volunteers to
    work with ex-offenders; and a coordinator to establish a consumer
    education bureau.

CAN I GET IN?
  Academic requirements: College student
  Length of commitment to internship: One or two years
  Special: Interest in community college services or administration

DO I GET PAID, EXPENSES, OR CREDIT?
  College credit: Sometimes is arranged

HOW DO I GET IN?
  Closing date for application: On-going   Interview required: Yes
  When will I know about application: Within two weeks of applying or before
    August 15.

WHERE CAN I GET MORE INFORMATION?
  Write: James W. Ratcliff, Coordinator, Community Services Program,
    Prestonsburg Community College, Prestonsburg, KY 41653
  Phone: (606) 886-3863

COUNCIL FOR RETARDED CITIZENS
Louisville, Kentucky

WHAT'S IT DO?
  Purpose and goals:
    The Council for Retarded Citizens is a voluntary advocacy organization, which promotes services for citizens who are mentally retarded. Further, the Council works to reinforce the respect, dignity, and rights due retarded citizens by helping to shape societal attitudes to value the strengths, abilities, diversity, and contributions unique to every person.
  Current projects and activities:
    In addition to public education, legislative review, service monitoring, and class advocacy, the Council provides the following direct services:
      Custom manufacturing service - provides evaluation, training, job placement, and long-term sheltered employment.
      Recreational services - includes basketball and bowling leagues, swim programs, summer camp and vacation trips.
      Citizen Advocacy Program - matches competent interested citizens with citizens who are mentally retarded. The relationship may provide friendship, practical assistance or legal responsibility.
      Parent outreach - matches concerned and knowledgeable parents of mentally retarded persons with new parents or parents of older children who are mentally retarded.
      Council and parent meetings - held regularly as are board and committee meetings. These activities provide an opportunity for community and parental input.
  Number of permanent staff: 14   Annual budget: $800,000
  Publications: 3 journals and numerous periodicals

WHAT CAN I DO?
  Internship descriptions:
    Social work internships are available. Others vary with the student. Students would be used to supplement existing programs and to work directly under the supervision of the council staff.

CAN I GET IN?
  Academic requirements: College student
  Length of commitment to internship: Semester or year
  Number of 1978 interns: 2
  Number planned for the future: 2 to 4 each semester

DO I GET PAID, EXPENSES, OR CREDIT?
  Expenses: Sometimes   College credit: Can be arranged

HOW DO I GET IN?
  Closing date for application: On-going   Interview required: Yes
  When will I know about application: Each one varies

WHERE CAN I GET MORE INFORMATION?
  Write: April Kerr, Council for Retarded Citizens, 1146 S. Third Street, Louisville, KY 40203
  Phone: (502) 584-1239
  Read: <u>Normalization Principle</u> by Wolfensberger

DAYTON BOARD OF EDUCATION

Dayton, Ohio

WHAT'S IT DO?
  Purpose and goals:
    The Board of Education sponsors a volunteer program which offers economically disadvantaged, unemployed, or underemployed youth between the ages of 14 and 21 an opportunity to have meaningful exposure and experience in a variety of occupational areas, thereby enhancing their employability and acquainting them with career options related to personal goals and interests. Successful completion of the volunteer service and learning experience affords the student on-the-job training, job references, and high school or college credit related to academic course work. With proper motivation and 5 to 10 hours per week at an assigned site, the high school student can earn up to one-half credit per semester, while the college student can fulfill a course requirement.
  Current projects and activities:
    1. Extending programs in private agencies.
    2. Extending work sites in new and varied areas.
  Number of permanent staff: 4   Annual budget: $39,000
  Publications: Research written by volunteers from the program

WHAT CAN I DO?
  Volunteer service and learning experiences are available in the following career areas: Accounting and bookkeeping, art, drafting and engineering, early childhood education (day care centers), tutoring, health, law and law enforcement, mental health, nursing homes, recreation and arts and crafts, secretarial and clerical, graphic arts, social services, communications and public relations, fire science, veterinary medicine.

CAN I GET IN?
  Academic requirements: High school student   Age: 15 to 20
  Length of commitment to internship: At least one semester
  Number of 1978 volunteers: 200
  Number planned for the future: 200 to 300

DO I GET PAID, EXPENSES, OR CREDIT?
  High school credit: Can be earned
  College credit: Can be arranged

HOW DO I GET IN?
  Closing date for application: February 30 and September 30 for each semester
  Interview required: Yes
  When will I know about application: After the interview

WHERE CAN I GET MORE INFORMATION:
  Write: Edward McGee, Dayton Board of Education, Volunteer Program, 348 West First Street, Dayton, OH 45402
  Phone: (513) 461-3850
  Read: <u>High School Volunteer Handbook</u>, from the above address

FRENCH LIBRARY

Boston, Massachusetts

WHAT'S IT DO?
  Purpose and goals:
    The French Library is an independent, non-profit organization incorporated in 1946 for the purpose of disseminating French language and culture throughout New England. In addition to traditional in-house services, its native French staff brings visual and other language-training materials from its "Médiathèque" into the classroom, ranging from interviews with literary personalities to popular songs, from documentaries to news shorts.
  Current projects and activities:
    The French Library sponsors regularly-scheduled lectures, films, book discussions, art exhibits, and musical programs, as well as other French cultural events. It recently started a pilot project of seminar-workshops which bring together French teachers and students to work on joint ventures.
  Number of permanent staff: 7   Annual budget: $106,000
  Publications: Bi-monthly calendar, <u>Le Bibliophile</u>

WHAT CAN I DO?
  Internship descriptions:
    Library internship. The student will assist the head librarian and will have the opportunity to utilize and improve French while, at the same time, gaining first-hand knowledge of a large and distinguished collection of French literature. Duties entail shelving, processing, and accessioning books. It also involves some shelf reading. All written material with which the intern comes in contact is in French.
    Media internship. The media aide helps staff in operating audio-visual equipment, such as slides, films, cassettes, and records, and in filling film orders from schools. The aide also may be called upon to assist with film rental orders and leasing of films, special showings, and recording albums or original cassettes onto other cassettes. A knowledge of audio-visual materials is helpful for this position. Of course, the student's French will benefit, as films, cassettes, and records are all in French.
    Clerical internship. The clerical aide helps with secretarial duties, such as typing correspondence and other written material and general office duties.

CAN I GET IN?
  Academic requirements: High school   Age: 16
  Special: Knowledge of French
  Length of commitment to internship: Negotiable
  Number of 1978 interns: 5   Number planned for future: Open

DO I GET PAID, EXPENSES, OR CREDIT?
  Negotiable

HOW DO I GET IN?
  Closing date for application: On-going
  Interview required: Not always

WHERE CAN I GET MORE INFORMATION?
  Write: Mrs. Mylo Housen, Director, The French Library, 53 Marlborough
    Street, Boston, MA 02116
  Phone: (617) 266-4354
  Read: <u>The French Library</u>, a brochure

GIRLS CLUB OF LYNN

Lynn, Massachusetts

WHAT'S IT DO?
  Purpose and goals:
    The Girls Club of Lynn is a non-profit organization whose purpose is to
    promote the education and welfare of girls ages 6 to 16 from the greater
    Lynn area. It is devoted to the educational, social, vocational, and
    recreational needs of girls and young women, and to family support for
    their clients. It is a member of the Girls Clubs of America and of the
    United Way of Massachusetts Bay.
  Current projects and activities:
    The Girls Club provides programs in recreation, social group development,
    and day care. The Club fosters both individual and group development.
    Its specific services include: an after-school day care program for
    children of working parents; an after-school recreation program for girls;
    a joint recreational program with the Boys Club of Lynn; and an adolescent
    girls' program.
  Number of permanent staff: 3 professional, 3 support, 2 para-professional,
    and 1 teen coordinator

WHAT CAN I DO?
  Internship descriptions:
    Group worker. Worker will develop and implement recreational and social
      group development activities for girls and boys, ages 6 to 12. Will be
      responsible for safety and discipline of all participants, as well as
      for administrative duties such as attendance forms and program evalua-
      tions. Worker will act as a "public relations" person for the Girls
      Club in the schools where programs are held and will attend and parti-
      cipate in staff training and planning meetings. Must be a self-starter
      and able to work independently.
    Public Relations Assistant. A student in photography and media is needed
      to prepare a slide presentation of the youth programs at the Girls Club
      of Lynn to be used in public relations events of the agency. Student
      should bring own camera; the agency will supply all materials and
      processing. This is a short-term project which could be used as a term
      project to satisfy a course requirement.
    Group Worker/Boys internship. Worker will develop and implement activities
      around small group development. Worker will work as part of a team with
      three other staff people. Worker will be responsible for the safety and
      discipline of a group and will also attend and participate in staff
      training and planning meetings. Boys participating in program are
      primarily inner city youth. Job requires a self-starter and mature
      individual.
  The Club does not usually have regular intern positions. Rather, if a person
    wants to do an internship, one will be developed around agency goals. Staff

training, written evaluations, and pre-work orientation are offered. The Club is very committed to helping potential youthworkers gain practical experience in a supervised setting.

CAN I GET IN?
   Academic requirements: College students with an interest in physical
      education, recreation, human services, or education.
   Age: 19
   Experience: Some work with children in a recreational setting
   Length of commitment to internship: Semester or longer
   Number of 1978 interns: Varies
   Number planned for the future: Open

DO I GET PAID, EXPENSES, OR CREDIT?
   College credit: Can be arranged

HOW DO I GET IN?
   Closing date for application: On-going
   Interview required: Yes

WHERE CAN I GET MORE INFORMATION?
   Write: Nancy Bartels, Girls Club of Lynn, 88 Broad Street, Lynn, MA 01902
   Phone: (617) 592-9744

INSTITUTE FOR RESPONSIVE EDUCATION

Boston, Massachusetts

WHAT'S IT DO?
   Purpose and goals:
      The Institute for Responsive Education is a private, non-profit organization created in 1973 to study and assist the process of citizen participation in educational decision-making. It believes that developing more effective citizen participation in all aspects of governmental and institutional life is essential if we are to have healthy communities.
   Current projects and activities:
      The Institute is currently involved in three national studies: 1) a study of citizen participation funded by the National Institute of Education, 2) a study of the role of citizens in educational collective bargaining, and 3) a study of school councils as mechanisms for citizen participation in local educational decision making. It publishes reports and periodicals of interest to parents and educators seeking a larger citizen voice in education.
   Publications: <u>Citizen Action in Education, Factual Politics-Five New Action-Research Publications</u>

WHAT CAN I DO?
   Internship description:
      Internship possibilities include communications (library work, publications work), business management, and research, if the intern has the appropriate background and skills. The business intern will learn the financial procedures needed to maintain and control a non-profit education-related organization.

CAN I GET IN?
  Academic requirements: Skills for the particular job
  Age: College age
  Length of possible commitment to internship: Negotiable
  Number of interns planned for the future: Open

DO I GET PAID, EXPENSES, OR CREDIT?
  College credit: Can be arranged

HOW DO I GET IN?
  Closing date for application: On-going
  Interview required: Yes

WHERE CAN I GET MORE INFORMATION?
  Write: Betsy Wachtel, Institute for Responsive Education, 704 Commonwealth
    Avenue, Boston, MA 02215
  Phone: (617) 353-3309
  Read: Citizen Action in Education

J. U. KEVIL MENTAL RETARDATION-MENTAL HEALTH CENTER

Mayfield, Kentucky

WHAT'S IT DO?
  Purpose and goals:
    The Kevil Memorial Foundation Center is a non-profit organization serving,
    but not limited to, the counties of Graves, Fulton, Hickman, and Carlisle.
  Current projects and activities:
  Mental Health. Mayfield Comprehensive Care Center is one of five centers
    which are a service of the Western Kentucky Regional Mental Health and
    Mental Retardation Board. It provides mental health services in the
    areas of prevention, direct outpatient services, and aftercare.
  Direct Services. Direct services are available on an outpatient basis
    dealing with any mental health problem ranging from minor adjustment
    problems to alcohol and drug problems to severe emotional problems.
  Inpatient Services. Inpatient services are made available to clients,
    when needed, by referring them to the Lourdes Psychiatric Unit in
    Paducah or Western State Hospital in Hopkinsville.
  Aftercare Services. Aftercare services, follow-up care after hospitali-
    zation, include a stimulating partial hospitalization program for
    clients in need of occupational/recreational therapy.
  Mental Retardation. The J.U. Kevil School operates five days a week and
    maintains five different classes for children and adults.
  Workshop. The Kevil workshop trains either mentally or physically
    handicapped boys and girls, men and women to become individuals with
    acceptable work habits, to provide long-term employment, and to provide
    a therapeutic work atmosphere for severely handicapped individuals.
    This is accomplished by doing work for industries in the community.
    The purpose is to assess the areas of strength and weakness of physi-
    cally and mentally handicapped men and women.
  Work Adjustment Training. The purpose is to improve the problem areas
    of each client, in order to achieve acceptable work habits that would

enable the person to be placed in sheltered or competitive employment.

Sheltered Employment. The purpose is to provide a place for long-term employment of handicapped individuals who would not be capable mentally and/or physically of entering competitive employment.

Work Activities. The objectives are to provide a therapeutic work setting plus concentrated instruction in the areas of self-help skills, basic motor skills, functional academics, home and community living skills, social skills, and use of leisure time.

Kentucky Bureau of Rehabilitation Services. This provides the services necessary to render disabled persons fit to engage in remunerative employment.

Number of permanent staff: 27   Annual budget: $300,000

WHAT CAN I DO?
  Internship descriptions:
    Work adjustment
    Speech therapy
    Work evaluation
    Recreational therapist

CAN I GET IN?
  Academic requirements: Background in social work, rehabilitation, industrial arts, or education.
  Length of commitment to internship: One year
  Number of 1978 interns: 2
  Number planned for the future: Unlimited

DO I GET PAID, EXPENSES, OR CREDIT?
  College credit: Can be arranged

HOW DO I GET IN?
  Closing date for application: On-going
  Interview required: No
  When will I know about application: No formal procedure

WHERE CAN I GET MORE INFORMATION?
  Write: Larry G. Knight, J.U. Kevil Mental Retardation-Mental Health Center, South 10th Street, Mayfield, KY 42066
  Phone: (502) 247-5346

KENTUCKY COMMUNITY EDUCATION OFFICE
Mt. Sterling, Kentucky

WHAT'S IT DO?
  Purpose and goals:
    The community education program operates from a central office serving eight schools and a community center. It provides recreation, enrichment, social and adult basic education services to all age persons in the community with special emphasis on the handicapped, disadvantaged, and minority groups.
  Current projects and activities:
    Serving 7,000 persons in after-school and night recreation, enrichment, and adult programs, plus aging, in-school youth, and vocationally disadvantaged persons during the school day.

WHAT CAN I DO?
  Duties include proposal writing, promotion, supervision, and evaluation of community education classes and activities including adult education programs. In addition there is a volunteer coordinator who trains recreation and counseling volunteers throughout all our programs.

CAN I GET IN?
  Academic requirements: None
  Length of commitment to internship: Semester or longer
  Number of 1978 interns: 3
  Number planned for the future: 4 to 6

DO I GET PAID, EXPENSES, OR CREDIT?
  College credit: Can be arranged

HOW DO I GET IN?
  Closing date for application: On-going
  Interview required: No
  When will I know about application: No formal plan

WHERE CAN I GET MORE INFORMATION?
  Write: Director, Community Education Office, 19 Trojan Avenue, Mt. Sterling, KY 40353
  Phone: (606) 498-5864
  Read: Material available on request.

KENTUCKY SCHOOL FOR THE DEAF
Danville, Kentucky

WHAT'S IT DO?
  Purpose and goals:
    Provides educational and residential services for students who, because of their hearing loss, cannot be educated in the regular public school system. Students are from 6 to 18 years old. Curriculum is similar to that of the public schools.
  Current projects and activities:
    Academic and vocational classroom instruction. After school hours athletics, recreational, social and cultural enrichment programs.

WHAT CAN I DO?
  Internship description:
    Four openings for recreation aides. Duties would include assisting in after-school activities to include athletics, drama, and art. Materials and scheduling will be provided.

CAN I GET IN?
  Academic requirements: Background in education, art, physical education, or counseling.
  Experience: An interest in working with handicapped children with some knowledge of child development.
  Length of commitment to internship: Semester or year
  Number of 1978 interns: 7
  Number planned for the future: Open

DO I GET PAID, EXPENSES, OR CREDIT?
  College credit: Can be arranged

HOW DO I GET IN?
  Closing date for application: On-going
  Interview required: No
  When will I know about application: No formal procedure

WHERE CAN I GET MORE INFORMATION?
  Write: Edward Peltier, Principal, Kentucky School for the Deaf, South Second Street, Danville, KY 40422
  Phone: (606) 235-5132

LOUISVILLE YWCA

Louisville, Kentucky

WHAT'S IT DO?
  Purpose and goals:
    The Association draws together into responsible membership women and girls of diverse experiences and faiths, that their lives may be open to new understanding and deeper relationships and that together they may join in the struggle for peace and justice, freedom and dignity for all people. The Louisville-Jefferson County YWCA works together to improve the lives of women and their families.
  Current projects and activities:
    Rape center, day care program, creative employment project, shelter for battered wives, recreation classes and activities.
  Number of permanent staff: 87
  Publications: Quarterly newsletter

WHAT CAN I DO?
  Help the staff with any of the programs above. Write a plan of your own, as they have not had many interns but would like some ideas for what particular young women would like to do for these or related programs.

CAN I GET IN?
  Academic requirements: Background in physical education, child development, social work, recreation or community organization.
  Age: 18
  Special: Committed to principles of the YWCA
  Length of commitment to internship: Six months or a year

DO I GET PAID, EXPENSES, OR CREDIT?
  Negotiable

HOW DO I GET IN?
  Send a letter with a resume stating what you would like to do, your interest in the program and the place.
  When will I know about application: No formal plan

WHERE CAN I GET MORE INFORMATION?
  Write: Bobbie Bateman, YWCA, 604 S. Third Street, Louisville, KY 40402
  Phone: (502) 585-2331
  Read: Newsletter from above address

MUHLENBERG COUNTY OPPORTUNITY CENTER

Greenville, Kentucky

WHAT'S IT DO?
  Purpose and goals:
    To train handicapped people to compete in competitive labor market, and to meet their own needs. Provides rehabilitation, vocational and other training workshops to help the severely handicapped get back into society.
  Current projects and goals:
    Sheltered workshop, activities center, and vocational development
  Number of permanent staff: 17

WHAT CAN I DO?
  Interns needed to help with the above projects and for social work rehabilitation. Flexible internships will be negotiated.

CAN I GET IN?
  Educational requirements: College level   Age: 21
  Length of commitment to internship: Semester or longer
  Number of 1978 interns: 1   Number planned for the future: Open

DO I GET PAID, EXPENSES, OR CREDIT?
  College credit: Can be arranged

HOW DO I GET IN?
  Closing date for application: On-going
  Interview required: Yes
  When will I know about application: As soon as you are interviewed

WHERE CAN I GET MORE INFORMATION?
  Write: Don Rose, Director, Muhlenberg County Opportunity Center,
    P. O. Box 15, Greenville, KY 42345
  Phone: (502) 338-0301

NATIONAL STUDENT LOBBY

Washington, D.C.

WHAT'S IT DO?
  Purpose and goals:
    The National Student Lobby is a student-financed and controlled, independent organization advocating specific student issues and concerns in the government. NSL remains non-partisan and refrains from endorsing candidates, but takes stands on specific legislation.
  Current projects and activities:
    Legislative projects which concern students such as tax credit for college tuition, student right-to-work bill, foreign affairs and international education. Also, child care centers on campuses, student discount travel, and women and minority issues in education.
  Number of permanent staff: 8
  Annual budget: $150,000
  Publications: Student Lobbyist, a monthly magazine

WHAT CAN I DO?
  Internship descriptions:
    Although duties will focus around the area of work particularly suited to the individual intern, a certain amount of general labor will be required. It should be noted that all staff members do their share of phone answering and typing; the same is expected of NSL interns. A prospective intern must indicate for which of the three programs described below he or she is applying, according to personal interests and background.
    Legislative internship. An applicant should be familiar with the legislative process and also with current issues, both education and non-education related. He or she should have good analytical and communication skills.
    In consultation with the legislative director, the intern will choose one legislative issue and work primarily in that one area. The intern will be responsible for carrying out lobbying activities on that issue, under the direction and guidance of the legislative director. The intern will be responsible for writing statements and analyses of the issue for the use of the Lobby. When appropriate, the intern will attend Congressional hearings and floor debates, as well as meetings of other educational associations. Besides the chosen area of concentration, the intern will have ample opportunity to become versant in a wide variety of issues, and to become well acquainted with the Federal government and its workings.
    Press internship. Persons interested in an internship in this area should be able to write clearly and concisely and also display originality and creativity. Experience in journalism--working on the school newspaper or other publication--would also be helpful. A press intern would assist in the publication of the monthly Student Lobbyist newsletter. The intern would also share the responsibility for writing

news releases and other correspondence with legislative interns and staff members. Assistance might be needed on any phase of the publications--writing, editing, layout, printing, and mailing. As needed, he or she might be called on to write an occasional press release. The intern would help to maintain NSL's contacts with the media by keeping its representatives informed of the Lobby's activities. During the spring and fall, it is necessary to keep in constant communication with campus newspapers. This might be a responsibility of the press intern.

Administrative internship. An administrative intern should be knowledgeable about business management, and should also have good organizational ability. Having held a position of leadership in a club or organization would be useful background experience. Possible assignments for an administrative intern are extremely varied. One duty might be the writing and development of NSL organization and legislative manuals for distribution to membership. Another responsibility might be to search for and develop potential sources of funds for the Lobby. This would include establishing relationships with foundations and developing communication with potential individual donors and business contacts. Another duty might be recruitment of individual and institutional NSL members. Administrative interns help in planning the NSL Annual Lobbying Conference, including arranging for speakers, working on press and publicity, making appointments with Congresspersons for students who will be attending the conference, and handling much of the detail work at the conference central office itself. This would be especially true of the spring semester.

CAN I GET IN?
The Lobby is seeking college students who are self-directed, able to accept responsibility, and to make decisions. Preference in choosing interns will be given to those students who attend NSL full-member schools, second priority to students from subscribing members.
Length of commitment to internship: Semester or year
Number of 1978 interns: 8
Number planned for the future: About the same

DO I GET PAID, EXPENSES, OR CREDIT?
College credit: Can be arranged; most students do receive credit.

HOW DO I GET IN?
Closing date for application: On-going
Interview required: Preferred
When will I know about application: No formal plan

WHERE CAN I GET MORE INFORMATION?
  Write: Sheila McRebey or Ellen Vollinger, 2115 S Street, N.W., Washington, DC 20008
  Phone: (202) 234-5774
  Read: Student Lobbyist, available from above address

NORTH AMERICAN STUDENT COOPERATIVE ORGANIZATION

Ann Arbor, Michigan

WHAT'S IT DO?
  Purpose and goals:
    NASCO is an association of consumer cooperatives located in the U. S. and Canada. It provides technical, consulting, and publications services to its members, most of whom are student housing co-ops. In addition, it acts as a clearinghouse for information on co-ops and answers requests for information from the general public. Finally, NASCO publishes a journal entitled The New Harbinger that covers the entire cooperative movement.
  Number of permanent staff in main office: 2
  Annual budget: $35,000
  Publications: The New Harbinger (a 64 page quarterly journal), Monthly News of Co-op Communities (a monthly newsletter), Member News (three times per year, tabloid), Leadership Directions (six times per year, mimeo)

WHAT CAN I DO?
  Internship descriptions:
    NASCO is extremely open to volunteer internships. It would be willing to utilize volunteers in a wide range of capacities and would tailor the program to suit his or her needs and interests. NASCO is willing to work with stopouts who might be interested in doing an internship project at one of its members (currently 15). The members are predominantly student housing co-ops and they utilize internships in a multitude of different projects including business operations, energy conservation, member education, advertising, maintenance, financial affairs, and accounting. Member co-ops are currently located in Ontario, Canada (including Toronto); as well as Berkeley, California; Madison, Wisconsin; Minneapolis, Minnesota; Oberlin, Ohio; Ann Arbor, Michigan; Austin, Texas; and East Lansing, Michigan.

CAN I GET IN?
  Academic requirements:
    No requirements other than serious interest in learning about, and working on behalf of, the cooperative movement.
  Length of commitment to internship: Semester or year

Number of 1978 interns: None
Number planned for the future: Depends on number of qualified applicants

DO I GET PAID, EXPENSES, OR CREDIT?
College credit: Can be arranged

HOW DO I GET IN?
Closing date for application: On-going
Other procedures: Interested students should write or call NASCO and should be prepared to state their interest and previous involvement in co-ops.
When will I know about application: No formal plan

WHERE CAN I GET MORE INFORMATION?
Write: Stewart Kohl, Coordinator, North American Student Cooperative Organization, Box 7239, Ann Arbor, MI 48107
Phone: (313) 663-0889
Read: Applicants should refer to our journal, The New Harbinger, for more information.

NORTHWEST COLLEGE AND UNIVERSITY ASSOCIATION FOR SCIENCE

Richland, Washington

WHAT'S IT DO?
Purpose and goals:
The program is supported financially by the U.S. Department of Energy and offers participants an introduction to science and technology as well as an opportunity to develop a better comprehension and appreciation of research methods in industry. Students selected for the program work under the guidance of senior research scientists. The program is designed for undergraduate students who possess the potential for a successful career in engineering, mathematics, or the sciences as indicated by their record of scholastic achievement, aptitude, and interests. They work in one of six Department of Energy laboratories in the Richland area.
Current projects and activities:
Engineering, mathematical and science research in energy.
Annual budget: Financed by the U.S. Department of Energy

WHAT CAN I DO?
Internship description:
A student will work with the senior scientists in various disciplines. The intern is requested to specifically state interests when completing the application.

CAN I GET IN?
Academic requirements: Junior standing in college with a strong engineering, science, or mathematical scholastic achievement, aptitude, and interests.
Special: Open only to U.S. citizens from U.S. educational institutions
Length of commitment to internship: Semester
Number of 1978 student trainees: 68
Number planned for the future: About the same

DO I GET PAID, EXPENSES, OR CREDIT?
  Pay: A stipend of $125 per week
  Expenses: Round-trip travel between the trainee's home and the site will be provided.
  College credit: Can be arranged

HOW DO I GET IN?
  Closing date for application: January 15 of the year in which the student hopes to participate
  Interview required: No
  Other procedures: Completed application form endorsed by an academic official (including a statement from the student outlining current and long-range plans for a career in engineering, mathematics, or the sciences.)
  A character reference form.
  A listing of courses currently being taken.
  Two confidential reference forms sent individually (or letters of recommendation).
  Transcripts of all college work.
  When will I know about application: Usually by March 1

WHERE CAN I GET MORE INFORMATION?
  Write: Bryan B. Valett, Program Director, NORCUS, 100 Sprout Road, Richland, WA 99352
  Phone: (509) 946-3588

ST. PAUL'S SCHOOL

Concord, New Hampshire

WHAT'S IT DO?
  Purpose and goals:
    Founded in 1856, St. Paul's School is a four-year co-educational boarding school of the highest academic standards and achievements. Equally important, it is a community of 495 boys and girls; 80 teachers and their families; and over 160 members of the staff. Teachers and students come from all parts of the country as well as from foreign countries, and they represent various economic, racial, and religious groups. Although the school has a traditional but informal relationship with the Episcopal Church, it welcomes--as it always has--faculty and students of all faiths and creeds. The school has a diversity that is a powerful and constructive force in its life, and it continues to seek people of conviction and commitment.

WHAT CAN I DO?
  An intern program is sponsored by St. Paul's School for young men and women interested in the teaching profession, yet without experience. Interns participate in all of the activities of boarding school life, from the classroom, to athletics, to dormitories, to the multiple activities of the school community. An intern is assigned his or her academic work through one teacher, generally the head of the department for the subject in which the intern is interested. The intern attends many classes given by many

different teachers in all academic subjects and discusses with them thereafter the strengths and weaknesses of those classes. From time to time in the course of the fall term the intern teaches a single class on a given day or may teach a given class for several days running, with the regular teacher present, and later, with the regular teacher absent. By the winter term, if in the judgment of the teacher and the intern it is appropriate, the intern may take on his or her own class or classes, being responsible for all of the activities, including the grading of the students. Naturally enough, such teaching would be under close supervision. An intern is expected to help with the athletic program of the school and, generally, to help with the supervision of dormitories. Each intern is also expected to accept other significant responsibilities of the faculty, such as regular attendance at Chapel and the presiding over a table in one of the dining rooms four nights each week.

CAN I GET IN?
  Academic requirements: Upper college level
  Length of commitment to internship: One school year

DO I GET PAID, EXPENSES, OR CREDIT?
  An intern is furnished living quarters (including all utilities except telephone), meals in the school dining room, and a stipend of $3,400, as well as coverage under the "usual and customary" and major medical health insurance of Blue Cross/Blue Shield.

HOW DO I GET IN?
  Closing date for application: Interns should send a resume and letter stating their interests in January or February.
  Interview required: Yes
  When will I know about application: Late April or May

WHERE CAN I GET MORE INFORMATION?
  Write: Philip Burnham, Vice Rector, St. Paul's School, Concord, NH 03301
  Read: Teaching at St. Paul's School, a brochure

POLITICAL DISCOVERY

Boston, Massachusetts

WHAT'S IT DO?
  Purpose and goals:
    Political Discovery is a state-funded education program designed to bring together about 60 students and 6 teachers from urban, suburban, private, public and parochial junior high and high schools into a government center to learn first-hand about the political process as they learn about each other. For one week, students will meet with government officials, lobbyists, media people and community organizers, using government buildings, banks, insurance companies, and art galleries as classrooms. Eight programs are conducted between November and May.
  Current projects and activities:
    Political Discovery is running eight programs with emphasis on law and courts, legislative process, women in politics, and legislative level.
  Number of permanent staff: 4   Annual budget: $139,315
  Publications: Resource Book

WHAT CAN I DO?
  Internship descriptions:
    The duties and responsibilities of this job will vary from administrative to personal contact with students and teachers. More specifically, the work includes: pre-program tasks--scheduling in-school orientations, phone contact with teachers, gathering information from the participating schools, and keeping portfolio materials up-to-date; during-program tasks--assuming the role of a small group discussion leader, assisting to plan large group discussions and activities, maintaining constant interaction with students and teachers and meeting with speakers in advance of sessions; post-program tasks--writing a brief analysis of the program and tallying evaluation results. Telephone skills are essential and typing helpful. If you are not experienced, you will be able to learn on the job. Interns can expect to learn how an educational program is put together, about politics in Boston, and about dealing with people--while having fun in the process.

CAN I GET IN?
  Academic requirements: Junior in high school   Age: 15
  Length of commitment to internship: Semester or year
  Number of 1978 interns: 4   Number planned for the future: About the same

DO I GET PAID, EXPENSES, OR CREDIT?
  College credit: Can be arranged

HOW DO I GET IN?
  Closing date for application: January   Interview required: No
  When will I know about application: Within two weeks of your request

WHERE CAN I GET MORE INFORMATION?
  Write: Albie Davis, Political Discovery, 7 Marshall Street, Boston, MA 02108
  Phone: (617) 742-0180
  Read: Resource Book, Staff Profiles, available upon request from above address

UNITED STATES NATIONAL STUDENT ASSOCIATION

Washington, D.C.

WHAT'S IT DO?
  Purpose and goals:
    The United States National Student Association (USNSA) is the oldest and largest confederation of student governments in the United States. Educational programs and services are coordinated by student officers and professional staff at the national headquarters in Washington. The USNSA, a registered Federal lobby, engages in an ongoing, year 'round effort to provide information, resources, and support services to students working for change on educational and social issues.
  Current projects and activities:
    Legislation. The lobbying director keeps a legislative watch on Congress for pending legislation which will affect students.
    Congress and Conferences. Each year, USNSA sponsors a lobbying conference in April and a Congress in August.
    Information Service. Collection, analysis, and dissemination of current accurate information on a regular basis is one of the primary jobs of the Association.
    Third World Desk. Conducts research, lobbying, and organizing efforts to combat racial discrimination.
    Women's Deak. Designed to develop publications, research, and lobby to combat sexism in higher education.
  Number of permanent staff: 4   Annual budget: $275,000
  Publications: <u>National Student Association Magazine</u>, a monthly

WHAT CAN I DO?
  Internship descriptions:
    Each intern is assigned to a regular staff person or officer to work on projects which will provide the student with a basis in which to place her or his previous classroom experience. The range of activities with which interns may become involved is virtually limitless. You will have plenty of opportunities to lobby on Capitol Hill if you are working on current legislation. You will have the chance to observe "mark-up" sessions in Congress (where bills are literally all marked-up) and to help develop testimony to be delivered at Congressional hearings. You can research issues using all the resources the city of Washington has to offer: George Washington University, the Library of Congress, the Center for Law and Social Policy. More specifically, some of the projects interns have been involved in include lobbying members of Congress on the minimum wage bill, re-organizing the National Student Association Information Service, and working with the Coalition for Women and Girls in Education. USNSA leaders and staff continue the Association's long and proud tradition of fighting for open and equal access to education, combatting sexism, racism, and economic exploitation, and supporting struggles for human rights and dignity around the world and in the United States.

CAN I GET IN?
  Academic requirements: College student
  Length of commitment to internship: Semester or year
  Number of 1978 interns: 12   Number planned for the future: About the same

DO I GET PAID, EXPENSES, OR CREDIT?
  College credit: Can be arranged and most interns receive credit

HOW DO I GET IN?
  Closing date for application: On-going
  Interview required: Preferred
  When will I know about application: No formal plan

WHERE CAN I GET MORE INFORMATION?
  Write: Diane Hamlin, Internship Coordinator, U.S. National Student Association, 2115 S Street, N.W., Washington, DC 20008
  Phone: (202) 332-8428
  Read: National Student Association Magazine

THE ENVIRONMENTAL CLUSTER

Chesapeake Bay Center for Environmental Studies
Defenders of Wildlife
Environmental Action Foundation
Environmental Learning Center
Friends of the Earth
National Parks and Conservation Association
National Wildlife Federation
National Wildlife Federation Raptor Information Center
Nature Conservancy
Rachel Carson Trust for the Living Environment
Student Conservation Program

CHESAPEAKE BAY CENTER FOR ENVIRONMENTAL STUDIES

SMITHSONIAN INSTITUTION

Edgewater, Maryland

WHAT'S IT DO?
  Purpose and goals:
    Encompassing 2,600 acres, the Chesapeake Bay Center is on the Rhode River seven miles south of Annapolis, Maryland. The Center is engaged in a long-range study of the Rhode River watershed and its estuary. This research program includes both aquatic and terrestrial studies and is concerned with the impact of humans upon the functioning of the ecosystem. An expanding environmental education program focuses on research in outdoor centered learning, as well as serving adult groups, school children, and college students.
  Current projects and activities:
    Upland ecology, estuarine ecology of environmental research, and watershed studies, plus an information transfer program.
  Number of permanent staff: 42   Annual budget: $606,000

WHAT CAN I DO?
  Upland Ecology Program:
    This describes and interprets ecological patterns characteristic of an area that once was entirely covered by deciduous forest, but which now is a complex mosaic of cropland, pasture, and regenerating forest.
      Project 1. Structure and function of ant communities. This research seeks to quantify the relationship between community diversity, abundance, and trophic organization on the one hand and biotic and physical factors on the other. In addition to making field observations of behavioral interactions within and between ant species, the student will conduct a standardized sampling program to monitor ant activity and abundance of ants, will help in the statistical analysis of data and will be expected to present a discussion of her or his work to an informal seminar group toward the end of the project period.
      Project 2. Upland plant ecology. The student will participate in planning ecology projects at either the populations, community, or ecosystem level.
  Estuarine Ecology:
    This develops a better understanding of the biotic responses to physical/chemical factors in given sections of the Rhode River estuary.
      Project 1. The structure and function of microbial communities in a terrestrial-aquatic ecosystem. The goal of the overall program is to determine the effects of environmental changes on phytoplankton and bacteria, especially those changes resulting from artificial perturbations. Current projects include investigations of the Rhode River estuary and its watershed. The student will be responsible for collecting and processing water samples and quantitatively estimating population density of bacteria and algae, using appropriate techniques for identification.
      Project 2. Estuarine fish population. A study of the population dynamics of selected indigenous fish of the Chesapeake Bay will be made. The fish will be studied during their spawning period and a

variety of parameters investigated including sex, age, weight, length and previous growth rates. A seminar in which these activities are summarized and related to environmental studies in general will be required.

Project 3. Chemistry of air-water interface. The purpose of this project is to undertake a comparative study of concentrations of certain chemical material at the water microsurface and in bulk water solutions. A screen sampling technique for surface water will be used. Depending on the individual project, students will be able to learn and operate analytical instruments such as atomic absorption, gas chromatograph or u.v.-visible spectrophotometer.

Project 4. Estuarine Ecology - U.S. Geological Survey Potomac River Program. In the laboratory, where most of the time will be spent, benthic samples will be sorted, species identified and specific biomass determined. Some preliminary preparation work for future chemical analyses of the fauna will be performed. Biological and physical-chemical data will be processed and statistically analyzed.

Environmental Education:
Three objectives characterize the major thrusts of this program: 1) to improve the quality and effectiveness of outdoor-centered environmental education through research and experimentation in curriculum design; 2) to convey the results and implications of the Center's scientific research efforts to the general public and agencies involved in environmental decision making; and 3) to achieve a better understanding of human behavior in outdoor settings. A number of projects have been planned to investigate the psychological effects of experience in the out-of-doors. This work should result in a better understanding of how people respond to outdoor settings, and consequently suggest ways to improve outdoor environmental education programming.

Student-Generated Projects:
The Center's Work/Learn program is not primarily designed to sponsor independent projects. It will consider, however, applications from mature students who wish to pursue a more independent course of study within the projects outlined in these pages.

CAN I GET IN?
  Academic requirements: Upperclass college students, competitive abilities, and interest
  Length of commitment to internship: Semester or year
  Number of 1978 interns: Several in each project
  Number planned for the future: Same

DO I GET PAID, EXPENSES, OR CREDIT?
  Pay: Interns will receive a stipend of $40 per week and living accommodations.
  College credit: Can be arranged

HOW DO I GET IN?
  Closing date for application: For projects starting in September, deadline is previous July 1; for projects beginning in February, deadline is previous December 1.
  Special procedures: The completed material should consist of an application, transcripts from the indicated schools, an essay, and two

referee letters. Referees will be asked to comment on the essay and add any additional appropriate comments. As part of the application, each applicant will be asked to submit a short essay (4-6 pages) outlining past and present interests and academic and nonacademic experience.

WHERE CAN I GET MORE INFORMATION?
  Write: Work/Learn Program, Chesapeake Bay Center for Environmental Studies, Smithsonian Institution, Route 4, Box 622, Edgewater, MD 21037
  Phone: (301) 798-4424

DEFENDERS OF WILDLIFE

Washington, D.C.

WHAT'S IT DO?
  Purpose and goals:
    Defenders of Wildlife is a Washington-based, national environmental organization devoted to protecting wildlife. Its first goal is to represent the best interests of wildlife before national decision-makers. It strongly advocates an ecological approach to wildlife conservation, in which every animal species is regarded as an indispensable part of an interdependent ecosystem. Defenders is a quick-acting, responsive organization capable of generating media attention to critical and timely wildlife issues.
  Current projects and activities:
    In the legislative arena, Defenders fights to protect the Endangered Species Act; to set aside new national parks, national wildlife refuges, and other wild lands in Alaska; and for passage of trapping reform, predator protection and non-game wildlife legislation. Defenders is currently represented on national citizen's task force efforts to analyze and reform the National Wildlife Refuge System and predator control practices.
  Number of permanent staff: 18   Annual budget: $1,462,800
  Publications: <u>Defenders</u>, bimonthly magazine

WHAT CAN I DO?
  Internship descriptions:
    Interns are requested to initiate one or more projects of their own choosing aimed at benefitting wildlife. Project areas have included analysis of Federal regulations concerning endangered species, marine mammals, and waterfowl hunting; studying Federal budget plans for the National Wildlife Refuge System; and preparing (possibly delivering) position statements for congressional hearings. In general, intern projects will help the individuals involved learn the workings of the national conservation and environmental movement and demonstrate citizen influence on governmental decision-making. Results of student progress will be evaluated continually by Defenders' staff. Most interns initiate projects to mitigate or resolve some threat to wildlife, or to promote positive changes beneficial to wildlife. The issues may involve existing legislation, Federal regulations and enforcement, or the need for research and effective protection. In the course of the project, activities may include attendance at meetings or hearings, completion of research and

reports or formal comments to government agencies, lobbying and public awareness campaigns (press releases and action alerts) to influence legislators or administrators.

CAN I GET IN?
  Academic requirements: Two years of college experience is preferred
  Length of commitment to internship: One semester or year considered
  Number of 1978 interns: 8
  Number planned for the future: About the same

DO I GET PAID, EXPENSES, OR CREDIT?
  Expenses: Some transportation expenses are covered while at work.
  College credit: Can be arranged

HOW DO I GET IN?
  Closing date for application: On-going
  Interview required: No
  Other procedures: A cover letter should include the following: 1) reasons for wanting to pursue an internship with us, and goals of the experience; 2) major areas of interest; 3) academic background and previous experience with conservation activities; 4) familiarity with environmental laws such as the Endangered Species Act, Marine Mammal Protection Act, and National Environmental Policy Act.
  When will I know about application: As soon as possible

WHERE CAN I GET MORE INFORMATION?
  Write: Toby Cooper, Wildlife Programs Director, Defenders of Wildlife, 1244 19th Street, N.W., Washington, DC 20036
  Phone: (202) 659-9510
  Read: Back issues of Defenders

ENVIRONMENTAL ACTION FOUNDATION

Washington, D.C.

WHAT'S IT DO?
  Purpose and goals:
    Environmental Action Foundation is a tax-exempt, public interest organization which has gained a national reputation as a source of quality research and educational materials on a wide variety of environmental issues. Over the past seven years, EAF has worked to give citizens the tools they need to understand and actively participate in complex environmental debates. The organization has maintained a strong local orientation, unique among national environmental groups, by providing technical and organizational expertise to community activists and groups. At the same time, EAF has a broad enough focus to examine the public policies which underlie environmental problems and to integrate environmental concerns with work on energy and resource shortages, threats of job loss, and consumer needs.
  Current projects and activities:
    EAF projects now focus on electric utilities, solid waste and materials conservation, deposit legislation, the B-1 bomber, transportation, water

quality, solar energy, and nuclear power.
Number of permanent staff: 9   Annual budget: $250,000
Publications: The Powerline, a monthly; Garbage Guide, irregular; many reports.

WHAT CAN I DO?
　Internship descriptions:
　　Utility Project internship. Now in touch with over 1,000 citizens' groups across the country, the Project is helping to challenge nuclear plants and other power facilities, oppose higher rates and adjustment clauses, work for rate structure reform, and establish publicly-owned power systems. The internship is essentially a research and writing position in support of an existing project being done by the utility staff or in background preparation for a future staff project. It often involves research in Federal Power Commission files, utility industry data, information from local citizens, and synthesis of data in final written form for use by the utility staff and by local contacts. Useful background for this internship would be: 1) Knowledge of economics, finance, or accounting; 2) Previous work on utility or energy issues; 3) writing ability; 4) Experience with citizens' organizations.
　　Legislative Project internship. The intern will be working under the Field Director and Media Coordinator to increase constituent pressure, organize targeted districts, and assist in local and national media work. Ideal qualifications: a person with political and citizen organizing interests (not necessarily direct experience), who can write and communicate fairly well, and who does not mind a fair amount of support work. Major tasks: 1) Update Environmental Action's press list (calling and talking with about 500 Washington reporters); 2) Assist in writing news releases and in legwork associated with news releases (for example, hand-delivering to reporters, etcetera) 3) Compile materials on working with press and assist local citizens to develop press expertise in local districts; 4) Assist in editing and procuring op-ed pieces or features; 5) Collect, compile, and combine lists of activists from various sources and contact activists in key Congressional districts; 6) Assist in mobilizing these coalitions when important environmental votes are about to occur in Congress.
　　Solid Waste Project internship. EAF's Solid Waste Project serves as the national clearinghouse for citizen organizations concerned about solid waste issues. In October 1976, Congress passed the new Resource Conservation and Recovery Act. Provisions in the Act call for the consideration of low technology approaches in dealing with solid waste regionally. The project staff is in an ideal position to utilize its expertise, communication network and experience in this issue to see that the provisions become a working reality. While monitoring the various stages of development of guidelines and studies mandated under the new law, "A Citizen's Guide to the Act" will be written to encourage public participation at the local and state level. The intern will survey and compile available information on low technology source separation systems (separation of recyclables at the home/office/business). This would take the form of setting up resource files, generating fact sheets on the concept in general, and writing up more detailed information sheets on current projects and success stories of various communities. Previous work on environmental, specifically solid

waste issues, would be helpful. Writing ability as well as research (information-seeking) skills and experience with citizen organizations is desirable.

Deposit Legislation Clearinghouse internship. Where can someone in Hawaii get information on a Michigan law concerning throwaway bottles and cans? The National Clearinghouse on Deposit Legislation helps environmentalists implement returnable beverage container programs in their communities or states. The clearinghouse intern will answer correspondence; compile material for the newsletter; and research new developments in the bottle bill controversy. Closely involved with several different state efforts to pass legislation, the intern will learn a great deal about campaign strategy, an essential skill for both grass roots organizers and environmentalists. Writing and research skills are essential, graphic skills desirable. Knowledge of campaign tactics and familiarity with grass roots organizing would also be helpful.

CAN I GET IN?
  Academic requirements: College student   Age: 18
  Length of commitment to internship: Semester or year
  Number of 1978 interns: 12
  Number planned for the future: Same

DO I GET PAID, EXPENSES, OR CREDIT?
  College credit: Can be arranged

HOW DO I GET IN?
  Closing date for application: On-going
  Interview required: No
  When will I know about application: About one month before start of internship

WHERE CAN I GET MORE INFORMATION?
  Write: Dick Munson, Environmental Action Foundation, 724 DuPont Circle Building, Washington, DC 20036
  Phone: (202) 659-9682
  Read: Send for list of publications at above address including three newsletters.

ENVIRONMENTAL LEARNING CENTER
Isabella, Minnesota

WHAT'S IT DO?
  Purpose and goals:
    Each year thousands of Minnesota school children spend a full week of their normal school time at the Environmental Learning Center. With their own teachers and frequently parents, as well as the help of Center staff, they participate in courses which depend primarily on the out-of-doors as a classroom. A major goal is to provide environmental education opportunities for as many people as possible. The Center believes that a substantial program of environmental education, with outdoor education as the focus, will result in people living in greater harmony with nature.
  Current projects and activities:
    Resident environmental education programs, weekend environmental education programs for adults, intern program for college students.
  Number of permanent staff: 5

WHAT CAN I DO?
  There is no one typical week that can be described. One week may see an intern working by helping with a canoeing lesson, going on an overnight hike with 12 students and their teacher, teaching rock climbing, then helping with orienteering and perception lessons. That weekend the same intern may be liaison for an adult program dealing with wild foods or timber wolves. The work interns do falls into four primary areas, and a few minor areas also. The primary areas are: 1) To serve as a liaison for school groups and for weekend adult groups. 2) To aid teachers. The teachers have worked out their schedule and lessons but need help so that there are not large groups of students all trying to see, feel and touch the same item. 3) To teach. There are some activities that can be taught very effectively at the Center that teachers are unfamiliar with. In these cases teachers usually ask an intern to conduct the lesson, and the teacher serves as an aide. 4) To work on a Center directed project. Interns generally assume responsibility for some aspect of the Center's operation. This ranges from being in charge of trail food, to keeping track of, and repairing, equipment.

CAN I GET IN?
  Academic requirements: Most are upperclass college students. Majors in recreation, outdoor education, biology are helpful but not necessary.
  Length of commitment to internship: Semester or quarter
  Number of 1978 interns: 23
  Number planned for future: Up to 30

DO I GET PAID, EXPENSES, OR CREDIT?
  Expenses: Board and room provided
  College credit: Yes, intern must get college credit.

HOW DO I GET IN?
  Closing date for application:
    Fall (September 5 through November 15): apply by April 15
    Winter (January 2 through March 20): apply by November 1
    Spring (March 15 through May 31): apply by February 1
    Summer (June 1 through August 15): apply by April 1

Interview required: No
When will I know about application: About 10 days after closing dates above

WHERE CAN I GET MORE INFORMATION?
  Write: Dr. John Y. Jackson, Program Coordinator, Environmental Learning
    Center, Box 191 A, Isabella, MN 55607
  Phone: (218) 293-4345 or 293-4185

FRIENDS OF THE EARTH

Washington, D.C.

WHAT'S IT DO?
  Purpose and goals:
    The Legislative Office of the Friends of the Earth is coordinated with
    grassroots action throughout the United States. It has four registered
    conservation lobbyists and expends a major part of its funds in advocating
    good environmental legislation and urging public support of it. FOE is
    dedicated to advocating the rights of nature, to enhancing conservation
    in the United States and internationally and to preserving, restoring and
    initiating a more rational use of the earth.
  Current projects and activities:
    The lobbying office of FOE focuses on national legislation on energy,
    Alaska public interest lands, recombinant DNA, Endangered Species Act.
  Number of permanent staff: 9   Annual budget: $150,000
  Publications: a newsletter

WHAT CAN I DO?
  Intern descriptions:
    Friends of the Earth is not an envelope stuffing opportunity--internships
    entail lobbying, researching, as much as you personally want to make of
    this opportunity. In the past people who have interned for FOE have gone
    on to secure employment either directly in the environmental field or with
    Congressmen or Senators. Interns are placed under the personal supervision
    of staff members. There is an effort to match the intern's interests with
    the needs of the staff. The work varies.

CAN I GET IN?
  Academic requirements: None
  Length of commitment to internship: Semester or year
  Number of 1978 interns: 6   Number planned for the future: Open

DO I GET PAID, EXPENSES, OR CREDIT?
  College credit: Can be arranged

HOW DO I GET IN?
  Closing date for application: April 1   Interview required: No
  Other procedures: Write a resume and cover letter expressing your specific
    environmental interests, and a general idea of when you will be available.
  When will I know about application: As soon as possible

WHERE CAN I GET MORE INFORMATION?
  Write: Jeffrey Knight, Friends of the Earth, 620 C Street, S.E., Washington,
    DC 20003
  Phone: (202) 543-4312

NATIONAL PARKS AND CONSERVATION ASSOCIATION

Washington, D.C.

WHAT'S IT DO?
  Purpose and goals:
    NPCA is a private, non-profit environmental organization concerned with
    the protection and preservation of the national parks as well as with the
    conservation of the whole environment. NPCA is not a government agency.
    Rather it is a monitor organization, unencumbered by special interest
    pressures. NPCA is the major bulwark in resisting pressures for over-
    development and commercialization of our parks and monuments, because it
    believes that the natural values and wilderness ecosystems are the greatest
    assets of the National Park System.
  Current projects and activities:
    Activities include a magazine which has a circulation of over 60,000;
    testimony presented on invitation before Congressional committees; and
    pressure on the executive branch of the government by its members and
    staff. Past activities and projects include the opposition to construction
    of ecologically unsound dams. NPCA was instrumental in the successful
    campaign to scuttle 13 out of the 16 dams planned by the Army Corps of
    Engineers on the Potomac.
  Number of permanent staff: 25
  Publications: The Environmental Journal, a monthly magazine

WHAT CAN I DO?
  Interns attend Congressional hearings and governmental meetings, take part
  in meetings and projects with other environmental groups, review environmental impact statements and legislation, write reports and testimony for
  submission to Congressional or executive committees, handle general correspondence, brief NPCA staff on activities and projects, and, of course, the
  nitty-gritty work that everyone in public service organizations must do.
  They are supervised in their work by the NPCA staff member in charge of the
  area to which they are assigned. Internships are usually tailored to the
  individual capabilities and experience. Some of the issue areas that interns
  have handled are national parks, wildlife, water resources, endangered
  plants, energy, international environmental affairs, and outer continental
  shelf development.

CAN I GET IN?
  Academic requirements: College student   Age: 19
  Length of commitment to internship: Semester or year; "the longer the intern
    is with NPCA, the more she or he learns and is able to contribute."

DO I GET PAID, EXPENSES, OR CREDIT?
  College credit: Can be arranged
  Expenses: Work-related expenditure

HOW DO I GET IN?
  Closing date for application: July 15 for fall internship and February 1
    for spring internship
  Interview required: Preferred

Other procedures: In addition to a letter or telephone call, the applicant should send a resume that includes past environmental experience, either practical or academic, any skills that would be useful to the internship, description of areas of special expertise and an indication of the time period during which the intern would be available. Writing samples are required from interns wishing to work with the magazine staff.

When will I know about application: Within a week after the application is completed.

WHERE CAN I GET MORE INFORMATION?
  Write: Rita Molyneaux, Administrative Assistant, National Parks and Conservation Association, 1701 18th Street, N.W., Washington, DC 20009
  Phone: (202) 265-2717
  Read: National Parks and Conservation Magazine: The Environmental Journal

NATIONAL WILDLIFE FEDERATION

Washington, D.C.

WHAT'S IT DO?
  Purpose and goals:
    The National Wildlife Federation is a nongovernmental, nationwide conservation education organization concerned with conserving natural resources and preserving a quality environment. It is non-profit and tax-exempt. The Federation has 3,500,000 members and supporters. This broad membership provides direction and strength.
    As an instrument of democracy in a free society, the National Wildlife Federation is organized to stimulate a proper public attitude and appreciation regarding the wise use and management of all natural resources. If the United States is to maintain a position of world leadership and survive, its citizens must be competent to appraise the values and importance of all resources, and learn to husband and wisely manage them in perpetuity. Environmental education, therefore, is recognized by the National Wildlife Federation as the principal tool to reach these objectives.
  Current projects and activities:
    Publishing the magazines National Wildlife, International Wildlife, and Ranger Rick's Nature Magazine. A separate guide helps teachers integrate Ranger Rick's into the instructional program.
    Using the law, through litigation if necessary, to guard the public interest in wise resource management. Wetlands drainage, destructive Federal highways and dams, ocean pollution, coal development, and public land use are among fields in which the Federation has taken legal action.
    Preparing slide programs and audiovisual materials for use in environmental education programs by schools and individual organizations.
    Publishing an Environmental Quality Index, an annual assessment of the quality of life.
    Preparing and distributing annually, without charge or for nominal fees when requested in quantity, over two million pieces of educational

literature (including Wildlife Week material) to children, teachers, and others.
Preparing and distributing, upon request and without charge, Conservation News, a semi-monthly publication on conservation issues.
Preparing and distributing to Associate Members, on request and without charge, Conservation Report, a weekly digest of the status of environmental legislation and analysis of some of the major environmental issues facing the nation.
Publishing annually the Conservation Directory, a listing by name, address, and title of personnel engaged in conservation work at national and state levels, government and nongovernment, American and Canadian.
Publishing bimonthly a Club Program Bulletin that suggests program ideas and meeting material items for local conservation club activity.
Providing a family nature vacation, the Conservation Summit, a week of outdoor activities and recreation in mountain settings; also sponsoring 12-day environmental education camps and backpack trips, for boys and girls aged 8 to 16.
Operating a Raptor Information Center to protect bald eagle habitat, increase communication among people interested in raptors (birds of prey), and encourage support of priority research.
Sponsoring, since 1938, the annual observance of "National Wildlife Week."
Annually distributing millions of sheets of Wildlife Conservation stamps and nature-related items authentically depicting natural subjects, such as birds, mammals, fish, insects, and flowers, with educational messages.
Maintaining a staff of conservationists to coordinate Federation efforts on regional, state, national, and international levels.
Certifying backyards of homeowners who provide wildlife habitat by consistently furnishing food, water, shelter, and nesting places for birds, small mammals, and amphibians.
Maintaining a wildlife library in Washington, D.C., open to the public.
Giving individuals the opportunity to contribute land or funds to perpetuate wildlife and the quality of nature through "Planned Giving" and "Land Heritage" programs.
Preparing annually, for free distribution, the booklet Compensation in the Fields of Fish and Wildlife Management.

Number of permanent staff: 20 in conservation division
Annual budget: $20 million
Publications: National Wildlife, Ranger Rick's Magazine, International Wildlife, Conservation News, Conservation Report, and many more.

WHAT CAN I DO?
Internship descriptions:
Most of an intern's time is spent researching environmental policy issues. The kind of research undertaken by interns depends on their ability, background, interests, and the needs of the Federation and the environmental community. The results of this research appear in the Conservation

Report, published weekly during periods when the Congress is in session. This requires attending hearings and observing floor debates on environmental issues before Congress. Other responsibilities include monitoring environmental policy decisions, attending briefings and seminars, helping draft testimony to be presented by the Federation to Congressional and executive panels, writing for some of the Federation's other publications, and assisting generally in the activities of the Conservation Division. In some cases, interns will be registered as lobbyists and will work to influence specific pieces of environmental legislation in the Congress. Only a small part of an intern's time is spent in routine office work. Interns are given as much responsibility as they can handle and are considered for most purposes as professional staff members by the Federation.

CAN I GET IN?
  Academic requirements: No special background required but usually upper-class college students in the social sciences, journalism and natural resources related majors have the best chance of acceptance.
  Length of commitment to internship: 12, 20, or 26 weeks
  Number of 1978 interns: 15 stipend internships and 3 non-stipend
  Number planned for the future: About the same with a few more non-stipend interns

DO I GET PAID, EXPENSES, OR CREDIT?
  Pay: 15 interns will receive $105 per week for undergraduates
  College credit: Can be arranged; most who intern do receive college credit.

HOW DO I GET IN?
  Closing date for application: April 1 is the application deadline for a 26 week internship, and non-stipend interns may apply anytime.
  Interview required: No
  When will I know about application: Two weeks after the application deadline

WHERE CAN I GET MORE INFORMATION?
  Write: Sheldon Kinsel, Director, Conservation Intern Program, National Wildlife Federation, 1412 16th Street, N.W., Washington, DC 20036
  Phone: (202) 797-6862
  Read: Publications published by the Federation listed above.

NATIONAL WILDLIFE FEDERATION RAPTOR INFORMATION CENTER
Washington, D.C.

WHAT'S IT DO?
  Purpose and goals:
    The National Wildlife Federation is organized to stimulate a proper public attitude and appreciation regarding the wise use and management of all natural resources.
  Current projects and activities:
    1) Identification of critical bald eagle habitat.
    2) Creation of keyworded, computer-based bibliography on bald eagles.
    3) Identification of sources of raptor literature, with emphasis on unpublished or hard-to-find references.
    4) Creation of a reference source, by state, dealing with bald eagle historic nestings, environmental problems, and non-breeding roosts.
  Number of permanent staff: Part of National Wildlife Federation staff of 20 in conservation division.
  Annual budget: Part of National Wildlife Federation budget of $20 million

WHAT CAN I DO?
  Internship descriptions:
    Interns perform literature-oriented functions which are supportive to the Center's overall goals to conserve our birds of prey. Projects vary with individual program objectives and the qualifications of the intern; however, some potential projects that interns can work on include the 4 listed above.

CAN I GET IN?
  Academic requirements: Applicants should be upperclass college students, but more importantly, they should be particularly capable of independent work. Some background in biology, computer programming, information speciality, bibliographic research or an avid interest in the welfare of birds of prey is desirable.
  Length of commitment to internship: Open-ended and up to a year

DO I GET PAID, EXPENSES, OR CREDIT?
  College credit can be arranged; most who intern do receive college credit.

HOW DO I GET IN?
  Closing date for application: On-going, but internships start in January.
  Interview required: No.
  When will I know about application: Soon after it is completed with resume, references and cover letter.

WHERE CAN I GET MORE INFORMATION?
  Write: Dr. Jeffrey L. Lincer, Director, Raptor Information Center, National Wildlife Federation, 1412 16th Street, N.W., Washington, DC 20036
  Phone: (202) 797-6862

NATURE CONSERVANCY

Arlington, Virginia

WHAT'S IT DO?
  Purpose and goals:
    The Nature Conservancy is a national conservation organization whose object is to preserve and protect ecologically and environmentally significant lands and the diversity of life they support. The primary vehicle for achieving this goal is the acquisition of these unique areas. Although many of these natural areas have been transferred to other organizations for management, the Conservancy has retained direct stewardship responsibilities for approximately 660 preserves.
  Current projects and activities:
    1) Purchases land to promote intelligent land use.
    2) Develops comprehensive ecological land inventories to sound long range plans for development of these areas.
    3) Encourages state governmental acquisition and preservation of natural and historical sites.
  Number of permanent staff: 80
  Publications: On the Land, a monthly newsletter

WHAT CAN I DO?
  Internship descriptions:
    Annually, student interns are hired to conduct ecological evaluations and inventories on selected lands owned by the Conservancy. These students work on the preserves with the Conservancy's local volunteer stewardship committee.

CAN I GET IN?
  Academic requirements: College student
  Length of commitment to internship: Most are for the summer, but NC is receptive to a longer commitment.

DO I GET PAID, EXPENSES, OR CREDIT?
  Pay: Depending on experience and education, the interns are paid for their work.
  College credit: Most work for pay rather than credit, but college credit can be arranged.

HOW DO I GET IN?
  Closing date for application: On-going
  Other procedures: Send resume and letter to the main office and inquire about NC's other four regional offices.
  When will I know about application: No formal plan

WHERE CAN I GET MORE INFORMATION?
  Write: Anita H. Allen, Personnel and Administration, The Nature Conservancy, 1800 North Kent Street, Arlington, VA 22209
  Phone: (703) 524-3151

RACHEL CARSON TRUST FOR THE LIVING ENVIRONMENT

Washington, D.C.

WHAT'S IT DO?
  Purpose and goals:
    The Rachel Carson Trust for the Living Environment is an intelligence
    center focusing on chemical contamination of the environment, especially
    from pesticides. It gathers scientific data and interprets it for
    scientists, government committees and the public. Internationally, the
    Trust works with organizations and governments to alert them to the
    serious dangers of chemical pesticide use and to encourage the development
    of biological and integrated pest management programs.
  Current projects and activities:
    The Trust responds to public inquiries about pesticides. It prepares
    publications to inform the public of the danger of pesticides and other
    contaminants. It conducts conferences to disseminate accurate information
    to the concerned public, both here and abroad.
  Number of permanent staff: 3 professional staff members
  Annual budget: Around $10,000
  Publications: A Basic Guide to Pesticide Hazards; Down the Drain, a pamphlet

WHAT CAN I DO?
  Internship description:
    Work at the Trust differs from that of other environmental organizations.
    While alert to the broad implications of the global view, it is unique in
    its specialization on environmental effects of toxic chemicals. It
    functions as an intelligence and resource center for those taking direct
    action through hearings, law suits, education, and other pressures on
    public and private agencies and organizations. It collects and dissemi-
    nates information for its subscribers on subjects and in terms appropriate
    to the need of public understanding of the complex issues involved.
    Especially, it seeks to clarify misconceptions that often becloud them.

CAN I GET IN?
  Academic requirements: The Trust does not have an intern or volunteer
    program but it would like to have one in the future. Send in your resume,
    a letter stating why you are interested in this project and arrange for an
    interview and a plan of your own for an internship.

WHERE CAN I GET MORE INFORMATION?
  Write: Shirley A. Briggs, Executive Director, Rachel Carson Trust for the
    Living Environment, Inc., 8940 Jones Mill Road, Washington, DC 20015
  Phone: (301) 652-1877
  Read: A Basic Guide to Pesticide Hazards

STUDENT CONSERVATION PROGRAM

Charlestown, New Hampshire

WHAT'S IT DO?
  Purpose and goals:
    The Student Conservation Program was initiated in 1957 as a student response to the threatened over-use of America's park and forest resources. Through the program, thousands of young people have had the opportunity to offer assistance to the national parks and forests, providing services in wilderness conservation, historic preservation and visitor contact, which would not otherwise have been available.
  Current programs:
    High school and college students work with a number of agencies and organizations including 39 national forests and parks, the Merck Forest Foundation, the Appalachian Trail Conference and The Nature Conservancy.

WHAT CAN I DO?
  Job descriptions:
    High school students. You will live and work together with 10 to 15 other young people from different parts of the country and with experienced adult supervisors. You will be based at a remote campsite, where you will share in activities from routine camp duties to hiking several days with heavy packs. Resource people and environmentalists will come and share their knowledge and opinions with the group. It's a chance to learn, to work hard together, to have a good experience, and to help provide better care of the nation's parks and forests.
    If you are at least 18 years old, SCP offers the opportunity to be a Park or Forest Assistant in the national parks and forests, historic sites, seashores and monuments. You will be working directly with professionals, taking part in many of the same duties as the park or forest rangers. The particular projects differ with each site, but the program offers the chances to learn about the natural environment and to work with resource people in interpreting it to the public. It's a learning, growing experience that will require 30 hours of work a week, but also leaves you time to hike and explore on your own.

CAN I GET IN?
  Academic requirements: One program for high school students, and the other, the assistantship program, is for students after one year of college.
  Age: 16 for the high school group and 18 for the college group.
  Special: Good health and interested and willing to work in conservation.
  Length of commitment: Semester or year
  Number of 1978 assistants: 271 in the high school group and 208 were Park and Forest Assistants.
  Number planned for the future: Year-round volunteers are just starting and the program will be expanded.

DO I GET PAID, EXPENSES, OR CREDIT?
  Expenses: Volunteers are provided lodging and a food allowance plus their travel expenses to the site.
  College credit: Can be arranged for the year-round volunteer

HOW DO I GET IN?
  Closing date for application: Applications are due March 1 for a summer
    term, later for the fall term.
  Interview required: No
  When will I know about application: No formal plan

WHERE CAN I GET MORE INFORMATION?
  Write: Henry S. Francis, Jr., Executive Director, The Student Conservation
    Association, Inc., P.O. Box 550, Charlestown, NH 03603
  Phone: (603) 826-5206

THE GOVERNMENT-SPONSORED AGENCIES CLUSTER

Including city, state and Federal agencies

ACTION: Volunteers in Service to America
Alaska Bureau of Land Management
Atlanta Urban Corps
Boston City Council
California Coastal Commission
California Department of Alcoholic Beverage Control
California Department of Corrections
California Department of Education
California Department of Finance
California Department of Fish and Game
California Department of Food and Agriculture
California Department of Forestry
California Department of Health
California Department of Housing and Community Development
California Department of Motor Vehicles
California Department of Parks and Recreation
California Department of the Youth Authority
California Employment Development Department
California Highway Patrol
California Postsecondary Education Commission
California Public Utilities Commission
California State Library
California State Office of Substance Abuse
California State Water Resources Control Board
Connecticut General Assembly Legislative Intern Program
Kentucky Bureau of Corrections
Kentucky Office of Public Defender
Los Angeles City Volunteer Corps
Massachusetts Department of Corrections
Massachusetts Department of Food and Agriculture
Massachusetts Department of Mental Health
  Neighborhood Day School
Massachusetts House of Representatives -
  Representative James E. Smith
Metropolitan Washington Council of Governments
New York City Urban Corps
Rhode Island Intern Consortium
White House Fellowships

ACTION: VOLUNTEERS IN SERVICE TO AMERICA

Washington, D.C.

WHAT'S IT DO?
  Purpose and goals:
    Volunteers in Service to America (VISTA) was established in 1964 as a national corps of men and women to fight poverty in the United States. It began as a part of the Office of Economic Opportunity (the "War on Poverty"). Later, it was merged with the Peace Corps and several other volunteer service programs into ACTION.
  Current projects and activities:
    VISTA volunteers work in one of six general fields:
      1) Community Service. Most VISTA volunteers work in some area of improving community services to the poor. If assigned to a community organization project, the volunteer would be working with many different kinds of issues. They might include distribution of city or rural services, lack of health care facilities, utility rate reform, sub-standard housing, inadequate nutrition, women's rights, ethnic and cultural identity, or problems of crime. Volunteers might help with door-to-door organizing or spend much of their time researching regulations concerning one or more poverty issues. They might help develop more outreach programs to assist the poor. They could work with fund-raising efforts (anything from garage sales to grant proposals) or spend most of their time in public information work.
      2) Economic development. Volunteers work with low-income groups to help them become more economically self-sufficient. Some of the activities which this might involve are work with cooperatives, consumer stores, buying clubs, credit unions, handicraft production, and technical assistance to small business. Some of the projects require a sophisticated background in accounting, computer programming and the like. Other projects are geared to make use of volunteers who are interested in doing research, writing, and (in general) making available resource information.
      3) Knowledge/skills. Volunteers are not teachers, in the ordinary sense of the word. They are not in formal classrooms and teacher certification is not required. Some, however, work with Indian tribes to improve children's education. Others work in vocational education, youth services in Appalachia, physical education projects, programs for dropouts, and services to potential dropouts. VISTA's organize tutoring programs, alternative schools, and adult literacy classes.
      4) Health/nutrition. VISTA's, including nurses, work with grass roots organizations to help bring better health services to the poor. Malnutrition is a widespread problem among the poor. As a volunteer, one might help set up an outreach program for food stamp eligibility or help expand the services of a food club, or recruit volunteers for a meal program for the elderly.
      5) Legal rights. VISTA volunteers (mostly lawyers and some paralegals) are active in legal assistance projects nationwide. Among them are juvenile justice, civil legal problems of prisoners, legal services for the elderly poor, community legal education programs (including those for the Spanish speaking), assistance to cooperatives and

credit unions, and research regarding utilities.
6) Housing/energy conservation. VISTA's work with neighborhood groups on housing rehabilitation, tenants' rights, home repair, and energy conservation. VISTA architects and planners work in community design centers in many parts of the country.

Number of permanent staff: In the hundreds
Annual budget: Includes both ACTION funds and from cooperating agencies

WHAT CAN I DO?
There are almost as many options for services and different types of jobs as there are VISTA volunteers. Your background would be reviewed in terms of current project needs from one or more of the areas cited above.

CAN I GET IN?
Academic requirements: College training is helpful, but not required. Persons with special skills in health, accounting, law, group work are particularly desired but less experienced persons are picked for service each year. Spanish is helpful.
Age: 18
Length of commitment to program: Usual term is for one year; this may be extended where the volunteer wishes and the project is continuing.
Number of 1978 volunteers: 4,000
Number planned for the future: 4,000 a year

DO I GET PAID, EXPENSES, OR CREDIT?
College credit: Can be arranged
Expenses: VISTA volunteers receive a basic living allowance covering housing and food plus around $75 a month for incidental expenses.
Accrued allowance: VISTA volunteers receive an additional $50 for each month of service as a readjustment allowance.

HOW DO I GET IN?
Closing date for application: On-going   Interview required: No
When will I know about application: After references have been checked and application processed.
Training: Volunteers attend pre-service orientation sessions to prepare them for their assignments. Training often continues on the job.

WHERE CAN I GET MORE INFORMATION?
Write: Local ACTION recruiting offices. They are located in Boston; New York City; Rochester, New York; Washington; Atlanta; Philadelphia; Pittsburgh; Dallas; Denver; Austin; Chicago; Detroit; Columbus; Des Moines; Minneapolis; Kansas City, Kansas; Champaign, Illinois; Madison, Wisconsin; San Francisco; Los Angeles; Phoenix; Portland, Oregon; Seattle; and Honolulu. Look in the phone book, under "U. S. Government--ACTION."
Nationally: You may contact VISTA Recruiting Office, 1713 H Street, N.W., Washington, DC 20525
Phone: (800) 424-8580 (This is toll free, from any part of the country.)
Read: <u>VISTA: A Louder Voice for the Nation's Poor</u>

ALASKA BUREAU OF LAND MANAGEMENT

Anchorage, Alaska

WHAT'S IT DO?
  Purpose and goals:
    Each year the Bureau of Land Management appoints approximately 250
    applicants to seasonal fire fighting positions in Alaska.
  Current projects and activities:
    Seasonal projects to protect the land include the following positions:
    forestry aide technician, forestry technician, smokejumper, recreation
    technician, and biological technician.

WHAT CAN I DO?
  Forestry Aid Technician:
    Assists in forestry, range management, forest or range fire control work,
    or in related fields such as farming, ranching, fishing, or trapping for
    subsistence (Alaska only). The applicant must have some of the basic
    knowledges and skills related to the general fire control environment.
    Included is experience in warehousing, slash burning, handling fire equip-
    ment, and working around dispatching stations where the applicant could
    gain some basic knowledges and skills in the fire control field. The
    technician assists the staff with some combination of fire dispatching,
    fire prevention or presuppression, fire control or suppression.
  Recreation Technician:
    Assists the staff in such areas as forestry recreation, aquatic recreation,
    recreation area grounds maintenance, or wildlife recreation. The applicant
    must have a basic knowledge and understanding of natural resource manage-
    ment, as related to outdoor recreation: e.g., forestry, range management,
    forest and range fire control, farming or ranching, and surveying or
    engineering. This involves actual outdoor recreation management and
    conservation work similar to that performed to support professional
    scientific outdoor recreation programs. Activities include the management,
    regulation and use of public or Federally controlled outdoor recreation
    areas, research activities related to outdoor recreation use and manage-
    ment, or the leading and supervising of camping and nature groups in public
    use areas.
  Biological Technician:
    Assists the staff in fishery management, animal husbandry, range management,
    forestry, farming, ranching, and horticulture. This internship includes
    actual wildlife management and conservation work such as projects for the
    enhancement and protection of the wildlife resource and/or the mitigation
    of losses that result from environmental factors or other land used. Also
    habitat/land management studies or work that includes the impact upon the
    wildlife and fishery resource, or wildlife research activities.

CAN I GET IN?
  Academic requirements: Selection is made from the best qualified applicants,
    very competitive as many college students apply each year.
  Special: Students must be in sound physical and mental health.
  Length of commitment to internship: It varies according to forest fires,
    but the usual dates are from March through September.
  Number of 1978 seasonal employees: 300
  Number planned for the future: About the same

DO I GET PAID, EXPENSES, OR CREDIT?
  Pay: Ranges from $3.16 to $5.54 an hour for seasonal positions depending on qualifications.
  Expenses: Cost of living allowances are provided. Seasonal workers must live in government quarters and are assigned to duty stations where they are on 24-hour on-call status.
  College credit: No

HOW DO I GET IN?
  Closing date for application: Applicants will be accepted on a continuing basis beginning September 1. Those received from eligibles by the last day of each month will be referred to the selecting officials by the 10th of the following month with the first list issued January 10th. Applications will not be considered after March 15th.
  Interview required: No

WHERE CAN I GET MORE INFORMATION?
  Write: Sally R. Lohse, Personnel, Bureau of Land Management, Alaska State Office, 555 Cordova Street, Anchorage, AK 99501

ATLANTA URBAN CORPS

Atlanta, Georgia

WHAT'S IT DO?
  Purpose and goals:
    The Atlanta Urban Corps started as an idea of a group of student leaders in the city in 1967. They had heard of an "Urban Peace Corps" (which soon became the "New York Urban Corps"), started by John Lindsay, a few years earlier. The students started a long campaign for support, which resulted in funding from the City of Atlanta and the Southern Regional Education Board in late 1968. The purpose of the Corps is actually two-dimensional. First, it provides students with experiences that allow them to learn and grow at their own pace. An internship is an educational experience, and each intern can and must evaluate the learning benefits to him or her on a personal, individual basis. The second dimension is that of community service. Each internship is designed so that the intern, while gaining educational growth, can contribute in some concrete way or ways to the community. The agency assignment is only a starting point; each intern must carry it from there, and each supervisor must assist in the effort.
  Current projects and activities:
    Education, business, media and the arts, government, community services, community development projects, research and planning, health, mental health and special education, recreation, and counseling.

WHAT CAN I DO?
  In general, an internship is a work situation which has been structured to give a student the opportunity to gain experience related to his or her academic field of interest. An internship is oriented toward the student's gaining skills not ordinarily taught in a classroom, as well as toward providing needed services to the agency in which the internship assignment is carred out. Ideally, the experience is a balanced "service-learning"

one. AUC will place you in an internship position corresponding to one of the choices you list on your application. Placement is based on special skills, previous experience, academic background, personal interests and an interview with either an AUC staff member or (for non-local students) AUC representative. Frequently large numbers of students with basically the same skills and experience apply for the same types of internships. In these situations placement is often based on how early the application was received by AUC. GET YOUR APPLICATION IN EARLY!

CAN I GET IN?
  Academic requirements: College student   Experience: See above
  Length of commitment to internship: Semester or year
  Number of 1978 interns: 800 to 1,000
  Number planned for the future: Same

DO I GET PAID, EXPENSES, OR CREDIT?
  Pay: 60% of the students are funded through the College Work-Study program. A limited number of paid internships ($2.50 - $3.25 per hour) are available to students who do not qualify for CWSP funds.
  College credit: Can be arranged

HOW DO I GET IN?
  Closing date for application: Send it in as early as possible
  Interview required: If you can not come for a personal interview, a phone interview will be required.
  When will I know about application: One month before your arrival in Atlanta.

WHERE CAN I GET MORE INFORMATION?
  Write: AUC Internship Coordinator, Georgia State University, University Plaza, Atlanta, GA 30303
  Phone: Call person-to-person collect to the Internship Coordinator, (404) 658-3558.

BOSTON CITY COUNCIL

Boston, Massachusetts

WHAT'S IT DO?
  Purpose and goals:
    The Boston City Council is the legislative arm of the Boston City Government and performs a watch-dog function over the executive branch. The major power of the Council is the approval of the budget, but it also drafts and sponsors legislation affecting the City Government. Council members spend a large portion of their time responding to citizen complaints, meeting with various community groups, sponsoring hearings on City issues, and serving in a volunteer capacity on advisory boards.
  Current projects and activities:
    On a daily basis, the Council's nine members, with help of aides, handle varying constituent requests. Each member is responsible to every voter and resident in an at-large system. Pending issues, in addition to daily business, include such things as rent control changes, equalized property assessments, or replacement site for a jail involved in a Federal suit.
  Number of permanent staff: 9 plus 19 legislative aides to Council members
  Annual budget: $149,528 plus $269,352 for aides
  Publications: Annual reports of city agencies and copies of ordinances

WHAT CAN I DO?
  Internship descriptions:
    Legislative internship. A student working in this office will perform a wide variety of tasks, but will concentrate on handling constituent complaints and doing research. Students generally direct the constituent to the city agency which can help with the complaint or help reduce red-tape by personally contacting the agency. The research is both legal and issue oriented. Interns also spend time writing press releases and letters, attending committee hearings, drafting resolutions, and doing office work.
    Volunteer Researcher internship. Interns will help in carrying out regular and special assignments for a City Councillor, aides to Councillors, the chief of research or Council staff aides. Functions will be varied. Among them will be monitoring city, state or court agency hearings on public issues before the City Council or matters that might become business of the Council. Assistants may help in daily synopsizing newspapers to help inform Council members of governmental developments elsewhere and acquaint them with innovative trends in municipal affairs. From time to time they will have opportunity to observe City Council meetings and Council committee hearings. Many of the opportunities will depend upon the time of the year involved in the internship.

CAN I GET IN?
  Academic requirements: Usually college students   Age: 17 to 23
  Experience: Not necessary, but an interest in government is helpful
  Length of commitment to internship: Semester or year
  Number of 1978 interns: 13, some part-time
  Number planned for the future: About the same

DO I GET PAID, EXPENSES, OR CREDIT?
  Pay: Only those on college work-study programs
  College credit: Can be arranged

HOW DO I GET IN?
  Closing date for application: On-going
  Interview required: Almost always
  When will I know about application: At the interview unless references are
    not checked

WHERE CAN I GET MORE INFORMATION?
  Write: James Coyle, Staff Director, Boston City Council, Boston City Hall,
    Boston, MA 02201
  Phone: (616) 725-3041
  Read: Annual reports from the City Council office

CALIFORNIA COASTAL COMMISSION

San Francisco, California

WHAT'S IT DO?
  Purpose and goals:
    The California Coastal Act of 1976 establishes policies by which coastal
    conservation and development decisions are made. These policies deal with
    public access to the coast, coastal recreation, the California marine
    environment, coastal land resources, and coastal development of various
    types, including power plant and other energy installations.

WHAT CAN I DO?
  Internship description:
    Paid internships are available throughout the state on an on-going basis.
    Positions are filled as they are vacated or new projects are developed.
    They are usually three to six months in length and relate to land, water
    use, and planning.

CAN I GET IN?
  Academic requirements: Registered college students with backgrounds in
    energy, planning, ecology, urban and environmental studies are needed.
  Length of commitment to internship: Semester
  Number of 1978 interns: 20
  Number planned for the future: About the same

DO I GET PAID, EXPENSES, OR CREDIT?
  Pay: Yes, check rate with agency
  College credit: Can sometimes be arranged

HOW DO I GET IN?
  Closing date for application: Send state application form #678, a resume,
    and a cover letter. Include in the cover letter the type of job desired,
    activities of interest, why you wish to work for the agency, and your
    availability in time and location.

WHERE CAN I GET MORE INFORMATION?
  Write:
    Janet Mahoney   or   Susan Ishimaru
    2nd Floor   Intern Coordinator
    1540 Market Street   State Personnel Board
    San Francisco, CA 94102   801 Capitol Mall
    (415) 557-3144   Sacramento, CA 95814
                                           (916) 445-7236

CALIFORNIA DEPARTMENT OF ALCOHOLIC BEVERAGE CONTROL

Sacramento, California

WHAT'S IT DO?
  Purpose and goals:
    The Department administers the provisions of the Alcoholic Beverage Control Act, including the exclusive right and power to license and regulate the manufacture, sale, purchase, possession and transportation of alcoholic beverages within the state and, subject to certain laws of the United States, to regulate the importation and exportation of alcoholic beverages into and from the state.
  Current projects and activities:
    Licensing, compliance, and administration are the three major work activities.

WHAT CAN I DO?
  Internship description:
    The Department hires 6 to 10 paid interns per year in Sacramento, Los Angeles, Fresno, and Santa Rosa areas. Students with a criminal justice background in police science, law enforcement or criminology should direct their resume, cover letter and state application (Form #678) to the address below indicating which geographic region is desired, so that your application will be routed to the proper location.

CAN I GET IN?
  Academic requirement: Usually a registered college student
  Special: See academic background preferred as listed above
  Length of commitment to internship: One year
  Number of 1978 interns: 6 to 10
  Number planned for the future: Same

DO I GET PAID, EXPENSES, OR CREDIT?
  Pay: Yes, check rate with agency
  College credit: Can sometimes be arranged

HOW DO I GET IN?
  Closing date for application: Send state application form #678, a resume, and cover letter. Include in the cover letter the type of job desired--paid, full-time; your activities of interest--research, personnel, administration, budget; and why you wish to work in the agency (do some preliminary research on the agency). Also give your availability in time and location.

WHERE CAN I GET MORE INFORMATION?
Write:
  Mary Groppi   or   Susan K. Ishimaru
  Department of Alcoholic Beverage   Coordinator
    Control, Rm. 450   California Internship Program
  1215 O Street   California State Personnel Board
  Sacramento, CA 95814   801 Capitol Mall
  (916) 445-5898   Sacramento, CA 95814
                                          (916) 445-7236

CALIFORNIA DEPARTMENT OF CORRECTIONS

Sacramento, California

WHAT'S IT DO?
  Purpose and goals:
    The Department is organized into four line divisions: policy and planning, administration, institutions, and parole and community services, with support of various staff service functions such as legislative liaison, personnel management and training, and public information. Located throughout the state are 12 correctional institutions with three of these having reception centers.
  Current projects and activities:
    The principal programs of the Department of Corrections are the control, care, and treatment of men and women who have been convicted of serious crimes or those admitted to the civil narcotic program and committed to state correctional facilities. The Department's objectives also include supervision of men and women who have been paroled from correctional facilities and returned to the community.

WHAT CAN I DO?
  The Department uses limited numbers of paid and nonpaid student interns during the academic year. The bulk of these are students with legal academic qualifications and those currently connected with a work-study program. Interns will work with the staff on the projects listed above.

CAN I GET IN?
  Academic requirements: Registered college students with a legal background
  Length of commitment to internship: Semester or year

DO I GET PAID, EXPENSES, OR CREDIT?
  Pay: Some paid internships, check with agency for rate
  College credit: Can be arranged

HOW DO I GET IN?
  Closing date for application: On-going
  Other procedures: Send a resume, cover letter and state application form #678. Include in the cover letter the type of job desired, activities of interest, and your availability in time and location.

WHERE CAN I GET MORE INFORMATION?
Write:
  Department of Corrections   or   Susan K. Ishimaru
  Angie Mendoza   Intern Coordinator
  714 P Street   State Personnel Board
  Sacramento, CA 95814   801 Capitol Mall
  (916) 445-5692   Sacramento, CA 95814
                                                  (916) 445-7236

CALIFORNIA DEPARTMENT OF EDUCATION

Sacramento, California

WHAT'S IT DO?
  Purpose and goals:
    California's public education system is administered at the state level by the Department of Education and is concerned with the education of more than 5 million students from preschool age through adulthood. The Department's organizational structure, which emphasizes delivery of elementary, secondary, and adult programs, recognizes the organizational arrangement existing in schools as well as the particular needs of students at different age levels. At the same time the Department is aware of the need to integrate delivery of services across age spans to meet special student needs.
  Current projects and activities:
    Elementary education, secondary education, adult education, special programs and support services, administrative support services, department management and special services, library services, legislative mandates.

WHAT CAN I DO?
  Paid and nonpaid internships will be available to help the staff with all of the projects listed above. In addition there is a special project on the environmental education unit which utilizes a limited number of nonpaid interns on an on-going basis. To be considered for positions during the academic year, please direct a resume and cover letter to: Rudolph Schafer, Consultant on Environmental Education, State Department of Education, 721 Capitol Mall, 3rd Floor, Sacramento, CA 95814.

CAN I GET IN?
  Academic requirements: A registered college student with research or
    administrative skills.
  Length of commitment to internship: Semester or year

DO I GET PAID, EXPENSES, OR CREDIT?
  Pay: Some internships are paid; write to the agency for the rate.
  College credit: Can be arranged

HOW DO I GET IN?
  Send a resume, cover letter and state application form #678. Include type of job desired, activities of interest, and your availability in time and location.

WHERE CAN I GET MORE INFORMATION?
Write:

Jerry Cummings   or   Susan K. Ishimaru
Department of Education   Intern Coordinator
Room 524   State Personnel Board
721 Capitol Mall   801 Capitol Mall
Sacramento, CA 95814   Sacramento, CA 95814
(916) 445-4338   (916) 445-7236

CALIFORNIA DEPARTMENT OF FINANCE

Sacramento, California

WHAT'S IT DO?
Purpose and goals:
By statute, the director serves as the Governor's chief fiscal policy advisor with emphasis on the financial integrity of the state and maintenance of a fiscally sound and responsible administration.
Current projects and activities:
1) To assist the Governor in the development and enactment of the annual financial plan.
2) To assess and optimize the efficiency and effectiveness of resource utilization for state-administered and state-financed programs.
3) To provide economic, financial, and demographic information.

WHAT CAN I DO?
Limited numbers of paid graduate students will be hired to participate in projects involving budget analysis, research and auditing.

CAN I GET IN?
Academic requirements: Registered college students with academic backgrounds in business administration, public administration, sociology, education, or economics.
Length of commitment to internship: Semester or year

DO I GET PAID, EXPENSES, OR CREDIT?
Pay: Some internships are paid; write to the agency for the rate.
College credit: Can be arranged

HOW DO I GET IN?
Send a resume, cover letter and state application form #678. Include in the cover letter type of job desired, your interests in activities, and your availability in time and location.

WHERE CAN I GET MORE INFORMATION?
Write:

Terri Fontenette   or   Susan K. Ishimaru
Department of Finance   State Personnel Board
Room 456   801 Capitol Mall
1025 P Street   Sacramento, CA 95814
Sacramento, CA 95814   (916) 445-7236
(916) 445-4946

CALIFORNIA DEPARTMENT OF FISH AND GAME

Sacramento, California

WHAT'S IT DO?
  Purpose and goals:
  1) To maintain all species of fish and wildlife for their natural and ecological values as well as for their direct benefits to humans. The objective is to maintain, as a basic necessity, any species to be used in the future. This includes the principle that fish and wildlife should be preserved as a human environment necessity. The present generation must assume the obligation to pass on to future generations all of the species that now exist, whether or not they are now used and enjoyed. The present contribution that each species makes to the ecological balance is not always known and may well change in the future. We should not tamper with this balance without understanding fully the eventual result. The restoration of native species that no longer exist in California but still exist in other areas offers a chance for returning to an original natural balance. The introduction of new species compatible with existing species offers a chance to add desirable elements to the environment. Similarly, planning permits the exclusion of undesirable species as a part of this program.
  2) To provide for varied recreational use of fish and wildlife. This objective, "recreational use," embraces all the ways that people may enjoy fish and wildlife. This variety of recreational opportunity will enable each individual to select the most rewarding type of recreation, based on personal interests and type of available access. Single uses will not predominate, merely because they might attract the greatest number of users. This objective sees the maintenance of fish and wildlife "game" populations at levels that will provide harvestable surpluses so that recreational hunting and fishing will continue to be enjoyed, as two of California's leading and traditional forms of recreation. The diversity of geographical areas and climatic conditions in California provides an unusually wide range of options.
  3) To provide for an economic contribution of fish and wildlife in the best interests of the people of the state. The third objective, "economic contribution," covers several distinct interests concerned with utilization of fish and wildlife resources. These include the commercial harvesters of these resources and the people who are related to them, such as suppliers of goods and services. The objective is to provide the maximum economic benefits to the people of California within the limits of the resources and other objectives.
  4) To provide for scientific and educational use of fish and wildlife. This fourth objective, "scientific and educational use," proposes to insure the availability of fish and wildlife for study and research by both scientists and students. Some of this offered through cooperating institutions.
  All of the programs of the Department are directed toward the accomplishment of these objectives through the conservation, enhancement, and restoration of fish and wildlife resources and habitats and regulation of the use of resources.

WHAT CAN I DO?
  Paid graduate and limited numbers of upper division undergraduate student assistants will be hired for field placements that are statewide. Positions are limited and confined to technical backgrounds in wildlife management, zoology, fisheries, marine biology, water quality biology and microbiology.

CAN I GET IN?
  Academic requirements: Registered college student in one of the above technical programs.
  Length of commitment to internship: Semester or year, part-time basis for some programs.

DO I GET PAID, EXPENSES, OR CREDIT?
  Pay: Write to the agency for the rate of pay.
  College credit: Can be arranged for some student assistants.

HOW DO I GET IN?
  File a state application #678, resume and cover letter to your local Fish and Game Office or send directly to the address below.

WHERE CAN I GET MORE INFORMATION?
  Write:
    Stuart Lott   or   Susan K. Ishimaru
    Department of Fish and Game   Intern Coordinator
    1416 9th Street   State Personnel Board
    Sacramento, CA 95814   801 Capitol Mall
    (916) 445-3189   (916) 445-7236

CALIFORNIA DEPARTMENT OF FOOD AND AGRICULTURE
Sacramento, California

WHAT'S IT DO?
  Purpose and goals:
    To serve the citizens of California by promoting and protecting California agriculture in the interests of public health, safety and welfare. To maintain a viable food system which assures delivery of an abundant supply of wholesome food to domestic and export markets. To preserve and protect use of the state's natural resources to meet the present and future requirements for food and fiber. To provide effective and uniform administration of the Food and Agricultural Code and other laws over which the Department has jurisdiction.
  Current projects and activities:
    Projects are developed within the above goals in many areas of the state.

WHAT CAN I DO?
  Internship description:
    Most internships are part-time assisting the staff in crop science, entomology, biological sciences, plant sciences and management analysis.

CAN I GET IN?
  Academic requirements: Registered college student with skills in the above sciences.
  Length of commitment to internship: Semester or year

DO I GET PAID, EXPENSES, OR CREDIT?
  College credit: Can be arranged

HOW DO I GET IN?
  Students with an interest in management analysis in Sacramento should submit a resume, cover letter and state application #678 to: Vashek Cervinka, Department of Food and Agriculture, Management Analysis, 1220 N Street, Sacramento, CA 95814; Phone: (916) 322-2395;

  or students interested in other areas please submit a resume, cover letter and state application form #678 to: Lyn Hawkins, Department of Food and Agriculture, Room 301, 1220 N Street, Sacramento, CA 95814; Phone: (916) 445-5986;

  or write: Susan K. Ishimaru, State Personnel Board, 801 Capitol Mall, Sacramento, CA 95814; Phone: (916) 445-7236.

CALIFORNIA DEPARTMENT OF FORESTRY

Sacramento, California

WHAT'S IT DO?
  Purpose and goals:
    This department has as its principal objectives the prevention and suppression of fires occurring in forests and other lands, land management programs such as the administration and enforcement of forest practice rules, forest advisory services, range improvement programs, production of nursery stock, management of state forests, and underwriting forest and fire research programs.

WHAT CAN I DO?
  This department hires only a few paid interns to assist the staff in the programs described above.

CAN I GET IN?
  Academic requirements: Registered college student with background that reflects an interest in forestry.
  Length of commitment to internship: Semester or year

DO I GET PAID, EXPENSES, OR CREDIT?
  Pay: Yes; write to the agency for the rate.

HOW DO I GET IN?
  Interested students may submit a resume, cover letter, and state application form #678 to: or write:

Bob Anderson   Susan K. Ishimaru
Department of Forestry   Intern Coordinator
Room 1525   State Personnel Board
1416 9th Street   801 Capitol Mall
Sacramento, CA 95814   Sacramento, CA 95814
(916) 445-0217   (916) 445-7236

CALIFORNIA DEPARTMENT OF HEALTH

Sacramento, Bay Area and Southern California

WHAT'S IT DO?
  Purpose and goals:
    The objective of the Department of Health is to improve and sustain in a uniform manner the quality and quantity of services that affect the health of the people of California. Emphasis is placed on providing needed services to particular groups of the state's residents who have been traditionally underserved, such as farmworkers, American Indians, children from low-income families, senior citizens, and persons affected by unique genetic diseases.
  Current projects and activities:
    Services currently include health protection and care through the following: prevention and control of disease and disability; control of environmental health hazards; assurance of high quality health services through inspection and licensing; comprehensive planning for optimum use of health resources; coordination of direct treatment programs for the developmentally disabled, the mentally ill, and substance abusers; provisions of social services to economically and socially deprived citizens; administration of the Medical Assistance Program (Medi-Cal) so as to maximize the use of public funds to provide medical services to the economically deprived; and delivery of direct treatment services through the 11 hospitals in the state hospital system.

WHAT CAN I DO?
  Student assistant positions are sponsored through the work-learn internship program. This program seeks to place students in nonpaid, career-related positions with the intent of providing academic credits. Placements are usually available in Sacramento, the San Francisco Bay Area, and Southern California.

CAN I GET IN?
  Academic requirements: Registered college students with backgrounds in
    biological sciences, research, statistics, public health, public/business administration, social welfare, psychology, law, political science, and planning/public policy.
  Length of commitment to internship: Semester or year

DO I GET PAID, EXPENSES, OR CREDIT?
  College credit: Most interns receive college credit

HOW DO I GET IN?
  Interested students should submit a standard resume, state application form #678, and a cover letter. Include in your letter the type of job desired, your activities and your availability in time and location.

WHERE CAN I GET MORE INFORMATION?
  Write:
    Student Assistant Coordinator   or   Susan K. Ishimaru
    Department of Health, Room 892   Intern Coordinator
    744 P Street   State Personnel Board
    Sacramento, CA 95814   801 Capitol Mall
    (916) 322-6580   Sacramento, CA 95814
                                             (916) 445-7236

CALIFORNIA DEPARTMENT OF HOUSING AND COMMUNITY DEVELOPMENT

Sacramento, California

WHAT'S IT DO?
  Purpose and goals:
    To provide decent housing in suitable living environments for California citizens of all socioeconomic levels. To protect the public from inadequate construction, manufacture, repair or rehabilitation of buildings, particularly dwelling units, and from improper living environs through the establishment and enforcement of health and safety standards.
  Current projects and activities:
    Projects are related to the above goals of the department.

WHAT CAN I DO?
  Students assist the staff in their work, and internships are designed around the skills of the particular intern and the current projects at hand.

CAN I GET IN?
  Academic requirements: Registered colleges with academic backgrounds in government, political science, environmental planning, public administration, economics, and law. Bilingual ability is desirable.
  Length of commitment to internship: Semester or year
  Number of 1978 interns: 22 including summer internships
  Number planned for the future: About the same

DO I GET PAID, EXPENSES, OR CREDIT?
  Pay: Yes; write to the agency for the rate.

HOW DO I GET IN?
  Send a resume, cover letter and state application #678. Include in the letter the type of job desired, activities of interest, and your availability in terms of time and location.

WHERE CAN I GET MORE INFORMATION?
  Write:
    Department of Housing and   or   Susan K. Ishimaru
      Community Development   Intern Coordinator
    921 10th Street   State Personnel Board
    Sacramento, CA 95814   801 Capitol Mall
    (916) 445-4807   Sacramento, CA 95814
                                             (916) 445-7236

CALIFORNIA DEPARTMENT OF MOTOR VEHICLES

Sacramento, California

WHAT'S IT DO?
  Purpose and goals:
    1) To protect public interest by identifying ownership through the process of vehicle registration.
    2) To promote safety on highways by licensing and controlling drivers.
    3) To provide public protection by licensing and regulating occupations and business related to manufacture, transporting, sale, and disposal of vehicles and to the instruction of drivers in safe operation on the highways.
    4) To provide a source of compensation through the Compulsory Financial Responsibility Law to those who suffer injury or damage to property in automobile accidents.
    5) To provide services, not directly related to motor vehicles or drivers' licensing, to the public and to other state agencies as required by statute.
  Current projects and activities:
    The Department is sponsoring a program entitled "Exploring the Bureaucracy." The program will provide 30 unpaid student internships directed toward evaluation of departmental objectives, goals, and programs.

WHAT CAN I DO?
  Positions are available to students with a variety of interests, including public administration, government, communication studies, journalism, sociology, business management, ethnic studies, engineering, mathematics, and criminal justice. Internships are not limited to these disciplines; they are intended to provide any student with a meaningful career development experience in a bureaucratic setting by using the analytical and specialized skills throughout the program. Students interested in taking a critical look at the functioning of public agencies or in a future career in such agencies should apply for the program.

CAN I GET IN?
  Academic requirements: Registered college student with a background as described above.
  Length of commitment to internship: Semester or year

DO I GET PAID, EXPENSES, OR CREDIT?
  College credit: Can be arranged

HOW DO I GET IN?
  Send resume, cover letter and state application #678. Include in the letter the type of job desired, activities of interest, and your availability in terms of location and time.

WHERE CAN I GET MORE INFORMATION?
  Write:
    Dr. Dennis O'Brien   or   Luisa Menchaca
    International Office   Personnel Management Services Section
    California State University,   Department of Motor Vehicles
      Sacramento   2570 24th Street
    6000 J Street   Sacramento, CA 95809
    Sacramento, CA 95826   (916) 445-5002
    (916) 454-6686
  or
    Susan K. Ishimaru
    Intern Coordinator
    State Personnel Board
    801 Capitol Mall
    Sacramento, CA 95814
    (916) 445-7236

CALIFORNIA DEPARTMENT OF PARKS AND RECREATION

Sacramento, California

WHAT'S IT DO?
  Purpose and goals:
    The Department of Parks and Recreation acquires, designs, develops, operates and maintains units of the state park system. The Department also has the responsibility to administer both Federal and state local assistance programs. An ever-increasing population in California has resulted in accelerated urbanization which necessitates the establishment of park units and recreation areas accessible to the major population centers of the state. Technological advances have created a more affluent society with additional leisure time spent increasingly in pursuit of various forms of recreation. It is necessary to provide for the wise and constructive use of the state's natural resources for recreational uses and to preserve its cultural, historical, and natural heritage for future generations to enjoy.
  Current projects and activities:
    These activities are directed toward the accomplishment of seven principal objectives:
    1) To secure and preserve elements of the state's outstanding landscape, cultural, and historical features.
    2) To provide the facilities and resources which are required to fulfill the recreational demands of the people of California.
    3) To provide a meaningful environment in which the people of California are given the opportunity to understand and appreciate the state's cultural, historical, and natural heritage.
    4) To maintain and improve the quality of California's environment.
    5) To prepare and maintain a statewide recreational plan that includes an analysis of the continuing need for recreational areas and facilities.
    6) To encourage all levels of government and private enterprise throughout the state to participate in the planning, development and operation of recreational facilities.
    7) To meet the recreational demands of a highly accelerated, urban-centered population growth, through the acquisition, development, and operation of urban parks.

WHAT CAN I DO?
  Internship descriptions:
    Paid and nonpaid positions will be available. Projects will involve a wide variety of effort. Interns with the following academic backgrounds are needed: recreation, park and recreation administration, environmental resources, biology, anthropology, archeology, history, and ethnic studies.

CAN I GET IN?
  Academic requirements: Registered college student, with the academic backgrounds listed above, plus research and writing skills.
  Length of commitment to internship: Semester or year

DO I GET PAID, EXPENSES, OR CREDIT?
  Pay: Some internships are paid; write to agency for rate and description.
  College credit: Can be arranged

HOW DO I GET IN?
  Send a resume, cover letter and state application #678. Include in the cover letter the type of job desired, your interests, and your availability in terms of time and location.

WHERE CAN I GET MORE INFORMATION?
  Write:
    Dorothy Benjamin   or   Susan K. Ishimaru
    Department of Parks and   Intern Coordinator
      Recreation   State Personnel Board
    1416 9th Street   801 Capitol Mall
    Sacramento, CA 95814   Sacramento, CA 95814
    (916) 445-4822   (916) 445-7236

CALIFORNIA DEPARTMENT OF THE YOUTH AUTHORITY

Six California Areas

WHAT'S IT DO?
  Purpose and goals:
    The primary objective of the Youth Authority is "to protect society more effectively by substituting for retributive punishment, methods of training and treatment directed toward the correction and rehabilitation of young persons found guilty of public offenses." A related mission is to protect society from criminal and delinquent behavior by children and youth.
  Goals:
    Youth Development. Increase opportunities for all children and youth to participate as contributing members of society.
    Delinquency Reduction. Reduce probability of illegal behavior by children and youth not yet involved in the justice system, but who have exhibited antisocial characteristics.
    Offender Rehabilitation. Reduce continuing illegal behavior by offenders.
    Research. Systematically develop knowledge about delinquency reduction, youth development, and offender rehabilitation.
  Current projects and activities:
    The Department carries out this mandate to protect the public by:

1) providing residential and community rehabilitation programs which will help persons committed to the Youth Authority to become useful and productive citizens, and

2) accumulating a body of knowledge relative to the causes of delinquency and the treatment and control of those who engage in illegal behavior.

WHAT CAN I DO?
  Internship descriptions:
    There will be approximately six paid internships available throughout the state. Application is not limited to specific academic background. Assignments can range from administrative, counselor aide, parole aide, recreation assistant to tutor. The internships will be in one of the four branches: Parole and Institutions; Prevention and Community Corrections; Planning, Research, Evaluation and Development; and Management Services.

CAN I GET IN?
  Academic requirements: Registered college student
  Length of commitment to internship: Semester or year

DO I GET PAID, EXPENSES, OR CREDIT?
  Pay: Yes; send to the agency for rates.

HOW DO I GET IN?
  Send a resume, cover letter and state application form #678. Include in the cover letter the type of job desired, preferred geographic area, and availability.

WHERE CAN I GET MORE INFORMATION?
  Write:
    Darrell Bray
    Department of the Youth
      Authority
    Room 900
    714 P Street
    Sacramento, CA 95814
    (916) 322-9064

  or

    Susan K. Ishimaru
    Intern Coordinator
    State Personnel Board
    801 Capitol Mall
    Sacramento, CA 95814
    (916) 445-7236

CALIFORNIA EMPLOYMENT DEVELOPMENT DEPARTMENT

Sacramento, California

WHAT'S IT DO?
  Purpose and goals:
    The Employment Development Department provides comprehensive statewide and local manpower planning, improves the efficiency of and accountability for delivery systems for manpower programs, places job-ready individuals in suitable jobs, provides qualified job applicants to employers, assists potentially employable individuals to become job ready, creates employment opportunities, and pays unemployment and disability insurance benefits.
  Current projects and activities:
    The Department's overall program is designed to achieve five goals:
      1) Provide job placements.
      2) Furnish job placements and related services to low-income clients.
      3) Maintain an unemployment insurance and disability insurance benefit payment system.
      4) Provide services to employers.
      5) Place welfare recipients in jobs.
    Employment Development offers a broad spectrum of services to the employables and their potential employers, including current and localized labor market information, instructions in job and employer requirements, training and education in demand occupations, job development with employers and industries, placement services, and follow up to improve job retention.

WHAT CAN I DO?
  The Department hires a limited number of paid and non-paid interns to work with its staff in all of the projects listed above. Each year the internships vary as projects develop and qualifications of interns differ.

CAN I GET IN?
  Academic requirements: Registered college student
  Length of commitment to internship: Semester or year

DO I GET PAID, EXPENSES, OR CREDIT?
  Pay: Some internships are paid; write to the agency for the rate.
  College credit: Can be arranged

HOW DO I GET IN?
  Send a resume, cover letter and state application #678. Include in the cover letter the type of job desired, activities of interest to you, and your availability in time and location.

WHERE CAN I GET MORE INFORMATION?
  Write:
    Employment Development Department   or   Susan K. Ishimaru
    Personnel Section   Intern Coordinator
    800 Capitol Mall   State Personnel Board
    Sacramento, CA 95814   801 Capitol Mall
    (916) 322-3664   Sacramento, CA 95814
                                                 (916) 445-7236

CALIFORNIA HIGHWAY PATROL

Sacramento, California

WHAT'S IT DO?
  Current projects and activities:
    Projects are being considered for using college students in every phase of the highway patrol programs.

WHAT CAN I DO?
  Paid and nonpaid internships are anticipated during the academic year. Plans are not formalized at this writing; however, projects are being considered that will accommodate all academic backgrounds.

CAN I GET IN?
  Academic requirements: Registered college student
  Length of commitment to internship: Semester or year

DO I GET PAID, EXPENSES, OR CREDIT?
  Pay: Yes; check rate with agency.

HOW DO I GET IN?
  Closing date for application: Send a resume, cover letter and state application form #678. Include in the cover letter the type of job desired, your activities of interest, and your availability, both time and location.

WHERE CAN I GET MORE INFORMATION?
  Write:
  Sharon Smith   or   Susan K. Ishimaru
  Department of the California   Intern Coordinator
    Highway Patrol   State Personnel Board
  2611 26th Street   801 Capitol Mall
  Sacramento, CA 95814   Sacramento, CA 95814
  (916) 322-5380   (916) 445-7236

CALIFORNIA POSTSECONDARY EDUCATION COMMISSION

Sacramento, California

WHAT'S IT DO?
  Purpose and goals:
    The California Postsecondary Education Commission was established by Chapter 1187, Statutes of 1973. A successor to the Coordinating Council for Higher Education, it assumed its duties on April 1, 1974. It has 23 members; 11 are directly connected with public or private postsecondary education, 12 represent the general public.
  Current projects and activities:
    The Commission is responsible for developing and annually bringing up to date a comprehensive five-year plan for postsecondary education. It also reviews and integrates the long-range plans of the three public segments of higher education (University of California, California State University and Colleges, and California Community Colleges). Another primary duty is to advise the Governor and the Legislature on the need for and location of new institutions and campuses, and proposals for new programs. The Commission is a clearinghouse for information on higher education.

WHAT CAN I DO?
  Internship descriptions:
    Paid positions are available for students with most academic backgrounds. Descriptions of the internships are not available at this writing since the positions are dependent on projects still being developed. Interns will work with staff on the above projects.

CAN I GET IN?
  Academic requirements: Registered college students with writing and research skills.
  Length of commitment to internship: Semester or year

DO I GET PAID, EXPENSES, OR CREDIT?
  Pay: Yes; check with agency for rate of pay.
  College credit: Sometimes is arranged

HOW DO I GET IN?
  Send a resume, cover letter and state application form #678. Include in the cover letter the type of job desired, your activities of interest, and your availability in time and location.

WHERE CAN I GET MORE INFORMATION?
  Write:
    Dolores Dowdle   or   Susan K. Ishimaru
    California Postsecondary   Coordinator of Interns
      Education Commission   State Personnel Board
    2nd Floor   801 Capitol Mall
    1020 12th Street   Sacramento, CA 95814
    Sacramento, CA 95814   (916) 445-7236
    (916) 322-8019

CALIFORNIA PUBLIC UTILITIES COMMISSION

San Francisco, California

WHAT'S IT DO?
  Purpose and goals:
  1) To provide the public with the lowest reasonable rates for services by utilities, transportation, and warehouse companies.
  2) To make certain that utilities and transportation companies render adequate service and have sufficient facilities to meet the needs of the public.
  3) To ensure that the public has stable, efficient utilities and transportation services by controlling and limiting entry into the field to those applicants with financial responsibility and demonstrated capability to render adequate service.
  4) To promote public safety and accident reduction by establishing and enforcing safety regulations for utility and transportation companies.
  5) To determine the just compensation for the acquisition of utility or transportation company property by political subdivisions.

WHAT CAN I DO?
  Internship descriptions:
    Internships are developed around the above objectives. Only students with academic backgrounds in engineering, environment, law, or economics will be considered.

CAN I GET IN?
  Academic requirements: Registered college students with the above academic backgrounds.
  Length of commitment to internship: Semester or year

DO I GET PAID, EXPENSES, OR CREDIT?
  College credit: Can be arranged

HOW DO I GET IN?
  Send resume, cover letter and state application #678. Include in the letter the type of job desired, your interests, and your availability.

WHERE CAN I GET MORE INFORMATION?
  Write:
    Bob Smith
    Public Utilities Commission
    Room 5160
    455 Golden Gate Avenue
    San Francisco, CA 94102

    or

    Susan K. Ishimaru
    Intern Coordinator
    State Personnel Board
    801 Capitol Mall
    Sacramento, CA 95814
    (916) 445-7236

CALIFORNIA STATE LIBRARY

Sacramento and San Francisco, California

WHAT'S IT DO?
  Current projects and activities:
    Library services to the state of California.

WHAT CAN I DO?
  Internship descriptions:
    Numerous nonpaid intern positions are available in Sacramento and San Francisco. These positions include projects at the library assistant level including work with rare manuscripts, creation of a state agency library directory, legislation, legal environment, photography, statistics, educational librarianship, art and Spanish language materials.

CAN I GET IN?
  Academic requirements: Registered college students with academic backgrounds in geography, history, library science, law, industrial design, art, economics, mathematics, statistics, public administration or Latin American/Spanish studies.
  Length of commitment to internship: Semester or year

DO I GET PAID, EXPENSES, OR CREDIT?
  College credit: Can be arranged

HOW DO I GET IN?
  Send a resume, cover letter and state application form #678. Include in the cover letter the type of job desired, activities of interest, your availability in time and location.

WHERE CAN I GET MORE INFORMATION?
  Write:

Mareia Brown Field	or	Susan K. Ishimaru
California State Library		Intern Coordinator
P.O. Box 2037		State Personnel Board
Sacramento, CA 95809		801 Capitol Mall
(916) 445-5370		Sacramento, CA 95814
		(916) 445-7236

CALIFORNIA STATE OFFICE OF SUBSTANCE ABUSE

(Formerly Narcotics and Drug Abuse)

Sacramento, California

WHAT'S IT DO?
  Purpose and goals:
    The State Office of Substance Abuse was established in 1970. Few prevention and treatment services were available at that time and no state agency existed to plan, develop, and coordinate the services needed to combat the problem. During the past six years it has directed the creation of more than 450 community based drug abuse prevention and treatment programs throughout the state. A system consisting of a drug program coordinator in each county, a mechanism for local determination of drug program priorities, planning and program administration has also been established through legislation.

WHAT CAN I DO?
  Internship descriptions:
    Student assistants can work full time to analyze data collected by the department. Some knowledge of community mental health systems and drug abuse treatment is required.

CAN I GET IN?
  Academic requirements: Registered college student with any background will be considered.
  Length of commitment to internship: November, December and January are needed.

DO I GET PAID, EXPENSES, OR CREDIT?
  Pay: Students will be paid $3.67 an hour.

HOW DO I GET IN?
  Closing date for application: October 31
  Other procedures: Send a resume including previous work experience, age, race ethnicity, sex, year in college, and state application #678.

WHERE CAN I GET MORE INFORMATION?
  Write:
  Division of Substance Abuse   or   Susan K. Ishimaru
  Department of Health   Intern Coordinator
  Room 1000   State Personnel Board
  714 P Street   801 Capitol Mall
  Sacramento, CA 95814   Sacramento, CA 95814
  (916) 322-4445   (916) 445-7236

CALIFORNIA STATE WATER RESOURCES CONTROL BOARD

Sacramento, California

WHAT'S IT DO?
  Purpose and goals:
    The objectives and responsibilities of the Water Resources Control Board are to preserve and enhance the quality of California's water resources and to assure their conservation and effective utilization. These objectives are achieved through two action programs--water quality and water rights.

WHAT CAN I DO?
  Internship description:
    Paid and nonpaid positions are filled on an ongoing basis to assist the staff in water quality and water rights projects.

CAN I GET IN?
  Academic requirements: Registered college students with various backgrounds are considered.
  Length of commitment to internship: Semester or year

DO I GET PAID, EXPENSES, OR CREDIT?
  Pay: Some positions are paid; check with agency for rates.
  College credit: Can be arranged

HOW DO I GET IN?
  Send a resume, cover letter and state application #678. Include in the letter the type of job desired, your interests and availability for the job.

WHERE CAN I GET MORE INFORMATION?
  Write:
    Susan Birch   or   Susan K. Ishimaru
    Water Resources Control Board   Intern Coordinator
    2014 T Street   State Personnel Board
    Sacramento, CA 95814   801 Capitol Mall
    (916) 322-4141   Sacramento, CA 95814
                                                     (916) 445-7236

CONNECTICUT GENERAL ASSEMBLY

LEGISLATIVE INTERN PROGRAM

Hartford, Connecticut

WHAT'S IT DO?
  Purpose and goals:
    To provide a rich, rewarding experience for both intern and legislator, as well as providing critically needed staffing to a part-time legislator. This broad experience enables an intern to gain an insider's view of how the Connecticut state government operates and the role that a legislator plays in that process. It allows these students to lend their expertise in areas in which they have an interest and to perform assignments that legislators themselves perform.
  Current projects and activities:
    An orientation session is held for intern candidates the month prior to the convening of the General Assembly. Weekly seminars are conducted with governmental leaders from the Governor on down and with individuals from the private sector who come in contact with state government officials. Interns maintain a weekly journal of their activities during the program and prepare a summary at the conclusion of their responsibilities. Evaluations are also used to gauge the success of the working relationship between intern and legislator. Both are asked to complete such forms, and are used in the grading process.
  Number of permanent staff in main office:
    Two co-directors are hired on a part-time basis, one each from two higher education institutions in Connecticut, assisted by a full-time administrative assistant.
  Annual budget: $12,000
  Publications: Internship brochure, Orientation Handbook and materials

WHAT CAN I DO?
  Internship descriptions:
    Interns are assigned to work with individual legislators. That work may take the form of performing casework duties, conducting polls, research, attending hearings and meetings (also testifying if the need arises), correspondence, scheduling, and preparing testimony and press releases.

CAN I GET IN?
  Academic: Interns must be in their second year of an accredited college program.
  Experience: While there may be exceptions, students must have some theoretical or practical knowledge of Connecticut state government and political science or government courses.
  Length of intern commitment: Semester
  Number of 1978 interns: 35
  Number planned for the future: 40

DO I GET PAID, EXPENSES, OR CREDIT?
  Pay: Students are given a stipend for the semester.
  College credit: Is granted after completion of all requirements, and even though it is left up to institutions to decide, the Intern Committee

suggests that 15 credits be granted to a full-time student, and 6 credits to part-time students.

HOW DO I GET IN?
Closing date for application: October 15th of the year, to be received by the faculty advisors on their respective campuses. The faculty advisors are then asked to screen out any intern applicants that can't meet the academic requirements. The remaining applicants are sent on to the Intern Committee, at which point another screening takes place, based upon advisor comments, academic proficiency and extracurricular activities.
Interview required: Yes
When will I know about application: Selection takes place shortly after the last interview day has been completed, and assignments are made.

WHERE CAN I GET MORE INFORMATION?
Write: Legislative Intern Committee, c/o Legislative Management Committee, State Capitol - Room 314, Hartford, CT 06115
Phone: (203) 566-7778 during session; (203) 566-3117 out-of-session
Read: Strengthening the Connecticut Legislature, David B. Ogle, 1970; Lawmaking in Connecticut, Wayne R. Swanson, 1972 (update as of 9/78)

KENTUCKY BUREAU OF CORRECTIONS

Frankfort, Kentucky

WHAT'S IT DO?
Purpose and goals:
The Bureau of Corrections exists primarily to serve the community and to treat offenders. It is only when Corrections and the community form an alliance based on genuine concern for the delinquent individual and dedicated to promoting his or her growth, welfare, and productivity that Corrections will actually "correct." The volunteer program provides friendship and guidance to released offenders and a strong basis upon which to build the citizen support needed for future correctional programs.
Objectives:
To develop an "Awareness Program" on the Criminal Justice System to be presented to the community with emphasis on volunteerism.
To obtain greater citizen involvement in community-based and institutional correctional programs through public relations and recruitment.
To increase volunteer services to meet most of the basic living needs of clients while under supervision.
To recruit, train and match volunteer probation counselors (VPC's) and probationers on an on-going basis, within the existing budget.
To evaluate the effectiveness of the VPC program on an on-going basis.
To visit regularly public and private agencies which are or may be utilized by the officers in securing services for their clients.
To act as liaison between resource agencies and the officers.
Number of permanent staff: 2   Annual budget: $125,000
Publications: Volunteer Handbook

WHAT CAN I DO?
Internship descriptions:
There are several types of interns and volunteer programs. All help in

the goals of the Bureau with the current projects as listed above.

CAN I GET IN?
  Academic requirements: Depends on position of practicum, volunteer, or intern
  Age: 20 to 25
  Length of internship commitment: Semester or more
  Number of 1978 interns: 3 plus 12 practicum and 800 volunteers
  Number planned for the future: Same

DO I GET PAID, EXPENSES, OR CREDIT?
  College credit: Can be arranged

HOW DO I GET IN?
  Closing date for application: May 1
  Interview required: Yes
  When will I know about application: Soon after the interview

WHERE CAN I GET MORE INFORMATION?
  Write: Brett D. Scott, Deputy Commissioner, Bureau of Corrections, Kentucky Department of Justice, Frankfort, KY 40601
  Phone: (502) 564-4221
  Read: <u>Volunteer Handbook</u>, available upon request

KENTUCKY OFFICE OF PUBLIC DEFENDER

Frankfort, Kentucky

WHAT'S IT DO?
  Purpose and goals:
    The Office of Public Defender provides competent legal representation to all indigent persons accused of crime or mental state which may result in their incarceration, confinement or fine of more than $500.
  Current projects and activities:
    This office provides representation at both the trial and appellate levels, gives technical aid to local defenders requesting assistance, defends those accused of committing a criminal offense while incarcerated at a state penitentiary or reformatory, and is involved in research designed to improve the criminal justice system.
  Number of permanent staff: Approximately 60. This includes attorneys, investigators, legal aides, secretaries, and administrative assistants.
  Annual budget: $900,000
  Publications: <u>Counsel for the Defense</u>, a monthly newsletter; the <u>Public Defender Administrative Newsletter</u>; <u>Kentucky Criminal Law</u>, a book that deals with criminal procedures in Kentucky.

WHAT CAN I DO?
  Internship descriptions:
    Each student, meeting the minimum requirements, applies to his or her respective college. Each college may send three or four candidates for interviews in Frankfort. The interview panel consists of agency directors, campus coordinators and present interns. Approximately 15 students are

selected on a highly competitive basis to serve as administrative interns. The seven month internship combines academic and practical experience in public administration and government. It is recommended that only students with a definite interest in Kentucky state government apply. Upon acceptance into the program not only is the student placed in a state agency, but she or he must also attend weekly seminars that deal with Kentucky state government, its Constitution, and its administration. Monthly field trips to various parts of the state are also included into the program. These trips may last one to three days and include such things as visits to the Kentucky State Penitentiary, meetings with local officials, and viewing coal mines (underground and strip mining) and holding discussions with executives of the coal mines, reclamation officers and the coal miners themselves. Each intern is required to do a research project that is submitted to his or her respective college for credit to complete the internship. Each agency supervisor evaluates the intern's work.

CAN I GET IN?
  Academic: 2.6 or better grade point standing
  Age: Must have completed sophomore year in college--preference given to college seniors
  Special: Must attend a Kentucky university or college
  Length of intern commitment: Seven months
  Number of 1978 interns: 15
  Number planned for future: 15 per year

DO I GET PAID, EXPENSES, OR CREDIT?
  Pay: $436 per month
  Expenses: Traveling expenses provided for monthly field trips
  College credit: 15 to 18 hours

HOW DO I GET IN?
  Closing date for applications: Varies with each college; bulletins are posted on each college campus stating closing date plus general information about the internship.
  Interview required: 1) on campus, the student must first be chosen to represent his or her college; 2) chosen students must be present for 15 minute individual interviews in Frankfort, final selections are made upon conclusion of this set of interviews.
  When will I know about application: Day after Frankfort interview

WHERE CAN I GET MORE INFORMATION?
  Write: WIlliam Strunk, Department of Personnel, Office of Public Defender, State Office Building Annex, 3rd Floor, Frankfort, KY 40601
  Phone: (502) 564-6700
  Read: <u>Kentucky Criminal Law</u>

LOS ANGELES CITY VOLUNTEER CORPS

Los Angeles, California

WHAT'S IT DO?
  Purpose and goals:
    The City of Los Angeles has a volunteer program helping to develop citizen participation in government and in the local community. The City Volunteer Corps is a cooperative effort of the Mayor's Office and the City Council. CVC volunteers have the opportunity to work with city officials and community organizations on projects that directly contribute to improving social services for people in need.
  Current projects:
    Examples of volunteers who have participated in CVC: An accountant set up bookkeeping procedures for an organization which serves orthopedically handicapped children; a student intern explored possibilities for funding a day care center, found one, and obtained the center's funding; a telephone company employee led in creating a career development center for Chicano women; a team of volunteers and interns helped community groups develop brochures, slide shows and other public relations materials; a team of volunteers with farming backgrounds developed a city vegetable garden project for about 100 families; college interns provided the city with basic research on programs for seniors, the handicapped, sources of low-cost housing, solid waste recycling, and many other concerns; an intern provided Spanish language translations for hospitalized children.
  Number of permanent staff: 5

WHAT CAN I DO?
  You can volunteer any of the following skills which you have to contribute to the City of Los Angeles program:
    Accounting/taxes
    Advertising/public relations
    Arts/entertainment
    Banking/economic development
    Business management/systems design
    Career planning/career development
    Clerical services
    Community planning
    Consumer affairs/tenant rights
    Counseling/social services
    Data processing
    Day care development/day care operations
    Education/training
    Engineering
    Environment
    Foreign language
    Fund raising
    Landscaping/gardening
    Law/law enforcement
    Mathematics/sciences
    Medicine/health services
    Merchandising
    Physical activities
    Photography/graphic arts/printing
    Research/library sciences
    Skilled trades
    Transportation
    Writing

CAN I GET IN?
  Academic requirements: None   Age: No limit
  Length of commitment to internship: At least one semester
  Number of 1978 volunteers: 155
  Number planned for the future: 200

DO I GET PAID, EXPENSES, OR CREDIT?
  College credit: Can be arranged; many do receive credit.

HOW DO I GET IN?
  Closing date for application: On-going
  Interview required: Yes
  When will I know about application: No formal date

WHERE CAN I GET MORE INFORMATION?
  Write: Barry Smedberg, CVC, Room 2403, City Hall, Los Angeles, CA 90012
  Phone: (213) 485-4437

MASSACHUSETTS DEPARTMENT OF CORRECTIONS

Boston, Massachusetts

WHAT'S IT DO?
  Purpose and goals:
    The Department of Corrections has direct control over about 3,000 men and women. It is the obligation of the Department to return these men and women to the community as useful and law-abiding citizens. The Department has the duty to keep recidivism to a minimum, thus adding to the protection of the citizenry through reorientation. Its goal is to find meaningful employment for the ex-offender population of the area including persons on work-release, parole, probation, pre-trial diversion, and the ex-offender included in one of the above categories. Resources used are a job bank, job development, newspaper ads, seminars, and an Annual Job Mart for Ex-Offenders.
  Current projects and activities:
    Sponsoring the Annual Job Mart for Ex-Offenders in Boston and in Springfield.
  Number of permanent staff: 7
  Publications: "What is a Pre-Release Center?"; "The Department of Correction Office of Manpower Development"; "Pre-Employment Training Program."

WHAT CAN I DO?
  Internship descriptions:
    Caseworker internship. The division monitors daily population count, inmate movement, classification boards and procedures, and furlough process. The caseworker will assist in reviewing area classification boards, case checking furlough applications and answering correspondence from inmates and families. In addition, the caseworker will assist in special projects related to a number of topics including overcrowding and special classification boards. An effort will be made to expose the caseworker to the field through observation of boards and tours.
    Administrative internship. The intern acting in the capacity of administrative assistant will be primarily involved in aiding the Director of Administration in preparing for the next fiscal year budget submission for all area institutions.
    Planning internship. Development of a national data base regarding prison population (including making appropriate contacts, researching demographic trends, etc.); on the short-term, tasks would include responding to

citizen letters, monitoring population changes, and completing corollary research.

General clerical internship. The intern will learn office procedures, including typing, filing, answering phones, record management, and receptionist duties in an office that deals with clients from all areas of the criminal justice field.

Career speicalist internship. The intern will learn the principles, methods, and techniques of job and vocational counseling, including vocational evaluation.

CAN I GET IN?
  Academic requirements: We are not particularly concerned that an intern be studying criminal justice, and are convinced that any student interested in state government or public policy development can find this a highly valuable experience.
  Age: 18
  Length of commitment to internship: Negotiable
  Number of 1978 interns: 3
  Number planned for the future: Flexible

DO I GET PAID, EXPENSES, OR CREDIT?
  Expenses: Sometimes travel expenses on the job are reimbursed.
  College credit: Can be arranged

HOW DO I GET IN?
  Closing date for application: Open   Interview required: Yes
  When will I know about application: After interview

WHERE CAN I GET MORE INFORMATION?
  Write: Edward Gallagher, Director of Manpower Development, Department of Corrections, 100 Cambridge Street, Boston, MA 02202
  Phone: (617) 727-3950
  Read: Publications listed above

MASSACHUSETTS DEPARTMENT OF FOOD AND AGRICULTURE
Boston, Massachusetts

WHAT'S IT DO?
  Purpose and goals:
    To make state owned land available to the public for commercial farming and community gardening purposes. To protect, preserve and promote the use of land for agricultural purposes in the Commonwealth of Massachusetts.
  Current projects and activities:
    Working with a range of issues centered around agricultural land use, we are arranging the use of state owned land, connecting gardeners with garden plots, undertaking a systematic review of available state land, providing assistance to urban community gardening projects, and working with land use policy.

WHAT CAN I DO?
  Internship descriptions:
    Community gardens internship. Assist community garden program. This would involve collection of information useful to youth, elderly, and low-income gardening efforts, assistance to field agent investigating potential garden sites in highly populated areas. Help organize inner-city farmer's market. Student should 1) be fairly self-motivated and self-directed; 2) be knowledgeable of community organizations and neighborhood characteristics; 3) be able to work with a wide variety of people.
    Land inventory internship. 1) Inventory of state lands to determine existing food raising, food preservation, and food storage facilities. 2) Assist with inventory of state-owned land that could be offered for gardening or farming purposes through the division of agricultural land use.
    Researcher/urban pollution impact internship. Urban pollution as it affects urban gardeners (specifically trace element and metal poisoning like lead from atmosphere and soil). Duties might involve: 1) review of literature; 2) finding out who is currently working on it and what they are doing; 3) what does the above mean to community gardeners; 4) communication of relevant information and advice to community gardeners in Boston and other Massachusetts towns. This is a good opportunity for a science major who is also interested in urban problems.
    Urban composting and soil building internship. The student might 1) investigate feasibility of inner city compost building project; 2) help set one up; 3) find out what other city and urban gardening groups are doing; 4) explore possibilities of composting at the municipality level, and of intertown compost recycling (towns with excess ship to those that need it).

CAN I GET IN?
  Academic requirement: Related to the internship   Age: 18
  Length of commitment to internship: Semester or more

DO I GET PAID, EXPENSES, OR CREDIT?
  Expenses: Travel expenses are sometimes reimbursed.
  College credit: Can be arranged

HOW DO I GET IN?
  Closing date for application: No formal application procedures exist, but a letter expressing interest and a resume should be submitted.
  Interview required: Yes

WHERE CAN I GET MORE INFORMATION?
  Write: Susan Redlich, Director, Division of Agricultural Land Use, 100 Cambridge Street, 21st Floor, Boston, MA 02202
  Phone: (617) 727-6633

MASSACHUSETTS DEPARTMENT OF MENTAL HEALTH

NEIGHBORHOOD DAY SCHOOL

Boston, Massachusetts

WHAT'S IT DO?
  Purpose and goals:
    The Neighborhood Day School is a small preschool located in the Children's Unit of Massachusetts Mental Health Center. It enrolls children from the urban area immediately adjacent to the hospital. The program is designed to meet the needs of normal children ages three to five, and is also a demonstration of normal child development for residents training in child psychiatry. Interns participate in a weekly seminar with child psychiatry residents, consultations with the staff child psychiatrist and the director of social services, and an intensive discussion and record keeping session that follows each school day. Also, much emphasis is placed on work with parents.
  Current projects and activities:
    In addition to the school situation interns also are invited to participate in a wide variety of seminars, clinical presentations, and case studies which are part of the on-going training programs in both the Children's Unit and other parts of the hospital. An intern would be an assistant to the teacher, working toward having sole responsibility for the total group.

WHAT CAN I DO?
  Internship description:
    An intern is an assistant to the teacher-director, working toward having sole responsibility for the total group. The children's school hours are from 9:00 to 12:00 noon five days a week; an intern would be expected to be at school from 8:00 am to 1:00 pm. Flexible hours and days can be arranged. An intern will become familiar with the running of a pre-school; will develop a knowledge of child development, teaching techniques; and ways of presenting and implementing curriculum. There will be daily supervision sessions with the director.

CAN I GET IN?
  Academic requirements: College student   Age: 18
  Length of commitment to internship: One year

DO I GET PAID, EXPENSES, OR CREDIT?
  College credit: Can be arranged

HOW DO I GET IN?
  Closing date for application: On-going   Interview required: Yes
  When will I know about application: After the interview

WHERE CAN I GET MORE INFORMATION?
  Write: Ruth Misch, Director, Neighborhood Day School, 74 Fenwood Road,
    Boston, MA 02115
  Phone: (617) 734-1300 Ext. 316

MASSACHUSETTS HOUSE OF REPRESENTATIVES -

REPRESENTATIVE JAMES E. SMITH

Boston, Massachusetts

WHAT'S IT DO?
  Purpose and goals:
    This is a political activity; its goal is to elect Jim Smith to Congress.
    Individuals are needed, primarily volunteers, to perform a variety of
    tasks geared toward winning voter support. The work involves public
    opinion surveys; campaign funds solicitation and bookkeeping; scheduling
    candidate, policy and strategy development; research district, opponent
    and issues; correspondence; press relations; organization of volunteers
    by town. In a non-election year it services the needs of the people of
    the 22nd (Essex) District.

WHAT CAN I DO?
  Volunteer descriptions:
    1) Press. Write press releases, monitor press coverage, establish media
       contacts.
    2) Organizer. Identify Smith supporters in a given town, then develop an
       organization around them. Also needed are people to coordinate coffee
       parties.
    3) Bookkeeper. Regular updating of financial records--receipts and
       expenses, including filing of quarterly reports.
    4) Secretaries. People to type letters, memos, press releases and reports.
       Also to do filing.
    5) Receptionist. To answer phones, greet incoming volunteers and guests.
    6) Scheduler. Make the candidate's appointments, send follow-up mail,
       record information about the meetings.
    7) Research. Research a given topic for use in campaign theme, speeches,
       debates, etc.
    8) Graphics. Conceptualization and layout of campaign literature.
    9) Writer. Draft speeches, advertisements, literature, press statement
       and research documents.
    10) Advance person. Set up meetings, speeches, fund-raisers, conferences
        and other gatherings.
    11) Fund-Raiser. Work solely on developing financial contacts, soliciting
        contributions, and organizing fund-raising events.

12) Volunteer Recruiter. Identify, contact, and assign campaign volunteers.
Legislative researcher internship:
Participate in a variety of activities directed toward serving constituents. Assist in the research and final preparation of legislation, investigate constituent complaints and questions, and become thoroughly familiar with the legislation, investigate constituent complaints and questions, and legislative and executive processes and functions.

CAN I GET IN?
Academic requirements: No requirement, political science major preferred
Length of commitment to internship: Negotiable

DO I GET PAID, EXPENSES, OR CREDIT?
College credit: Can be arranged

HOW DO I GET IN?
Closing date for application: On-going
Interview required: Yes
When will I know about application: At interview

WHERE CAN I GET MORE INFORMATION?
Write: Representative James E. Smith, State House, Boston, MA 02133
Phone: (617) 727-3859

METROPOLITAN WASHINGTON COUNCIL OF GOVERNMENTS

Washington, D.C.

WHAT'S IT DO?
Purpose and goals:
The Metropolitan Washington Council of Governments (COG) is a voluntary association of the area's fifteen local governments, working cooperatively to solve mutual problems that are regional in scope and not confined by political or geographic boundaries.
Current projects and activities:
Include water quality, population growth, information center for citizens, environmental noise control, criminal justice, library program, commuter problems, housing and health projects.

WHAT CAN I DO?
Internship description:
During the past several years, COG has realized that many benefits were to be derived from employing student interns--from both the student and COG points of view. The interns' creativity, imagination, curiosity, and energy, applied to an organization's program, often give the regular staff new ideas, challenges, and incentives. Conversely, the internships provide an opportunity for the students to:
--test a career decision against the complexities of the profession;
--apply schoolroom theory to real world considerations (relationship of planning to political constraints);
--gain specialized training and practice under experts in current techniques, methods, and equipment;

--gain an overview of the activities, programs, and policies of the
  Council of Governments;
--gain familiarization with techniques being applied by the agency, and
  by other agencies in the metropolitan area who relate to the same
  problems and to new social, technical and economic concepts;
--obtain interdisciplinary work experience.

Students will be accepted to work in the housing, public safety, legal, regional planning, environmental, and administrative activities of COG. All participating interns work as an integral part of the COG professional staff meeting with management personnel, utilizing data resources, and attending meetings of policy and technical committees and the Board of Directors. Special seminars are also provided with professionals in government, private organizations, and the academic world.

Water quality internship. Assist in running computer programs on surface water hydrology, water quality reactions, and sewerage system hydraulics. Work will be primarily related to COG's water resources planning activities in preparation for an areawide waste treatment management plan for the Washington area. Work will involve conversion of raw data for input to these programs. Also, there will be data interpretation of results in the form of narrative descriptions, tables, graphs. Applicant should be graduate or upper class undergraduate student in Civil Engineering or Environmental Studies. Must have some exposure to computer programming applications. Some course work in water quality, hydrology and hydrologic desirable.

Areawide environmental noise internship. Work in conjunction with the noise staff in the collection of field data required in the analysis of various alternative noise control strategies. Individual needed in urban, city or transportation planning or civil engineering with an interest in environmental planning.

Criminal justice internship. Intern will assist criminal justice staff in data collection and analysis concerning evaluation of grants. Intern may conduct independent study or research as time permits. Intern should be in criminal justice, public administration, or related field.

Commuter club internship. Perform monitoring duties by telephone to determine the impact of commuter club activities on individual car pooling applicants. Their work might also include the canvassing of employers to convince them to help their employees car pool or form van pools. Students with an interest in transportation, urban studies or planning.

Housing internship. Monitoring the regional housing allocation plan; assisting in the development and execution of a regional demonstration effort under the Section 8 Housing Assistance Payments Program; providing support for the Department's extensive data collection and maintenance program. Students pursuing a degree in planning, urban affairs, public administration or a related field and have a familiarity with housing issues including basic research skills.

CAN I GET IN?
  Academic requirements: Applicants must be senior undergraduates enrolled in urban affairs, urban planning, transportation planning, public administration, health care administration, public finance, business administration, economics, library science and computer programming. Also, see internship descriptions.
  Length of commitment to internship: Semester or year

DO I GET PAID, EXPENSES, OR CREDIT?
  Pay: Some internships are paid at the rate of $3.50 per hour for undergraduates.
  College credit: Can be arranged

HOW DO I GET IN?
  Closing date for application: On-going
  Interview required: Only those selected will be asked for an interview, sometimes by phone.
  Other procedures: Send a resume and a copy of a paper, report, or work item that you have written in the past year. The subject need not be directly related to the position for which you are applying.
  When will I know about application: When the supervisors review all applications; date is not available.

WHERE CAN I GET MORE INFORMATION?
  Write: Intern Coordinator, Metropolitan Washington Council of Governments, 1225 Connecticut Avenue, N.W., Suite 201, Washington, DC 20036
  Phone: (202) 223-6800

NEW YORK CITY URBAN CORPS

New York, New York

WHAT'S IT DO?
  Purpose and goals:
    The New York City Urban Corps is the nation's largest public service internship program for university students in municipal government. It is sponsored cooperatively by the City of New York, the Federal government and participating colleges. Since the origin of the Urban Corps in 1966, college students from all over the United States have participated in its various employment and academic programs. These students come from over 125 colleges and universities each year under agreements drawn up between the individual school and the Urban Corps. The programs offer unique opportunities to learn from the special functions of operating city agencies.
  Current projects and activities:
    Over 125 city departments utilize the services of Urban Corps interns. The Urban Corps office is administered by Urban Corps interns under the direction of a small professional staff.

WHAT CAN I DO?
  Internship descriptions:
    Program development is guided by student interest and placement needs, along with a continuing effort to find the highest quality positions available. Urban Corps staff meets with designated coordinators in each city agency to determine how student skills may be best utilized. Written requests for college interns are then submitted to the Urban Corps office. Each request is reviewed on the basis of evaluation reports submitted by the Urban Corps Field Staff. The Urban Corps receives and processes over 6,000 job requests in this manner each year. Urban Corps interns have served as a valuable resource for the city by providing services which otherwise could not have been delivered. Among these have been: 1) rehabilitation therapy for post-psychiatric patients; 2) community information

centers for food stamps and welfare benefits; 3) prison legal assistants to act as liaisons between inmates and their attorneys; 4) assistance in production of street and indoor theatre in the Lower East Side; 5) research which affects transportation planning for the elderly and disabled.

- Academic credit internships. The program offers non-stipend, internship opportunities to undergraduate and graduate students who have obtained approval from their colleges to undertake off-campus projects. It is offered during the summer and the academic year.
- Creative artist public service internships. This program is open to undergraduate and graduate students who are interested in serving as an apprentice to an artist, photographer, or writer. The students must be eligible for Work-Study, and the program is operated year-round.
- Mobilization for Adolescent Student Health and Consumer Advocates Program. The program is open to undergraduate and graduate students who are interested in adolescent health needs or consumer problems. The program is funded by Action and provides a stipend and academic credit. The student is required to work for a full year.
- New York City urban fellowship program. Seniors in college or graduate students are provided an opportunity to study city government while receiving a stipend and academic credit during the school year. Interns are placed in positions of responsibility and attend weekly seminar sessions.
- Volunteer program. This program is open to any student who wants an opportunity to acquire experience in a specific field of study. It is operated on a year-round basis and the student must be prepared to commit at least ten hours a week to assignment.

CAN I GET IN?
  Academic requirements: College student
  Length of commitment to internship: Semester or year
  Number of 1978 interns and volunteers: 6,000
  Number planned for the future: About the same

DO I GET PAID, EXPENSES, OR CREDIT?
  Pay: The Urban Corps intern is an employee of the City of New York under the title of College Aide. As such, the intern is fully covered under Workmen's Compensation Insurance at the city's expense. Further, as a College Aide, the intern will not have Social Security deducted from her or his bi-weekly paycheck. The pay rates for the interns are: from freshman through completion of sophomore year - $2.50/hr.; from junior through completion of senior year - $3.00/hr.; all students in graduate level programs - $3.50/hr.
  College credit: Can be arranged; many interns do receive college credit rather than money.

HOW DO I GET IN?
  Closing date for application: On-going
  Other procedures: The placement of the student is based on the information filled out on the application and during the preliminary interview with the Urban Corps Placement staff. The student is then placed in a job assignment where an on-site interview with an agency supervisor is conducted to assure that the placement is most closely aligned with the needs of the student and the supervisor. If the assignment is not suitable, the student may be reassigned.

WHERE CAN I GER MORE INFORMATION?
  Write: Director, New York City Urban Corps, Office of the Mayor, 250 Broadway, New York, NY 10007
  Phone: (212) 566-3952

RHODE ISLAND INTERN CONSORTIUM

DIVISION OF YOUTH DEVELOPMENT

Providence, Rhode Island

WHAT'S IT DO?
  Purpose and goals:
    The State Division of Youth Development operates the Rhode Island Intern and Volunteer Consortium, which is a work experience program offering students a chance to apply academic curriculum and personal objectives to a viable work-learning experience in a non-profit, governmental or public sector agency. The Consortium presently maintains a clearinghouse of over 50 colleges and universities nationwide and over 300 agencies in the public, non-profit and private sectors.
  Current projects and activities:
    The Consortium programs offer internships and volunteer projects and activities in 70 different disciplines.
  Number of permanent staff: 2
  Annual budget: $74,000 (state and local only)
  Publications: The College Intern Book

WHAT CAN I DO?
  Internship descriptions:
    The Consortium deals with work-study, academic credit, and volunteer placements in over 70 field disciplines. These placements vary from full-time to part-time, and in length from a four-week intersession placement to a full year program. The needs of the student, relative to his or her academic and career goals are the main concern with the placement. If placements with the agencies listed in the directory are not suitable to the intern, an individualized placement will be developed. Duration is based on the student's availability.

CAN I GET IN?
  Academic requirements: None, but most interns and volunteers are Rhode Islanders, or college students in Rhode Island between the ages of 14 and 24.
  Length of commitment to internship: Varies up to a year
  Number of 1978 interns: 300
  Number planned for the future: 500

DO I GET PAID, EXPENSES, OR CREDIT?
  Pay: Only for those students on a college work-study program
  College credit: Can be arranged, and many students do receive credit.

HOW DO I GET IN?
  Closing date for application: On-going, but greatest number of placements

are at the beginning of each semester and the summer.
Interview required: Yes
When will I know about my application: Soon after the interview

WHERE CAN I GET MORE INFORMATION?
Write: Charles E. Totoro, Program Planner, Rhode Island Intern Consortium, Department of Community Affairs, Division of Youth Development, 150 Washington Street, Providence, RI 02903
Phone: (401) 277-3750
Read: <u>The College Intern Book</u>, from the address above

WHITE HOUSE FELLOWSHIPS

Washington, D.C.

WHAT'S IT DO?
Purpose and goals:
The White House Fellowship program provides gifted and highly motivated young Americans with some firsthand experience in the process of governing the Nation and a sense of personal involvement in the leadership of the society. The program seeks to draw exceptionally promising young people from all sectors of our national life--the professions, business, government, the arts, and the academic world.
Current projects and activities:
Each year, the 14 to 20 persons who are chosen as White House Fellows work as full-time employees of the Federal Government, working in a Cabinet level agency, in the Executive Office of the President, or with the Vice President.
Number of permanent staff: 7   Annual budget: $263,000
Publications: <u>White House Fellowship</u>, a brochure, and a newsletter

WHAT CAN I DO?
Rather than fit the Fellows to their pre-Fellowship specialities, the program aims at utilizing their abilities and developing their skills in the broadest sense possible. In most cases, a Fellow serves as a special assistant, performing tasks for a Cabinet Secretary, the Vice President, or as an assistant to the President. In this sense, the White House Fellow's year is a high-level internship in government--but it is also much more. In addition to the Fellow's full-time work assignment, an education program is a major element of the Fellowship year. During these education sessions the Fellows meet as a group with top-level government officials for off-the-record discussions and a question and answer period. An exchange of experiences in their respective agencies adds depth to the education program. At the end of his or her term each Fellow has had an intensive work experience as well as a broader insight into government through sessions with one another and with the Nation's leaders.

CAN I GET IN?
Academic requirements: No restrictions or requirements for age, education, sex, or race, but most Fellows are highly qualified young people in their early 30's and just starting their careers. Very competitive program.

Length of commitment to internship: One year
Number of 1978 interns: 14
Number planned for the future: 14 to 20

DO I GET PAID, EXPENSES, OR CREDIT?
Pay: Up to $36,171 a year

HOW DO I GET IN?
Closing date for application: December 1
Interview required: Several are required.
Other procedures: Regional finalists interviewed by selection panels in Atlanta, Boston, Chicago, Dallas, Denver, New York, Philadelphia, San Francisco, Seattle, St. Louis, or Washington, D.C.
When will I know about application: Regional finalists are notified January 31. National finalists are notified March 31. Announcement of White House Fellows is May 22.

WHERE CAN I GET MORE INFORMATION?
Write: W. Landis Jones, Director, PCWWHF, 1900 E Street, N.W., Washington, DC 20415
Phone: (202) 653-6263
Read: The White House Fellowships, from above address

THE HEALTH CLUSTER

American Cancer Society, Massachusetts Division
Andrew W. Johnson Alcohol Detoxification Center
Appalachian Regional Hospitals
Boston Coordinating Council on Drug Abuse
Central Kentucky Community Action Council
Coalition of Concerned Medical Professionals
Direct Relief Foundation
Health/PAC
Occupational Health Project

AMERICAN CANCER SOCIETY

MASSACHUSETTS DIVISION

Boston, Massachusetts

WHAT'S IT DO?
  Purpose and goals:
    The Massachusetts Cancer Information Service (CIS) is a state-wide, toll-free telephone resource on cancer-related matters. It is part of the National Cancer Insitute's nation-wide network of CIS's. Callers are cancer patients, their families, students doing research, people who suspect they may have cancer, and health professionals. The phone lines are open from 9 am to 4 pm on weekdays, and those are the hours for which coverage must be provided by a volunteer or intern. The goal of the CIS is to increase access to the medical world, for the layperson, and to provide a direct link with the National Cancer Institute and other Federal agencies, for laypeople and health professionals. It is a good place for one to become acquainted with the health care field.
  Current projects and activities:
    Update resource material for the phone calls. Answer 20 to 30 phone calls a day, answer letters, and write a newspaper column. The column, "Cancer Information," uses a question and answer format and covers issues raised in calls and letters received by the service.
  Number of permanent staff: 1½
  Annual budget: Funded by National Cancer Institute
  Publications: Newspaper column, Cancer Information

WHAT CAN I DO?
  Internship descriptions:
    After orientation to the office and its library of resources, the intern will:
      --answer telephone calls and correspondence about cancer and related issues;
      --research subjects such as causes, prevention, diagnostic methods, treatment, rehabilitation;
      --assist in tasks such as planning and evaluating;
      --assume responsibility for a project to be done for the resource files or public education work;
      --participate in training programs, which include formal workshops featuring cancer specialists and other health professionals, and which are held monthly.
    Based on the intern's interests, this experience could help to determine educational and employment goals, since one learns about psycho-social problems of cancer patients and learns to identify resources available to help people solve their problems. One also learns a bit of medicine. Students can concentrate on their areas of interest. For example, a science major may be responsible for gathering and updating the information on basic science and latest research on treatment or carcinogens. A social work or psychology student may concentrate on the aspects of counseling. Someone majoring in business or health care management might take on some aspect of evaluation and data collection. A student of physical therapy might update and expand resources on rehabilitation, or focus on rehabilitation counseling.

CAN I GET IN?
  Academic requirements: None   Age: 18
  Experience: Some knowledge of the health care field preferred
  Length of commitment to internship: Semester or longer
  Number of 1978 interns: 1   Number planned for the future: 3

DO I GET PAID, EXPENSES, OR CREDIT?
  College credit: Can be arranged

HOW DO I GET IN?
  Closing date for application: On-going   Interview required: Yes
  When will I know about application: Immediately after interview

WHERE CAN I GET MORE INFORMATION?
  Write: Anne Peckenpaugh Lund, Service Coordinator, Cancer Information
    Service, Box 462, Kenmore Station, Boston, MA 02215
  Phone: Toll-free 1-800-952-7420

ANDREW W. JOHNSON ALCOHOL DETOXIFICATION CENTER

Boston, Massachusetts

WHAT'S IT DO?
  Purpose and goals:
    To provide appropriate and professional acute care and detoxification of
    the alcoholic or problem drinker; and, initiate the process of alcoholic
    rehabilitation. The detoxification center is part of the John F. Kennedy
    Family Service Center whose basic purpose is to develop and execute
    programs in the Charlestown district of Boston and its environs to meet
    health, education, employment, recreation, and welfare needs. Its projects
    include training and placement of unemployed persons, family counseling
    services, programs for the strengthening of family life, and the prevention
    of juvenile delinquency.
  Current projects and activities:
    Several projects in the area of research and training.
  Number of permanent staff: 23   Annual budget: $287,250

WHAT CAN I DO?
  Internship descriptions:
    Medical, Social Service, or Administrative Aide internships. Intern works
    under supervision of the program director and nursing and counseling
    supervisors to provide care and social or administrative services to the
    clients in this 20-bed, in-patient, acute-care facility for the alcoholic.
    The detoxification center operates 24 hours each day, seven days a week.
    The intern must be self-directed in observing and participating in the
    agency and treatment dynamics and process.

CAN I GET IN?
  Academic requirements: College or specialized training
  Age: 18   Length of commitment to internship: Negotiable
  Number of 1978 interns: 5   Number planned for future: 6

DO I GET PAID, EXPENSES, OR CREDIT?
  College credit: Can be arranged

HOW DO I GET IN?
  Closing date for application: On-going   Interview required: Yes
  When will I know about application: Immediately

WHERE CAN I GET MORE INFORMATION?
  Write: Joseph H. Greene, Director, Andrew Johnson Alcohol Detoxification
    Center, 56 Havre Street, East Boston, MA 02128
  Phone: (617) 569-5478
  Read: Alcoholism Resources Directory, Director of Alcoholism, Department
    of Public Health, Boston, MA

APPALACHIAN REGIONAL HOSPITALS

Lexington, Kentucky

WHAT'S IT DO?
  Purpose and goals:
    Appalachian Regional Hospitals is a model, rural health care system of ten
    community health centers, embracing hospitals and related services, serving
    a mountainous region stretching 250 miles from Middlesboro, Kentucky to
    Beckley, West Virginia. Seven of the hospitals are in Eastern Kentucky,
    two in West Virginia, and one in Virginia. The ARH system is a non-profit
    humanitarian enterprise dedicated to providing high quality health care to
    many thousands of mountain folk who for decades had suffered from a lack
    of adequate medical and hospital services.
  Current projects and activities:
    The system's hospitals have 1,078 acute care beds, 67 skilled nursing beds
    and 26 intermediate care beds. The ARH system annually cares for more
    than 47,000 inpatients and provides more than 630,000 outpatient services.
    Its emergency rooms treat approximately 130,000 persons each year. Appa-
    lachian Regional Hospitals has entered new fields of service, including
    coronary and intensive care, rehabilitation, social services, emergency
    ambulance services, home care, skilled nursing care, and the servicing of
    health care centers and hospitals outside the ARH system.
  Number of permanent staff: 2,760 employees including 372 physicians
  Annual budget: More than $60 million a year

WHAT CAN I DO?
  Student employee training program:
    Appalachian Regional Hospitals will employ high school graduates, who have
    been accepted for admission into an accredited educational institution or
    program, or students of an accredited educational institution or program
    for the purpose of training and selecting future permanent employees.
    About 99% of the employees are those with health majors (most in nursing).

CAN I GET IN?
  Academic requirements: Allied health majors   Age: 18
  Experience: At least one year of academic program completed
  Special: Residents of Appalachia are given preference

Length of possible commitment to employment: Most employees work for the summer or during school holidays; however, longer times may be arranged.
Number of students employees in 1978: 55
Number planned for the future: Open

DO I GET PAID, EXPENSES, OR CREDIT?
Pay: From $2.65 to $3.30 an hour depending on the number of semester hours of credit the student has completed at the time of employment.

HOW DO I GET IN?
Closing date for application: April 1, for summer
Interview required: Usually not
When will I know about application: Within six weeks

WHERE CAN I GET MORE INFORMATION?
Write: Paul H. Pickering, Manager, Manpower Development, Appalachian Regional Hospitals, Box 8086, Lexington, KY 40503
Phone: (606) 255-4431
Read: Appalachian Regional Hospitals, a brochure

BOSTON COORDINATING COUNCIL ON DRUG ABUSE

Boston, Massachusetts

WHAT'S IT DO?
Purpose and goals:
The Boston Coordinating Council on Drug Abuse coordinates relevant city departments, advises the Mayor on measures to address the drug/alcohol abuse problem, and has provided expert testimony on matters pending before state legislative and Federal rulemaking panels. The Council also provides technical assistance and information to public health and safety professionals, employers, educators, private citizens and neighborhood organizations, in addition to drug abuse prevention programs. It was established in 1970 to facilitate the efforts of those public and private agencies in Boston which impact on the drug and alcohol abuse problem. Specifically, the 21-member board serves as a liaison between Boston's drug action community-based programs and government on the city, state, and Federal levels.
Current projects and activities:
Services to the public. A clearinghouse for information on drug and alcohol issues is provided via a resource library, film library, literature distribution and speaker's bureau.
Consultation with individuals such as school administrators and representatives of the media about substantive abuse issues.
Referral to drug/alcohol services in Boston.
Seminars and lectures for professionals and for business, elderly, and community groups.

Services to drug and alcohol treatment, rehabilitation and prevention programs. Publication of the "Directory of Boston Drug and Alcohol Programs"; ombudsman for governmental services; technical assistance and consultation (in-staff training, public relations, and fund raising); inter-agency personnel program (through CETA, over 125 personnel have been outstationed in more than 40 treatment, prevention and health care programs).

Research and planning. Preparation of annual city-wide substance and abuse management plan.
Survey of special prevention issues and treatment needs of high risk populations (women, elderly, youth, etc.) or settings (schools, industry, etc.)
Vocational rehabilitation and personnel needs survey for recovering substance abusers.
Public policy analysis.
Survey of public and private funds availability.

In addition to this broad responsibility, staff members are assigned specific areas of concentration in accord with the concerns of the Coordinating Council. Completed research and analysis is disseminated to the CCDA and to its committees (treatment and rehabilitation, education and prevention, administration of justice) and to its Alcoholism and Alcohol Abuse Advisory Panel. Results are also made available to the appropriate public agencies, treatment, rehabilitation and prevention programs, and are disseminated to the media and to the general public, upon request.

The Mayor's Office of Substance Abuse Activities also provides referral to treatment for residents of Boston.

Number of permanent staff: 11

Annual budget: $130,000

Publications: "Directory of Boston Drug and Alcohol Programs," "Annual City of Boston Substance Abuse Management Plan," assorted pamphlets

WHAT CAN I DO?

Internship descriptions:

Research internship. The intern's research assignments will help prepare a needs assessment which will culminate in Boston's annual "Drug Abuse Management Plan." This plan encompasses the fields of treatment, vocational rehabilitation, education, criminal justice, prevention and alternative youth programs.

Public information internship. The intern will help prepare public service campaigns and creation of drug abuse literature for neighborhood distribution. Also will assist the drug information director and public relations coordinator in their duties. The intern will be personally involved in a major public information effort to promote a critical public health and public safety issue. For students interested in a career in public relations, communications or public information, this internship should provide excellent on-the-job training. Writing and media liaison skills will be helpful for this internship.

Public policy analyst internship. This intern will work with senior staff members in the analysis of Federal, state and city public policy issues, related to human services in general and to drug abuse issues specifically. Assignments may range from oversight on a specific piece of legislation to in-depth analysis of the Federal drug abuse expenditures. This position offers a fine opportunity for interns considering a career in public service to get first hand experience dealing with government services, the law-making process, and the development of public policy.

CAN I GET IN?
  Academic requirements: College student
  Length of commitment to internship: Negotiable

DO I GET PAID, EXPENSES, OR CREDIT?
  Expenses: Travel expenses incurred as part of internship assignments
  College credit: Can be arranged

HOW DO I GET IN?
  Closing date for application: On-going
  Interview required: Yes
  When will I know about application: Within two weeks after interview

WHERE CAN I GET MORE INFORMATION?
  Write: Robert N. Downing, Deputy Director, Boston City Hall, 31 State Street, 6th Floor, Boston, MA 02109
  Phone: (617) 725-3260
  Read: Licity and Illicit Drugs, by Edward M. Brecher

CENTRAL KENTUCKY COMMUNITY ACTION COUNCIL
Lebanon, Kentucky

WHAT'S IT DO?
  Purpose and goals:
    A multi-purpose community action agency serving four rural counties just outside the Appalachian area, it operates information and referral, transportation, manpower, child development and aging programs.
  Current projects and activities:
    Programs for aging (meals and social services); development of coordinated district transportation program; operation of two day-care centers and 12 Head Start centers; winterization of houses in eight counties.
  Number of permanent staff: 5   Annual budget: $1,051,578
  Publication: <u>Bulletin</u>, a monthly newsletter and an annual report

WHAT CAN I DO?
  Internship descriptions:
    Opportunities include summer work as director of summer feeding program sites, director of youth recreational activities, chore services for the elderly throughout the year, and learning opportunities which could include work with the local community organizations and opportunities to form community-based groups. There is a need for legal services and for health services, particularly for physician-extenders.

CAN I GET IN?
  Academic requirements: No requirement   Age: 18
  Special: We will accept a volunteer on any basis as long as the volunteer makes an advance commitment to a specific time frame.
  Length of commitment to internship: Semester or longer
  Number of 1978 interns: 1
  Number planned for the future: Open for many more

DO I GET PAID, EXPENSES, OR CREDIT?
  Expenses: Travel is reimbursed while on the job. Occasional lodging is provided.
  College credit: Can be arranged

HOW DO I GET IN?
  Closing date for application: On-going
  Interview required: Yes
  When will I know about application: At the interview

WHERE CAN I GET MORE INFORMATION?
  Write: W. Terry Ward, Executive Director, Central Kentucky CAC, 406 West Main Street, Lebanon, KY 40033
  Phone: (502) 692-2136

COALITION OF CONCERNED MEDICAL PROFESSIONALS

New York, New York

WHAT'S IT DO?
  Purpose and goals:
    The Coalition of Concerned Medical Professionals is a community based organization dedicated to the provision of free comprehensive medical care to Americans whose economic position precludes their accessibility to such services in traditional settings. This includes farmworkers; domestic, service, and attendant care workers; independent contractors; welfare recipients; the elderly poor; and the unemployed--experiencing the greatest need for good medical care, but having the least access to traditional facilities. Faced with low wages, inadequate diet, lack of heat, lack of transportation, unsafe living and working conditions, these unrecognized workers meet numerous life threatening medical and medically related problems on an on-going basis.
  Current projects and activities:
    Volunteer health professionals, students, and other concerned community residents joined together with migrant and seasonal farmworkers in Suffolk County, New York to build an apparatus for the delivery of responsive and realistic health care. Based on the success of CCMP in Suffolk County and the need for such health care throughout the country coalitions were started in Pennsylvania, New Jersey, California, and Massachusetts. All of these organizations are connected to local organizing drives, and mutual benefits associations, seeking permanent solutions to the oppressive conditions faced by the low-income worker strata. CCMP does not accept governmental or corporate funding, but is reliant upon concerned community groups and individuals for its support.

WHAT CAN I DO?
  Medical Sessions and Follow-up volunteers. CCMP attempts to link together concerned health professionals and others with individuals with health care needs. Volunteers participate in medical sessions, notify patients of appointments, provide transportation, as well as make all necessary follow-up contacts. This follow-up includes the procurement, free of charge, of needed medications, medical supplies, and physical examinations; outreach into the community to recruit additional health professionals and other volunteers; necessary advocacy; and the training of newer volunteers in these activities.
  Medical Advocacy volunteers. Many low income workers are not familiar with available medical services due to the lack of publicity on the part on many service delivery systems. Volunteers work to collect information on existing medical services, including those requirements and restrictions that prohibit many low income workers from receiving the benefits of these services.
  Canvassing volunteers. Volunteers go to homes in low income communities to talk with patients and prospective patients to determine medical needs that CCMP should address, as well as to do follow-up including checking on the condition of patients, delivering prescriptions, and delivering emergency food, clothing, and blankets.
  Workers Benefits Council volunteers. In addition to canvassing, CCMP is able to determine the direction it should take by attending the weekly Workers

Benefits Council meetings of affiliated local organizing drives. In
Suffolk County, for example, the Workers Benefits Council directed CCMP
to expand its program to include special well child care medical sessions
so that the children of these workers could receive preventative health
care.

CAN I GET IN?
  Academic requirements: None
  Special: The only requirement to joining CCMP is a commitment to the
    delivery of free comprehensive health care to the unrecognized worker
    strata.
  Length of commitment to internship: Negotiable

DO I GET PAID, EXPENSES, OR CREDIT?
  Expenses: Full-time volunteers receive room, board, and necessary expenses.
  College credit: Can be arranged

HOW DO I GET IN?
  Closing date for application: On-going
  Interview required: No
  When will I know about application: No formal plan

WHERE CAN I GET MORE INFORMATION?
  Write: Helene Stillson, Coalition of Concerned Medical Professionals,
    76 West Main Street, Riverhead, NY 11901
  Phone: (516) 727-9380

DIRECT RELIEF FOUNDATION

Santa Barbara, California

WHAT'S IT DO?
  Purpose and goals:
    Direct Relief Foundation brings the means of restoration of health to
    continents where illness and malnutrition destroy people's energy potential
    to the detriment of the whole world. Aesculapian International, a division
    of Direct Relief Foundation, is dedicated to placement of concerned medical
    and paramedical personnel and students from all over the world. Its global
    scope includes hospitals and clinics in the U.S., the Caribbean, Africa,
    Central and South American, the Far East, and South Asia. All need medical
    help to treat patients, and many of them also require a medical instructor
    who can improve the capacities of local medical personnel. This may
    include clinical duty or training staff members with leadership qualities
    in health education, sanitation, and home nursing.
  Current projects and activities:
    DRF's health delivery system is curative, clinical, educational, and pre-
    ventive. Its programs are non-profit, non-sectarian and non-political, and
    are supported solely by private contributions. To complete an assignment
    costs DRF an average of $400. Although the office at headquarters is
    modest and the overhead is low, the work is regarded as a serious responsi-
    bility.
  Number of permanent staff: 14   Annual budget: $480,000
  Publications: Newsletter, "What's Up at DRF"

WHAT CAN I DO?
  Internship descriptions:
    Direct Action International arranges assignments of paramedical personnel. The office staff, specialists in their field, with 10 years of experience in arranging over 1,000 assignments, screen applicants, investigate institutions asking for assistance, catalog and file medical information, sociological data, status of education, personnel, weather and clothing on each location. The files at headquarters are full of complete professional, historical, cultural and pictorial information of such exotic places as American Samoa, Chichicastenango in Guatemala, and Dabou in the Ivory Coast. Files of both potential candidates and hospitals in need of their services are maintained.

CAN I GET IN?
  Academic requirements: College student
  Length of commitment to internship: One year

DO I GET PAID, EXPENSES, OR CREDIT:
  Pay: Transportation and some compensation is often paid medical personnel according to the economy of the location. Board and room are often supplied. Others receive an hourly wage depending on their college credits--$2.75 an hour for a first and second year college student.
  College credit: Can be arranged

HOW DO I GET IN?
  Closing date for application: On-going
  Interview required: Yes
  When will I know about application: At the interview

WHERE CAN I GET MORE INFORMATION?
  Write: Ruth E. Miller, Director of Assignments, Direct Relief Foundation, P.O. Box 1319, Santa Barbara, CA 93102
  Phone: (805) 966-9149
  Read: The Direct Relief Foundation newsletter

HEALTH/PAC

New York, New York

WHAT'S IT DO?

Purpose and goals:

Health/PAC is an independent, non-profit, public interest center, concerned with monitoring and interpreting the health system to change-oriented groups of health workers, consumers, professionals, and students. Health/PAC works toward providing:
- --A health system that provides low-cost, high-quality, relevant and accessible health services for all;
- --A health system which addresses the causes and prevention of illness, rather than one which is narrowly curative, overly technological and highly specialized;
- --A health system accountable to the communities which receive the care and the workers who provide it, and not to those who use the health system to enhance their power, profits, or prestige;
- --An end to all forms of discrimination, particularly those suffered by health workers and health consumers because of their age, race, sex, or class background.

Current projects and activities:

Publishes a bimonthly Bulletin bringing readers both facts and an understanding of important developments taking place in the health system at local, state, and national levels; produces and distributes educational materials on social, political, and economic issues in health care; maintains a resource center and offers a network for health activists to discuss, share and analyze their concerns and strategies with others across the country engaged in similar endeavors.

Number of permanent staff: 5   Annual budget: $110,000

Publications: Health/PAC Bulletin; Health/PAC books - *American Health Empire: Power, Profits and Politics* and *Prognosis Negative: Crisis in the Health Care System*; many pamphlets and issue packets.

WHAT CAN I DO?

Internships are organized around the on-going health projects in New York City. Some of the past accomplishments of health activists may give you further understanding about this agency. Throughout its ten-year history, Health/PAC has proven itself an effective voice for change in health care in America. Among its distinctive achievements are:
- --The first public challenge of the New York City Municipal Hospitals Affiliation Program, a program affiliating public to private hospitals. Once considered a solution to the crisis of public hospitals, the program is now widely recognized as a major part of the problem.
- --Publication of secret plans to close seven NYC municipal hospitals and the subsequent thwarting of those plans.
- --A key role in adoption of the landmark guidelines for sterilization procedures in NYC municipal hospitals--guidelines that mark the first attempt to protect women, especially low-income and minority women, from sterilization abuses. The guidelines are now being promoted as a model for women in all hospitals.
- --Expose showing that despite New York City's liberal reputation and ethnic diversity, its six medical schools lag behind the rest of the nation in

minority admissions, and their record is getting worse.
- --A 1974 analysis of prison health care that had major impact throughout the nation.
- --A major study of community mental health centers that provided ammunition for community organizations throughout the country struggling to increase the effectiveness of public, grass-roots control over mental health programs.

CAN I GET IN?
  Academic requirements: Prefer upperclass college students
  Length of commitment to internship: Negotiable

DO I GET PAID, EXPENSES, OR CREDIT?
  College credit: Can be arranged

HOW DO I GET IN?
  Closing date for application: On-going
  Interview required: Yes
  When will I know about application: Soon after resume and interview are completed

WHERE CAN I GET MORE INFORMATION?
  Write: Michael E. Clark, Health/PAC, 17 Murray Street, New York, NY 10007
  Phone: (212) 267-8891
  Read: American Health Empire: Power, Profits and Politics (Vintage); Prognosis Negative: Crisis in the Health Care System (Vintage)

OCCUPATIONAL HEALTH PROJECT

Bellport, New York

WHAT'S IT DO?
  Purpose and goals:
    The Occupational Health Project exists to address the harsh conditions and serious problems faced by domestic and service workers. The goals of OHP are two-fold: 1) provision of adequate compensation to those who have been injured and to the families of those who have been killed, and 2) elimination of dangerous and unhealthy working conditions from the lives of workers.
  Current projects and activities:
    Although over 1,500 laws have been put on the books since 1909 concerning the working conditions of farmworkers in the U.S., many farmworkers in Suffolk County lose their fingers in the potato graders, some receive fatal injuries while working with the potato combines, and tuberculosis, seizures, blood dyscrasias are prevalent among migrant farmworkers. The average life expectancy of farmworkers nationally is 49 years of age. OHP believes these problems to be a direct result of occupational related conditions-- constant exposure to toxic pesticides, dust, and faulty and dangerous machinery. Volunteer scientists, environmentalists, students, and other concerned community residents worked together with farmworkers to produce a report on their findings, "Working Conditions Among Farmworkers in Suffolk County," which has helped workers identify specific hazards as

they affect their health. Although farm labor ranks as the third most dangerous occupation in the United States, farmworkers in this county were not receiving Workmen's Compensation for the numerous injuries they receive. OHP won an historic victory in Suffolk County by demanding this compensation be made available to farmworkers according to their right by law. Currently OHP is in the process of expanding in both upstate New York where many farmworkers are employed, and Medford, Oregon where a large number of workers are employed in the lumber industry.

WHAT CAN I DO?
　Internship descriptions:
　　Specific activities for volunteers include: 1) filing and advocacy for workmen's compensation for workers and/or their families; 2) community canvassing to determine those occupational hazards most in need of address by OHP. To find out information on specific health problems workers face, and to advise workers of their right to safe and healthy working conditions and Workmen's Compensation; 3) research into various health hazards affecting unrecognized workers; 4) community outreach for the recruitment of volunteers for OHP; 5) attendance at the weekly Workers Benefits Council meeting of the affiliated local organizing drive to report on OHP progress and receive input and direction from representatives of various occupations and low income communities; and 6) attendance at classes on occupational health problems which affect the unrecognized workers strata and ways these problems can be solved.

CAN I GET IN?
　Academic requirements: None
　Special: The only requirement for volunteering with OHP is a commitment to adequate compensation for occupationally related injury and death and the need to eradicate the dangerous working conditions low income workers face.
　Length of commitment to internship: Semester or year

DO I GET PAID, EXPENSES, OR CREDIT?
　Expenses: Full-time volunteers receive board, room and necessary expenses
　College credit: Can be arranged

HOW DO I GET IN?
　Closing date for application: On-going
　Interview required: No
　When will I know about application: No formal plan

WHERE CAN I GET MORE INFORMATION?
　Write: Jim Reaven, The Occupational Health Project, 58 Beaver Dam Road, Bellport, NY 11713
　Phone: (516) 286-8004

THE PUBLIC INTEREST AND CONSUMER PROTECTION CLUSTER

    Association of Community Organizations for Reform NOW
    Bureau of Rehabilitation
    Center for Defense Information
    Center for National Security Studies
    Citizens for Participation in Political Action
    Citizens Organization for a Sane World
    Common Cause
    Community for Creative Nonviolence
    Consumer Federation of America
    Institute for Local Self-Reliance
    National Abortion Rights Action League
    National Committee Against Repressive Legislation
    National Labor Federation
    National Organization for the Reform of Marijuana Laws
    National Self-Help Resource Center
    National Taxpayers Union
    Oxfam-America
    Public Citizen
    Zero Population Growth

ASSOCIATION OF COMMUNITY ORGANIZATIONS FOR REFORM NOW (ACORN)

Little Rock, Arkansas

WHAT'S IT DO?
  Purpose and goals:
    ACORN is a multi-issue grassroots community organization, currently in Arkansas, Texas, Louisiana, Missouri, South Dakota, Tennessee, Florida, Colorado, Nevada, Pennsylvania, Iowa, and Massachusetts and with plans for further expansion. It is a membership organization made up of low and moderate income families organized into neighborhood groups, developing political and economic power through community action. Wholly supported by membership dues and local fund raising projects, it receives no government money.
  Current projects and activities:
    ACORN offers a unique alternative to the institutional mainstream. It trains new staff to become community organizers. Trainees generally go through an intensive eight to ten week apprenticeship-style training in the ACORN model of community and neighborhood organizing. Trainees conduct an organizing drive, learn how to build a neighborhood organization from scratch, develop leadership in the neighborhood people, recruit members, and research and develop strategy on local issues. After the initial training drive, an organizer is generally moved to another city and begins work with several existing local groups, coordinating campaigns, and continuing to build each group through increased membership and participation in ACORN actions. Illustrative of its programs is the Boston Acorn Child Care Center, a community-based day care program, serving 44 children. Families served are predominantly Chinese, but the Center seeks to maintain a balance of ethnic and racial backgrounds.
  Number of permanent staff in Boston: 6
  Annual budget in Boston: $105,000

WHAT CAN I DO?
  Internship descriptions:
    Persons who commit themselves to work for a minimum of one year receive a stipend. There are also non-paying internships for those who can't stay a full year. Applicants must demonstrate concern for economic justice, dedication to social change, willingness to move according to the needs of the organization, and ability to work well with people of varied backgrounds.
      Administrative Assistant internship (Boston). Help director with organizing office, from filing and running errands, to reporting center finances. It offers the opportunity to learn about administration of human services, possibly some training in bookkeeping and accounting.
      Teacher Aide (Boston). Works with director and teachers at Acorn in daily routine and in planning curriculum and activities for the children.

CAN I GET IN?
  Academic requirements: Related to your interests in internships
  Age: 16   Experience: Field experience helpful
  Special: Driver's license required
  Length of commitment to internship: Semester
  Number of 1978 interns: 0   Number planned for the future: 3 to 5

DO I GET PAID, EXPENSES, OR CREDIT?
  College credit: Can be arranged

HOW DO I GET IN?
  Closing date for application: On-going
  Interview required: Yes
  When will I know about application: 1 to 2 weeks after interview

WHERE CAN I GET MORE INFORMATION?
  Write: ACORN Internship Director, 523 West 15th, Little Rock, AK 72202 or
    Ann Lassen, Recruitment Coordinator, ACORN, 34 Oak Street, Boston, MA 02111
  Phone: Little Rock (501) 376-7151
         Boston (617) 482-9165
  Read: Acorn News (Little Rock, at above address, regular newspaper);
    Acorn: An Overview on its History, Structure and Philosophy as it Developed in Arkansas; "Acorn Calling," Working Papers, Summer, 1975, Vol. III, No. 2; "Lobby of Have-Nots Nettles the Southern Establishment," The New York Times, Wednesday, October 6, 1976; "They've All Gone to Look for America," Mother Jones, February/March 1976, Vol. 1, No. 1.

BUREAU OF REHABILITATION

Washington, D.C.

WHAT'S IT DO?
  Purpose and goals:
    The Bureau of Rehabilitation, a private correctional service agency, serves offenders and their families while they are in pre-trial, incarcerated, probation or parole status. Dedicated to the development of reasonable alternatives to confinement, the Bureau has developed services in community residential, drug abstinence and pre-trial programs. Particular concern has been directed toward improving community services for alcoholic offenders, and juveniles.
  Current projects and activities:
    Walk-In Social Service. The Bureau provides supportive counseling, material assistance, temporary lodging, job placement, vocational guidance, and limited financial and leisure time pursuits for clients and their families. Caseworkers and trained volunteers provide such services as specialized counseling and needed referrals to the families and inmates to prepare for return to the community. In cooperation with the Community Services Division of the Bail Agency, the Bureau supervises defendants conditionally released by the courts to the community prior to trial or sentencing. The primary goals of the program are to insure that defendants are in court as scheduled and refrain from criminal activity. The Drug Abuse Aftercare Unit continues to provide services to parolees and probationers with drug histories, who are under the supervision of the U.S. Probation Office of the U.S. District Court. In addition, there is a residential program which, through a complex of five halfway houses with a total bed capacity of 127, assists offenders in gaining or regaining those skills needed to lead crime-free, independent, and productive lives in the community.
  Number of permanent staff: 115   1976 Annual budget: $1,615,000
  Publications: Annual report

WHAT CAN I DO?
  Internship descriptions:
    Correctional institutional visitor. Visit men or women who are incarcerated and awaiting parole; help inmates prepare for return to the community; explore educational, training, employment and personal options; provide an "ear" and a link to the outside.
    Community specialist. Visit families of incarcerated and help prepare them for family member's return to the community; refer family to community services which would help meet their needs; help family members work together to prevent further involvement in criminal justice system; tutor children, counsel teenagers, talk with parents.
    Counselor aide. Counsel men and women who have been arrested and are awaiting trial; identify educational, vocational and other supportive resources in the community to meet needs of offenders; maintain contact with employers, probation officers, courts, families.
    Job counselor. Identify and develop employment resources for offenders; maintain contacts with private industry, public service employers.

CAN I GET IN?
  Academic requirements: College student   Age: Mature
  Special: Prefer academic work in counseling and community work
  Length of commitment to internship: Negotiable
  Number of 1978 interns: 25
  Number planned for the future: 50

DO I GET PAID, EXPENSES, OR CREDIT?
  College credit: Can be arranged

HOW DO I GET IN?
  Closing date for application: On-going
  Interview required: Preferred
  Other procedures: A resume and two letters of reference are required.
  When will I know about application: 30 days after application is completed

WHERE CAN I GET MORE INFORMATION?
  Write: Mona Asiner, Bureau of Rehabilitation, Suite 1100, 666 11th Street, N.W., Washington, DC 20001
  Phone: (202) 637-6932
  Read: Annual report

CENTER FOR DEFENSE INFORMATION

Washington, D.C.

WHAT'S IT DO?
  Purpose and goals:
    The Center for Defense Information (CDI) is a non-profit, non-partisan, public interest organization. It is dedicated to making available continuing, objective information and analyses of our national defense-- information which is free of the special interest of any government, military, political or industrial organization. The Center's policy supports a strong defense but opposes excessive expenditures or forces. It holds that strong social, economic, and political structures contribute equally to national security and are essential to the strength and viability of our country. The CDI was established to make independent, intelligent analyses of American defense policies available to government officials, scholars, the press, and the public. It educates the public about the domestic and global effects of American defense policies. Although it is not called a disarmament group, it is concerned with military needs and excesses.
  Current projects and activities:
    Testifying on the impact of U.S. military commitments and the overseas operations of the military. Expanding CDI's contact with students, public interest groups and the press. Conducting studies on the rationale for nuclear weapons. Preparing radio programs and television appearances. Leading conferences, seminars, meetings, and special courses on national security.
  Number of permanent staff: 10   Annual budget: $150,000
  Publications: 10 times a year, The Defense Monitor, and a book, Current Issues in U.S. Defense Policy

WHAT CAN I DO?
  Internship description:
    The Center offers an intern program to undergraduate students and recent graduates who have strong interests in U.S. military issues and related public policy questions. While prior course work in these areas is not required, high academic achievements are important. Writing skills are essential. Interns perform a variety of professional support functions, but their principal one is to serve as research assistants. They work closely with the Center staff, usually with considerable responsibility. Intern projects have included such diverse subjects as the military balance in the Mediterranean, cruise missile programs, other weapons proposals, and military lobbying.

CAN I GET IN?
  Academic requirements: No specific requirements or preferred background
  Length of commitment to internship: Semester
  Number of 1978 interns: 8   Number planned for the future: 8

DO I GET PAID, EXPENSES, OR CREDIT?
  Pay: $400 a month
  College credit: Can be arranged; no pay if receiving credit

HOW DO I GET IN?
  Closing date for application: November 15 for January semester and July 15
    for fall semester
  Interview required: No
  When will I know about application: One month after deadline for applications

WHERE CAN I GET MORE INFORMATION?
  Write: Jo L. Husbands, Intern Coordinator, Center for Defense Information,
    122 Maryland Avenue, N.E., Washington, DC 20002
  Phone: (202) 543-0400
  Read: The Defense Monitor, a newsletter

CENTER FOR NATIONAL SECURITY STUDIES

Washington, D.C.

WHAT'S IT DO?
  Purpose and goals:
    The Center's primary objective is to contribute to a public reappraisal
    of the purposes and policies of our national security institutions. The
    Center works with other groups and with concerned citizens in exposing
    secret policies to public debate. Its goal is to be the public watchdog
    of the CIA, and FBI, the National Security Council, and the Law Enforce-
    ment Assistance Administration.
  Current projects and activities:
    The Center conducts research and produces information on issues of
    national security; it provides information and expertise to concerned
    groups, individuals, the press and Congress and sponsors conferences and
    public meetings; it coordinates the efforts of citizens' groups and
    individuals concerned about the issues. It develops reform proposals to
    hold national security institutions accountable to the Congress and
    responsive to the people and assists individuals and groups seeking
    information under the Freedom of Information Act and coordinates litiga-
    tion in related ateas.
  Number of permanent staff: 15
  Publications: First Principles, a monthly

WHAT CAN I DO?
  Internship descriptions:
    Legislation internship. While the Center does not lobby, it follows
      legislation pertaining to intelligence issues. An intern would attend
      hearings, analyze bills, and generally monitor legislative reforms to
      control the intelligence agencies. This intern would also provide
      support for informal groups organized around intelligence issues.
    Newsletter internship. The Center publishes First Principles, which
      explores the relationship between national security prerogatives and
      civil liberties. An intern would be responsible for searching out and
      preparing summaries of current literature on intelligence issues for
      inclusion in the newsletter.
    Library internship. The Center is currently in the process of gathering
      materials for an intelligence library. A library intern would assist
      in the collection and dissemination of these materials, especially

those documents received as a result of Freedom of Information Act requests.

Research internship. Several assistants are needed for work on the following projects: 1) An intern would assist in the research for a book on the CIA's drug testing and behavior modification programs; and 2) An intern would do general research on the Center's publications, particularly on a revision of the Center's <u>Freedom of Information Act</u> pamphlet. In addition to research on a specific project, each intern will be required to devote one day per week to administrative tasks such as typing, filing, and copying.

CAN I GET IN?
  Academic requirements: College student
  Length of commitment to internship: Semester or year
  Number of 1978 interns: 6 per semester
  Number planned for future: Same

DO I GET PAID, EXPENSES, OR CREDIT?
  Expenses: Some travel expenses are paid
  College credit: Can be arranged

HOW DO I GET IN?
  Closing date for application: On-going
  Application procedures: Students should send a writing sample (an excerpt from previous work is acceptable) and a one to two page letter explaining why they are currently interested in the work of the Center. If possible, a personal interview in Washington should be arranged. Inevitably, preference is given to those students able to interview at the Center but allowance is made for distance and time considerations. Students may be requested to call CNSS for a telephone interview. Students should make initial contact at least six weeks prior to the beginning of the program, and indicate their preference among the different projects of the Center. We will try to make selections based on the student's preference, placing the student in a position that meets the needs of the student and the Center.

WHERE CAN I GET MORE INFORMATION?
  Write: Intern Program, Center for National Security Studies, 122 Maryland Avenue, N.E., Washington, DC 20002
  Phone: (202) 544-5380
  Read: <u>The Lawless State</u> by Morton H. Halperin (NY: Penguin, 1976) $2.95

CITIZENS FOR PARTICIPATION IN POLITICAL ACTION
Boston, Massachusetts

WHAT'S IT DO?
  Purpose and goals:
    CPPAX is a multi-issue, statewide political organization, dedicated to meaningful social change. It is a progressive, public information and political action organization, working on issues, candidates, and legislation. Main interests are social justice, economic democracy, peace and foreign policy, and election and citizen control. There are 2,500 members statewide with both local chapter and statewide activity.
  Current projects and activities:
    CPPAX has divided its issue areas among four working groups, or task forces: economic democracy, elections and citizen control, social justice, and peace action. CPPAX employs a broad spectrum of tactics to advance its issues. These tactics may range from picketing jewelry stores which sell the Krugerrand, to coordinating a major effort to elect progressive candidates to the Massachusetts Legislature.
  Number of permanent staff: 4   Annual budget: $50,000
  Publications: Monthly newsletter

WHAT CAN I DO?
  Volunteer description:
    Everything from general office work to researching voting records of public officials, writing leaflets, organizing public forums, helping to organize demonstrations, and lobbying. There is much flexibility in the organization both in terms of issues and organizing activities. One specific project is to monitor CPPAX sponsored legislation as it proceeds through the legislature. This will entail spending time at the State House speaking with legislators and attending various hearings and committee meetings. A later step in this project will involve taking on the responsibility for mobilizing support for specific legislation at critical points in its history. This step will encompass lobbying, organizing people to testify at hearings, contact with other concerned special interest groups and use of the media. Another project will involve organizing support for serious challenges against certain targeted "bad" incumbent legislators. This project will entail organizing community meetings, doing research into the political background of state legislators, and speaking in particular communities. A volunteer could also assist any of four task forces in its on-going work. The Task Force on Elections and Citizen Control will be working primarily on the statewide and state legislative races. The Economic Democracy Task Force is working on attaining both statewide and nationwide full employment, anti-redlining legislation, and the implementation of a state linked deposit banking system for Massachusetts. The Social Justice Task Force is attempting to alleviate the very divisive problems of racism and sexism through its rigorous support of Metco and strong affirmative action programs. The Peace Action Task Force is directing its energies toward enactment of a transfer amendment to transfer funds from the military budget to human services, nuclear disarmament, and black majority rule in South Africa. CPPAX views volunteers as a very valuable resource and can provide a volunteer with valuable political experience. In turn, that person will be making a positive contribution to the organization and its goals.

CAN I GET IN?
  Academic requirements: Commitment to progressive issues
  Age: No requirement
  Length of commitment to internship: Negotiable
  Number of 1978 interns: 3   Number planned for the future: Open

DO I GET PAID, EXPENSES, OR CREDIT?
  College credit: Can be arranged

HOW DO I GET IN?
  Closing date for application: On-going
  Interview required: No, but helpful
  When will I know about application: Soon after applying

WHERE CAN I GET MORE INFORMATION?
  Write: Tom Boreiko, CPPAX, 35 Kindston Street, Boston, MA 02111
  Phone: (616) 426-3040
  Read: Requested CPPAX literature

               CITIZENS ORGANIZATION FOR A SANE WORLD

                          Washington, D.C.

WHAT'S IT DO?
  Purpose and goals:
    SANE is a citizens' organization committed to an end to the international
    arms race. The world's superpowers spend enormous amounts of money build-
    ing arsenals that do not enhance significantly their own national security
    and bring the nations of the world closer to war. SANE does public
    education and lobbying on disarmament, national priorities and peace
    questions.
  Current projects and activities:
    Lobbies against weapons and for arms agreements that reduce arms. Broad-
    casts a radio program "SANE Views the World." Gives lectures, slide shows,
    newspaper articles and TV appearances. Analyzes the performance of
    members of Congress and presidential candidates. Supplies background
    information to public officials. Conversion project with major unions.
  Number of permanent staff: 4   Annual budget: $150,000
  Publications: Sane World

WHAT CAN I DO?
  Internship descriptions:
    Interns work on the above current projects. The interns have been polled
    about the time they have spent on the job and have broken it down in the
    following ways: 25% routine office work - stuffing envelopes, addressing,
    membership file work, running messages, clipping newspapers, etc.;
    50% researching/writing - for some interns this has been one large research
    project, and for others several smaller ones; 25% other - attending con-
    ferences, meetings, and Congressional hearings, making telephone calls,
    working on issues, etc.

CAN I GET IN?
   Academic requirements: SANE looks for interns who write well and who need
      little supervision. Preference is given to interns who have academic
      backgrounds in any of the following: 20th century history, political
      science, government, peace studies, journalism, or economics. Applicants
      who have an interest in politics, political action, and/or the issues of
      disarmament are preferred.
   Length of commitment to internship: Semester or year
   Number of 1978 interns: 4
   Number planned for future: 6

DO I GET PAID, EXPENSES, OR CREDIT?
   Pay: Interns are given a weekly stipend of $15
   College credit: Can be arranged

HOW DO I GET IN?
   Closing date for application: 3 months before semester begins
   Interview required: No
   When will I know about application: Within two months

WHERE CAN I GET MORE INFORMATION?
   Write: David Cortright, SANE, 318 Massachusetts Avenue, N.E., Washington,
      DC 20002
   Phone: (202) 546-4868
   Read: Sane World, from above address

COMMON CAUSE

Washington, D.C.

WHAT'S IT DO?
   Purpose and goals:
      The primary purpose of this group is to make government more responsive
      to the needs of the public. It is a national citizens movement working
      for public interest at all levels of government--opening up the way
      government works and how decisions are made so that each citizen can see
      what's going on or driving corruption out of the political finance field
      so that politicians are accountable to the people instead of the big
      campaign contributors. That is what Common Cause is all about: no more
      "buying politicians" and no more "doing public business behind closed
      doors."
   Current projects and activities:
      To bring accountability to government, Common Cause has worked for and
      continues to work for: the citizen's right to know; opening Congressional
      committee and Federal agency meetings to the people and the press; finan-
      cial disclosure by political candidates and office holders to lay bare
      conflict of interest; extending the $1 tax check-off to Congressional
      campaigns to take dirty money out of all our elections. Current priority
      issues include: public financing of Congressional elections, tax reform,
      conflict of interest legislation, "sunset" (mandatory review of government
      programs to justify their continued existence), ratification of the ERA,
      energy conservation, and lobby disclosure.

Number of permanent staff: 60 to 70
Annual budget: $6 to 8 million
Publications: <u>Frontline</u>, a newsletter

WHAT CAN I DO?
  Internship descriptions:
    Washington Connection internship. The national office in Washington is
      the pressure point for Common Cause action on national issues--both with
      Congress and with the executive branch of government. It is here that
      volunteers work closely with the national staff to form the frontline
      link between the national office, the 50 Common Cause state organizations
      and the 270,000 concerned citizen-members across the nation. They are
      known as the Washington Connection. When citizen pressure on members of
      Congress is necessary, these volunteers activate the Common Cause national
      telephone network connecting 435 Congressional districts. This turns on
      a barrage of telephone calls, letters to the editor, and extensive TV and
      newspaper coverage--all geared to letting members of Congress know
      exactly where citizen-taxpayers stand. An intern's role in the Washing-
      ton Connection is to act as a liaison between the national office and
      the local organizations in the Congressional districts. Consequently,
      an ability to be both informative and persuasive over the phone is
      necessary.
    Press office internship. The job consists basically of routine administra-
      tive and clerical duties: updating press lists; filling requests for
      studies, press releases; working with the field organization to figure
      out the liaison needs for press clips; being a messenger to take
      releases around the city to DC bureaus; reading <u>New York Times</u>, <u>Washing-</u>
      <u>ton Post</u>, <u>Wall Street Journal</u>, and <u>Washington Star</u> every day for stories
      on Common Cause, and distributing them in the office; acting as a back-
      up to the volunteers on the Common Cause information desk. When needed,
      drafting releases and other written material.
    Issue development internship. Interns in issue development will research
      and write on Common Cause national and state on-going and possible
      future issues. Projects include memoranda, reports, term papers,
      statistical compilations, and support work for investigative studies.
    ERA internship. Thirty-four of the needed 38 states have ratified the
      Equal Rights Amendment. A key element of the ERA activities will be
      the assistance and resource that Common Cause in Washington can provide
      to organizations in Florida, Indiana, Illinois, Missouri, Nevada, Okla-
      homa, and North Carolina. Interns are needed to assist the state and
      local organization in lobbying both in the state house and around the
      state. This may include calling members in targeted districts to
      generate their support and contacting the media around the states to
      place ERA materials.
    Case study internship. Political science background (if not actual major),
      writing experience, journalism experience particularly helpful. Intern
      would be given one of Common Cause's issue battles as his or her project
      and would be responsible for first organizing the files on the subject,
      preparing a chronology of Common Cause action on the issue, interviewing
      lobbyist issue manager, and finally drafting a case study of Common
      Cause's strategy and activity on the issue.
    Operations and case studies internship. Organizing materials for a
      chronology of the political battles involved and Common Cause's role in

those battles. Indexing so that appropriate materials can be sent to Princeton University for Common Cause archives and for use in preparing case studies and a history on campaign financing reform.

Legislation internship. Interns will participate in two projects: Congressional monitoring and monitoring of agency observance of the government in the Sunshine Law.

Action information internship. Interns will work part-time in the office of action information, writing and editing materials. These include: membership flyer (pamphlet); editing Common Cause materials; writing Frontline, news stories, and in-depth feature stories; writing promotional copy.

Issue mail internship. Interns assigned to issue mail prepare responses to correspondence which the organization receives from its members and the general public. They are also responsible for maintaining an ongoing survey of membership sentiment as expressed in the correspondence for the benefit of the management staff.

CAN I GET IN?
Academic requirements: College student
Length of commitment to internship: Semester
Number of 1978 interns: 160 a year
Number planned for the future: About the same

DO I GET PAID, EXPENSES, OR CREDIT?
Expenses: Interns are reimbursed for daily out-of-pocket transportation expenses.
College credit: Can be arranged

HOW DO I GET IN?
Closing date for application: Fall applications are due August 15; spring applications are due December 1
Interview required: No
Other procedures: An application which should include a resume, two recommendations, a writing sample (research or term paper), and a cover letter indicating length of stay, number of days a week available, and interests.
When will I know about application: As soon as it is completed and references checked

WHERE CAN I GET MORE INFORMATION?
Write: Volunteer Office, Common Cause, 2030 M Street, N.W., Washington, DC 20036
Phone: (202) 833-1200
Read: Frontline, newspaper

COMMUNITY FOR CREATIVE NONVIOLENCE

Washington, D.C.

WHAT'S IT DO?
  Purpose and goals:
    Community for Creative Nonviolence is a volunteer group of people committed to exploring nonviolence as a way of life, who are involved in community living and in nonviolent direct action. CCN is also involved in educational work. It seeks to confront the violence and injustices of our society, and also to heal the victims of violence and to live with some fidelity to the demands of nonviolence, both personally and politically. Volunteers live in community, and welcome others to join them in their work. The great questions of human survival are interconnected--the nuclear arms race, economic injustice and military control cannot be separated from the problems of environment, pollution, sexism, unemployment, technology--and that they are all tied to racism and to the struggle between the "haves" and the "have-nots."
  Current projects and activities:
    On-going poverty work includes a free soup kitchen, medical clinic, housing, pretrial release program, urban land trust, and training for the unskilled in printing.
  Number of permanent staff: The number of people in the community changes often. Presently there are 35.
  Publications: A Catholic pacifist quarterly, <u>Gamaliel</u>

WHAT CAN I DO?
  Join with CCN for as long as you can, through any internship program. It would be mostly unstructured, and the "internship" would consist of people living and sharing the work and community life. At various times in the past, interns have had academic projects to work on while in the community.

CAN I GET IN?
  CCN never turns anyone away, but students visit first to get some firsthand experience of how they would live.

DO I GET PAID, EXPENSES, OR CREDIT?
  Expenses: People usually get their room and board.
  College credit: Some students have arranged to get credit from their own colleges.

HOW DO I GET IN?
  Letters and visits to the community are necessary before your decision to join the community.

WHERE CAN I GET MORE INFORMATION?
  Write: Rachelle Linner, Community for Creative Nonviolence, 1335 N Street, N.W., Washington, DC 20005
  Phone: (202) 232-9533
  Read: <u>Peace and Nonviolence</u>, edited by Edward Guinan, Paulist Press, 1973.

CONSUMER FEDERATION OF AMERICA

Washington, D.C.

WHAT'S IT DO?
  Purpose and goals:
    The Consumer Federation of America is the nation's largest consumer organization. The CFA is a federation of over 225 national, state and local organizations which have joined together to help affect public policy as it is formulated by Congress, the President, regulatory agencies, the courts and industry. CFA provides a well-reasoned and articulate voice for consumers by gathering facts, analyzing issues and disseminating information to the public, legislators and regulators. CFA also organizes consumers at national, state and local levels and provides a national resource center to assist them with special projects. As a leading advocate for consumer concerns, CFA is the largest consumer organization that lobbies regularly before Congress.
  Current projects and activities:
    CFA's recent legislative actions before Congress include: leading the fight for the creation of an independent Agency for Consumer Protection; urging legislation for the establishment of a National Consumers Cooperative Bank to lend money for the creation and improvement of consumer cooperatives; spearheading the campaign for legislation which authorizes Federal government agencies to reimburse eligible citizens and citizen organizations for the expenses they incur when participating in agency proceedings; fighting for strengthening of credit legislation, no-fault auto insurance, and visible price labelling of retail items; actively supporting legislation to create a national Office of Clinical Laboratories to formulate minimum standards for clinical laboratories; monitoring the appointment process by supporting only nominees who are highly qualified by reason of a demonstrated sensitivity to the public interest, as well as a knowledge of the subject matter relevant to the position. CFA's Energy Policy Task Force (EPTF) is a coalition of 35 organizations established to represent the consumer viewpoint in energy policy debates before Congress, the administration and the public. Through its State and Local Organizing Project, CFA encourages the creation of local, regional, and state consumer organizations and the continuing success of existing organizations. The Project provides background information and support to new and established groups, and acts as a resource clearinghouse on a wide variety of consumer issues.
  Number of permanent staff: 12   Annual budget: $300,000
  Publications: <u>CFA News</u>, <u>How to Conduct a Candidate Survey</u>, <u>How to Activate Small Claims Courts</u>, <u>How to Prepare a Lifeline Proposal</u>, <u>How to Form a Consumer Complaint Group</u>.

WHAT CAN I DO?
  Internship descriptions:
    Work closely with staff members in research, drafting testimony for Congress, comments for agencies. Office support work and assist in preparation of the <u>CFA News</u>, and vote charts. Help with conference coordination. All of the current projects and activities listed above can use the help of interns.

CAN I GET IN?
  Academic requirements: College student
  Special: Political science, economics, law, journalism courses help, but are not required.
  Length of commitment to internship: Semester or year
  Number of 1978 interns: 1 to 5 at various times of year
  Number planned for the future: Same

DO I GET PAID, EXPENSES, OR CREDIT?
  College credit: Can be arranged

HOW DO I GET IN?
  Closing date for application: On-going
  Interview required: Yes, phone is OK
  Other procedures: Send letter, resume, and writing sample with application
  When will I know about application: No formal date

WHERE CAN I GET MORE INFORMATION?
  Write: Irene Kessel, CFA, Rm. 901, 1012 14th Street, N.W., Washington, DC 20005
  Phone: (202) 737-3732
  Read: CFA News, sent upon request

INSTITUTE FOR LOCAL SELF-RELIANCE

Washington, D.C.

WHAT'S IT DO?
  Purpose and goals:
    The Institute for Local Self-Reliance was established to investigate the technical feasibility of community self-reliance in high density living areas. The staff of the Institute is committed to urban life and to the resolution of some of the problems which face the 75% of Americans who do live in urban areas. It is also committed to exploring the potential for self-reliance, of humanly-scaled cooperative communities, of neighborhoods and cities. It is on this level that people can take control over their own lives and wealth and begin to effect a transition away from the concentration of political and economic power which characterizes American democracy.
  Current projects and activities:
    Municipal Waste Management. Investigating and developing community-based solid waste collection and recycling systems; examining the possibilities for solid waste processing and manufacturing facilities and for sewerless toilet systems.
    Municipal Finance. Exploring the role of credit within a city and evaluating the possibilities for community-controlled banking and credit institutions in our cities and neighborhoods.
    Urban Energy Resources. Emphasizing decentralizing technologies such as solar collectors for thermal energy and solar cells for electrical generation.
    Urban Food Production. Examining food production systems appropriate to high density population areas, among them rooftop hydroponics, green-

house design, intensive organic gardening, basement sprout and earthworm production; evaluating the impact of air pollution on urban agriculture.
Community Housing. Evaluating and developing programs for community self-help housing and cooperative ownership.
Number of permanent staff: 11   Annual budget: $150,000
Publications: <u>Self-Reliance</u>, a newsletter and many pamphlets on issues

WHAT CAN I DO?
  Internship descriptions:
    Internships (for unlimited number of interns).
      1) Researching articles for newsletter and other publications.
      2) Outreach work for hands-on projects.
      3) Researching background information for projects in any of the fields in which we work.
      4) Hands-on work on projects, including running greenhouse, running or starting recycling system, installing or building solar heating systems.
      5) Editing or laying-out publications.
      6) Expanding book and periodicals library.

CAN I GET IN?
  Academic requirements: College student   Age: 18
  Length of commitment to internship: Semester or year
  Number of 1978 interns: 8
  Number planned for the future: Open

DO I GET PAID, EXPENSES, OR CREDIT?
  College credit: Can be arranged

HOW DO I GET IN?
  Application procedures: No formal application; interested students should send a letter citing projects of interest and explaining their background in that area, when they are available for work and why they would like to work for the Institute. This letter will be relayed to the appropriate project director who will then correspond directly with the prospective intern.

WHERE CAN I GET MORE INFORMATION?
  Write: David Morris, Institute for Local Self-Reliance, 1717 18th Street, N.W., Washington, DC 20009
  Phone: (202) 232-4108
  Read: <u>Neighborhood Power</u>, by David Morris and Karl Hess; please send a stamped, self-addressed envelope for a copy of our current publications list and project descriptions.

NATIONAL ABORTION RIGHTS ACTION LEAGUE

Washington, D.C.

WHAT'S IT DO?
  Purpose and goals:
    The National Abortion Rights Action League is a national membership organization registered as a lobby with the U.S. Congress for the issue of abortion. It works to preserve the 1973 and 1976 Supreme Court decisions legalizing abortion and defining a woman's right to choose abortion and opposes all attempts to restrict or outlaw legal abortion. NARAL was the first single-issue organization concerned solely with guaranteeing every woman the legal option of abortion. The League recognizes that the rich have always been able to have abortions and that it is the poor, and especially the very young, who have been forced either to bear children they are unable to care for, or to resort to illegal or self-induced abortions.
  Current projects and activities:
    Lobbying Congressional offices on the abortion issue in general and on specific legislation that has been proposed, such as Constitutional amendments to prohibit abortion and riders intended to restrict the provision of abortion such as the Medicaid ban; writing newsletters to members; researching the issue and preparing press releases; organizing state chapters; and analyzing the voting records of members of Congress.
  Number of permanent staff: 10   Annual budget: $150,000
  Publications: Newsletter, fact sheets and brochures

WHAT CAN I DO?
  Internship descriptions:
    Interns who work with NARAL should be prepared to work as project director in one area and as support staff in another--as all staff do. You might find yourself lobbying Congress in the morning and stuffing envelopes in the afternoon--with the Executive Director. The office is informal and tries to share both the policy making and the less attractive routine work.

CAN I GET IN?
  Academic requirements: No special education requirements   Age: 18
  Special requirement: Intern must favor a woman's right to choose. Active feminists and students with an interest in political science, government and health are preferred.
  Length of commitment to internship: The busiest period runs from October to May, although interns are accepted at other times.
  Number of 1978 interns: 6
  Number planned for the future: 10 a year

DO I GET PAID, EXPENSES, OR CREDIT?
  College credit: Can be arranged

HOW DO I GET IN?
  Closing date for application: On-going
  Interview required: Preferred
  Other procedures: Send a resume and recommendations and call for an interview if you are in Washington.
  When will I know about application: No formal plan

WHERE CAN I GET MORE INFORMATION?
  Write: Kay Harrold, Coordinator of Volunteers and Interns, NARAL, 825 15th
    Street, N.W., Washington, DC 20005
  Phone: (202) 347-7774
  Read: Newsletters sent upon request

NATIONAL COMMITTEE AGAINST REPRESSIVE LEGISLATION

Washington, D.C.

WHAT'S IT DO?
  Purpose and goals:
    The National Committee Against Repressive Legislation is a small civil
    liberties organization that opposes legislation that poses threats to
    First Amendment rights of free speech, press and assembly. It provides
    information on such legislation to Congress, to other national organiza-
    tions and to grass roots community groups across the country. NCARL has
    worked through its history to eliminate inquisitorial Congressional
    committees. In recent years, NCARL has led the struggles to repeal anti-
    riot, no-knock, preventive detention, wiretapping and immunity statutes
    and is recognized as the organizer of the mass public movement to defeat
    S 1, the Criminal Justice Reform Act, a recodification of Title 18 of the
    U.S. Code. NCARL is one of the founders of the Campaign to Stop Govern-
    ment Spying, a national coalition to halt intelligence abuses. NCARL has
    regional offices in New England, Northern California, the Midwest, and
    the South, and two national offices, the headquarters in Los Angeles and
    the legislative office in Washington, D.C.
  Current projects and goals:
    Opposition to S 1437, Criminal Code Reform Act of 1977 (actually leading
    the opposition); agitation for passage of controls on FBI investigative
    authority and abolition of CIA.
  Number of permanent staff: 3 in Los Angeles, 1 in Washington
  Annual budget: $50,000
  Publications: Pamphlets on specific legislation

WHAT CAN I DO?
  Internship descriptions:
    The Washington office has had an intern program since 1971. The NCARL
    interns work under the supervision of the Washington Coordinator, and
    attend hearings and committee meetings, research legislation and court
    decisions, write analyses and articles for the press, and watch Congres-
    sional floor debates. Interns also take part in the organizational work
    of NCARL. This includes answering requests for information from people
    around the country who write in, keeping NCARL staff and officers informed
    of latest legislative developments, getting information to national and
    local organizations who are working with NCARL on various issues,
    primarily criminal code reform and control of intelligence-gathering
    agencies, and attending meetings and assisting in the growth of various
    coalitions in which NCARL plays a leadership role. Interns help with the
    office work and, if the student works with NCARL long enough to develop an
    expertise on an issue, he or she may assist in the lobbying.

CAN I GET IN?
  Academic requirements: Prefer junior or senior in college
  Age: 20
  Special: Must be able to write. An interest in politics and a commitment
    to the defense of Constitutional liberties are absolute prerequisites for
    the job. Self-motivation, independence and an inquiring mind are
    necessary skills for an NCARL intern.
  Length of commitment to internship: Semester
  Number of 1978 interns: 2   Number planned for the future: 3

DO I GET PAID, EXPENSES, OR CREDIT?
  College credit: Can be arranged

HO DO I GET IN?
  Closing date for application: About 2 months before session
  Interview required: No, but it would help
  When will I know about application: No formal procedure

WHERE CAN I GET MORE INFORMATION?
  Write: Esther Herst, Washington Coordinator, NCARL, 510 C Street, N.E.,
    Washington, DC 20002
  Phone: (202) 543-7659
  Read: NCARL pamphlets and position papers

NATIONAL LABOR FEDERATION

New York, New York

WHAT'S IT DO?
  Purpose and goals:
    The National Labor Federation is a group of community based and supported
    grassroots organizing drives across the country that are united to achieve
    a common goal: the organization of that strata of the U.S. workforce
    which has been traditionally denied access to trade unions and similar
    structures. Workers specifically excluded from the coverage of the
    National Labor Relations Act and the Taft-Hartley Act--farmworkers,
    domestic and attendant care workers, independent contractors, seasonal
    workers, and the unemployed--are banding together through new types of
    organization, mutual benefits associations, in an attempt to gain control
    over their own living and working conditions.
  Current projects and activities:
    Organizing drives are now operating in New York, New Jersey, Massachusetts,
    Pennsylvania, Oregon, and California, and all of them are currently
    collectivizing resources and undertaking preliminary work to begin new
    organizing drives in twelve locations. With plans to double the size of
    the Federation, the need for full-time organizers to replace those leaving
    existing organizing drives to begin new ones is particularly great. Some
    of the projects that are associations affiliated with the NLF include the
    Eastern Service Workers Association in New Brunswick and Princeton, New
    Jersey; Rochester, New York; and Philadelphia, Pennsylvania. Also the
    Eastern Farmworkers Association in Wayne County and in Bellport and River-
    head, New York; the Northwest Seasonal Workers Association in Medford,

Oregon; and the Western Service Workers Association in Sacramento, Oakland, Santa Cruz and Santa Ana, California.
Number of permanent staff: 120 full-time volunteers

WHAT CAN I DO?
  Internship descriptions:
    All of the work of the organization, whether it be the simplest or the most difficult, is done by volunteers who receive no salary or stipend for their services. Through systemic organizing, new volunteers are trained by professional organizers in the skills necessary in a grassroots organizing drive. Once volunteers have learned these basic skills, they will be able to take on other assignments that involve a greater degree of responsibility. Below is a list of a few of the systems of each local association which make possible places for new volunteers.
    The membership system is responsible for the recruitment of members to the association. As the workers have no common place of employment or are often unemployed due to their lack of job security, the canvass is used as a means to contact potential members. The membership system coordinates house meetings in members' homes, and coordinates the work of the Workers Benefits Council, a body of representatives of the membership who meet each week.
    The benefits system is responsible for meeting the urgent day-to-day needs of the membership as expressed by the Workers Benefits Council. National Labor Federation benefits, which are currently provided free of charge to members, include medical care, dental care, emergency food, clothing and furniture, legal and welfare advocacy, an information and referral service, and an Occupational Health Project.
    The fundraising system is responsible for acquiring the donations of funds necessary to maintain and expand each local association. Since NLF accepts no government funding or grants with strings attached in order to function solely in the interest of its membership, community donations are obtained through such activities as bake sales, dance parties, dinners, and coffee houses.
    The procurement system is responsible for acquiring the donated resources needed by each association and its benefits program. This system coordinates such tactics as food and clothing drives and canvassing of stores.
    The cadre system is responsible for the recruitment and training of full-time organizers (cadre). The cadre system holds regular meetings with volunteers who work with the association on a regular basis, coordinates volunteer classes and training programs, and acts as a liaison to field placement directors of local colleges.
    The volunteer system coordinates the recruitment of part-time volunteers through literature tables, bucket drives in front of local stores and speaking engagements in local schools. This system is also responsible for orienting new volunteers to the purpose and functions of the organization and setting up their schedules to meet their specific interests and needs.
    The operations system is responsible for the coordination between these and other systems of each association and ensuring that the organization as a whole moves further toward its goals of alleviating the current situation faced by low income workers.
  Volunteers are also taught the theory behind the NLF organizing through

regularly scheduled classes encompassing such topics as the history of U.S. labor organizing, strata organizing, and the genesis of labor laws that affect its membership and organizing.

CAN I GET IN?
   Academic requirements: A commitment to the advancement of unrecognized workers, and the desire to learn the skills and structure necessary to the development of a grassroots organizing drive are needed.
   Length of commitment to internship: Semester or year
   Number of 1978 interns: 200   Number planned for the future: 1000

DO I GET PAID, EXPENSES, OR CREDIT?
   Expenses: Board and room and necessary expenses are provided for full-time volunteers.
   College credit: Can be arranged

HOW DO I GET IN?
   Closing date for application: On-going, accepted year around
   Interview required: No, but preferred
   When will I know about application: No formal plan

WHERE CAN I GET MORE INFORMATION?
   Write: Mary Tong, National Labor Federation, 200 West 20th Street, New York, NY 10011
   Phone: (212) 924-8402 and leave message on the answering service for the National Labor Federation

NATIONAL ORGANIZATION FOR THE REFORM OF MARIJUANA LAWS

Washington, D.C.

WHAT'S IT DO?
   Purpose and goals:
   NORML is a social-action group, working to decriminalize possession of marijuana. It educates the public and functions as a support organization for other groups, throughout the country, working for the same goal. NORML provides these groups with information, strategy and occasional financial assistance. They have encouraged professional people to testify before state legislatures in support of NORML's position.
   Current projects and activities:
   The main program includes lobbying with the state and Federal legislatures, filing lawsuits challenging the constitutionality of marijuana laws, and compiling information on how the laws are being enforced.
   Number of permanent staff: 8   Annual budget: $400,000
   Publications: a newsletter, The Leaflet

WHAT CAN I DO?
   Interns assist directly in projects and in general office work (mailing, telephone and xeroxing). Some of the projects that interns have worked on include: played a leading role in decriminalizing marijuana in Oregon, Alaska, Maine, Colorado, California, Ohio, South Dakota, and Minnesota; assisted in the successful landmark constitutional challenge of marijuana

laws in Alaska, and are mounting challenges in Arizona, California, the District of Columbia, Florida, Illinois, Missouri, New York, Pennsylvania, Tennessee, and Washington; brought legal action against the Federal Drug Enforcement Administration, seeking to make marijuana legally available for medical uses; obtained unpublished marijuana research and testing data from U.S. intelligence and defense agencies through the Freedom of Information Act; provided nationally known experts at legislative hearings across the country; aided hundreds of individuals arrested on marijuana-related charges to find legal counsel.

CAN I GET IN?
  Academic requirements: College student; research and writing skills are needed.
  Length of commitment to internship: Semester or year
  Number of 1978 interns: 4
  Number planned for the future: About the same

DO I GET PAID, EXPENSES, OR CREDIT?
  College credit: Can be arranged

HOW DO I GET IN?
  Closing date for application: On-going
  Other procedures: There is no special form to use in applying for an internship. Interested students should send a letter indicating their interest in working with NORML. This letter should indicate the date the student can begin, and the desired period of internship. Also include any other information the student thinks is important. A resume is fine, but it is not required. A short (ten pages or less) writing sample from the student would be helpful.
  When will I know about application: No formal date

WHERE CAN I GET MORE INFORMATION?
  Write: Peter H. Meyers, Chief Counsel, NORML Internship Program, 2317 M Street, N.W., Washington, DC 20037
  Phone: (202) 223-3170
  Read: The Leaflet, available from the above address

NATIONAL SELF-HELP RESOURCE CENTER

Washington, D.C.

WHAT'S IT DO?
  Purpose and goals:
    The National Self-Help Resource Center (NSHRC) is a non-profit, tax-exempt, national resource and technical assistance broker for community self-help initiatives. The NSHRC is also the developer and administrator of a new citizen involvement process, "community resource centers" (CRC's), and is the coordinator of the National CRC Network. Additionally, the NSHRC acts as a catalyst for dialogue within the voluntary sector so that mutually-shared problems can be resolved through the cooperative exchange of information and resources. The staff of the National Self-Help Resource Center has expertise in communications and public relations, community organizing and planning, survey research, program management, and direct involvement with grassroots community programs.
  Current projects and activities:
    A CRC serves both citizen needs and the needs of government and institutions by providing greater access to information and to volunteer technical skills. It helps legislators and public officials by being a vehicle for citizen feedback and by facilitating citizen input into public policy decisions. It provides an opportunity for citizens to learn how to assist themselves by joining with others in community dialogues and working together on common problems. The Center's organizers conducted the first nationwide study of the low-income self-help movement. Nearly 1,000 self-help projects were surveyed and 114 representative projects were exhaustively case studied.
  Number of permanent staff: 4   Annual budget: $250,000
  Publications: <u>Uplift: What People Themselves Can Do</u>, $5.00; <u>Community Resource Centers, The Notebook</u>, $8.00; <u>Program Planning and Evaluation</u>, a pamphlet; <u>Exchange</u>, a newsletter; <u>Network Notes</u>, a newsletter.

WHAT CAN I DO?
  Help the staff in the development of a thesaurus and national information system for use by the local community resource centers. Special project to work with local resource centers on their individual needs--anywhere in the country.

CAN I GET IN?
  Academic requirements: A college student with skills in research, library and information science, community organization, publication relations or social policy is not required but preferred.
  Age: 20   Length of commitment to internship: Negotiable
  Number of 1978 interns: 2
  Number planned for the future: About the same

DO I GET PAID, EXPENSES, OR CREDIT?
  Expenses: Sometimes, depending on community

HOW DO I GET IN?
  Closing date for application: April 30th
  Interview required: Yes, can be by phone
  When will I know about application: May 25

WHERE CAN I GET MORE INFORMATION?
  Write: Susan Davis, Executive Director, The National Self-Help Resource
    Center, Inc., 2000 S Street, N.W., Washington, DC 20009
  Phone: (202) 338-5704
  Read: Books listed above. Materials will be sent upon request.

NATIONAL TAXPAYERS UNION

Washington, D.C.

WHAT'S IT DO?
  Purpose and goals:
    The National Taxpayers Union is a registered lobby working to reduce taxes
    and to cut what it feels is wasteful government spending. The Union is
    working to amend the Constitution so as to require a balanced Federal
    budget.
  Current projects and goals:
    The balanced Federal budget proposal has been introduced in both the House
    and the Senate. In an effort to stir Congress to act on this proposal
    NTU has initiated a nationwide petition campaign which has collected
    thousands of signatures. Soon, there will be millions. Then, Congress
    will be virtually forced to act upon this proposal. NTU is also working
    to call a convention to amend the Constitution. Working with state and
    local taxpayers groups, the legislatures of 14 states have approved the
    Balance the Budget resolution. Maryland, Delaware, Virginia, South
    Carolina, Indiana, Louisiana, North Dakota, New Mexico, Mississippi,
    Florida, Nebraska, Oklahoma, and Georgia have all passed the resolution.
    When 34 states have passed the resolution, the Balance the Budget Amend-
    ment will be enacted.
  Number of permanent staff: 15   Annual budget: $400,000
  Publications: Dollars and Sense, a monthly newsletter

WHAT CAN I DO?
  Internship description: Involves research, lobbying, writing articles for
    the newsletter, and general office chores

CAN I GET IN?
  Academic requirements: College student
  Length of commitment to internship: One semester
  Number of 1978 interns: 11
  Number planned for the future: 10 to 15

DO I GET PAID, EXPENSES, OR CREDIT?
  Pay: $75 per week   College credit: Can be arranged

HOW DO I GET IN?
  Closing date for application: February 1 for spring internship and
    September 15 for fall internship
  Interview required: Preferred
  Other procedures: Submit resume and writing sample with application.
  When will I know about application: Within two weeks of closing date for
    application

WHERE CAN I GET MORE INFORMATION?
 Write: Stephen Chapman, National Taxpayers Union, 325 Pennsylvania Avenue, S.E., Washington, DC 20003
 Phone: (202) 546-2085
 Read: <u>Dollars and Sense</u>

OXFAM-AMERICA

Boston, Massachusetts

WHAT'S IT DO?
 Purpose and goals:
  Oxfam-America is a private, non-profit organization which sends money to developing countries for self-help projects. It is part of an international family of Oxfams (Belgium, Canada, Australia, UK and US). There are no religious or political affiliations and support is entirely by private donations. Oxfam is committed to funding self-help projects in Africa, Asia, and Latin America--projects which will enable the people to gain more control over their own lives, in their own way. The projects help some of the poorest rural people in the world. They mainly deal with agriculture, health and nutrition and the status of women in developing countries.
 Current projects and activities:
  Our three main activities are general fund raising, a nutritional cookbook, and general educational projects.
 Number of permanent staff: 14   Annual budget: $600,000
 Publications: A newsletter

WHAT CAN I DO?
 Internship descriptions:
  Community organizer internship. There are several positions open for assistants to the people organizing the annual Fast for a World Harvest, which is held the Thursday before Thanksgiving. This job requires community organizing, speaking before groups, and helping to get information to other organizers across the country about the event.
  Office internship. This is not a straight secretarial job nor is it one devoted entirely to stuffing envelopes for three months. Instead, this person (or persons) would help devise new systems for Third World project classifications and other types of organizational projects.
  Nutrition internship. Nutrition and the world food situation: for those interested in learning more about why people in other countries eat the way they do and how worldwide food policies are affected by decisions made in this country and by the governments of other countries, Oxfam-America is putting together a Third World cookbook called <u>Recipes for a World Harvest</u>. It will contain recipes and bits of information on what the other 90% of the world's population eats (in 18 countries where Oxfam-America has sponsored projects).
  General research internship. Need at least two good research assistants who will be able to help find things at the library and through phone interviews. Topics needing research include medical care in Third World countries, appropriate technology in Third World countries, and agriculture in developing countries.

Third World internship. One intern is needed who has skills and interests in helping obtain background information on countries where Oxfam-America has projects.

CAN I GET IN?
  Academic requirements: High school graduate   Age: 16
  Special: An interest in learning about Third World people
  Length of commitment to internship: Flexible
  Number of 1978 interns: 10
  Number planned for future: Up to 4 at a time

DO I GET PAID, EXPENSES, OR CREDIT?
  College credit: Yes   Stipend: Sometimes available

HOW DO I GET IN?
  Closing date for application: On-going   Interview required: Yes
  When will I know about application: Immediately after interview

WHERE CAN I GET MORE INFORMATION?
  Write: Su Kaneda, Volunteer Coordinator, OXFAM-AMERICA, 302 Columbus Avenue, Boston, MA 02116
  Phone: (617) 247-3304
  Read: Food First by Frances Moore Lappe and Joe Collins

PUBLIC CITIZEN

Washington, D.C.

WHAT'S IT DO?
  Purpose and goals:
    Headed by Ralph Nader, Public Citizen groups litigate, research and participate before Federal agencies, courts and Congress on behalf of citizen interests and foster citizen action in communities across the United States. Public Citizen advocates structural reforms in tax policy, antitrust enforcement, corporate accountability, freedom of information, health care delivery, occupational health, safe energy production, consumer choice in the marketplace and citizen participation in government decision-making.
  Current projects and activities:
    Health Research Group. The Health Research Group's (HRG) staff works for consumers in the areas of cost and quality of health care delivery, on-the-job safety and health, food, drug, and product safety, pesticides, and the environment. HRG works to present the consumer, patient, and worker's point of view by monitoring the enforcement of health and safety legislation, preparing Congressional testimony on health matters, presenting scientific data to government agencies, consumer organizations and the general public, and assisting consumer action with research and project materials. Annual budget: $146,972
    Tax Reform Research Group. The Tax Reform Research Group (TRRG) works for reform of Federal and local taxes, the IRS, and local administration of tax laws. TRRG activities include advising Congress, accumulating data, publishing studies on tax issues, testifying before legislative and

executive bodies, and promoting local citizen action. Annual budget: $85,382

Congress Watch. Congress Watch, with seven full-time advocates, scored some major successes in Congress. In addition, the groundwork was begun for major, structural reforms in the next Congress. Four bills of major importance to consumer rights were enacted following energetic advocacy by Congress Watch. Annual budget: with Critical Mass, $159,952

Litigation Group. The Litigation Group continued its success in the Supreme Court of the United States this year by winning two major victories for consumers. Coupled with its prior accomplishments, the Litigation Group has now won four of the six cases it has argued before the Supreme Court. Each of the cases which the Group lost has since been overruled by statutes passed by Congress largely due to the efforts of Litigation Group attorneys and the staffs of Congress Watch and the Tax Reform Research Group. Annual budget: $148,322

Public Citizen Visitors Center. During the Bicentennial year, the Public Citizen Visitors Center (PCVC) provided more than 15,000 visitors to Washington, D.C. with a diversity of interesting ways to learn about, and contribute to, their Federal government. To assist in the process of changing tourists from sightseers to participating public citizens, the PCVC opened an "annex" adjacent to the Supreme Court. Personalized tours of Capitol Hill are now conducted twice daily while Congress is in session. Annual budget: $36,725

Aviation Consumer Action Project. The aim of the Aviation Consumer Action Project (ACAP) is to represent the interests of passengers and other members of the public in improved air safety, lower fares, elimination of passenger abuse, reduction of jet noise and pollution, and the open and honest formulation of regulatory decisions. ACAP is the only non-profit organization devoted full time to advocating the interests of all passengers. Annual budget: $27,000

Critical Mass. Critical Mass, a part of the grassroots movement against nuclear power, is confronting a multi-billion dollar industry/government complex which commands a vast public relations apparatus that has concealed the dangers of atomic power for thirty years. Critical Mass' monthly newspaper has become the organ of the safe energy movement. Because each story is thoroughly researched and documented, Critical Mass is relied on by many members of Congress and reporters who cover the nuclear power controversy.

Capitol Hill News Service. Most daily newspapers cannot afford their own Washington correspondent and rely, instead, on press releases from their Senators and Representatives for news stories on activity in Congress. This lack of unbiased information on the U.S. Congress prompted the formation, in 1973, of the Capitol Hill News Service (CHNS) to provide objective, comprehensive, localized coverage of Congress at a cost feasible to even the smallest paper. Seven reporters write stories for 50 newspapers in eight states and over 20 broadcasting stations from Pennsylvania to California.

Citizen Action Group. The Citizen Action Group (CAG) supplies information and occasionally staff to assist citizens and students in organizing projects to assure greater consumer protection and effect social change. CAG has helped to create and train public interest advocacy groups at the community and statewide levels, including student-financed and directed Public Interest Research Groups (PIRG's) in 30 states and the

District of Columbia, and citizen support groups in Connecticut, California, and West Virginia. These groups employ professional staffs of attorneys, scientists, engineers, journalists and organizers to work full-time on issues of public concern. Annual budget: $142,848

Number of permanent staff: Litigation Office: 80; Visitors Center: 2

Publications: People & Taxes, the monthly newspaper of Public Citizen's Tax Reform Group; Critical Mass, the monthly newspaper of the citizen's movement to stop nuclear power; Inside the Capitol, the Public Citizen Visitors Center bi-weekly calendar of events for visitors to Washington; Public Citizen, a newspaper reporting on the activities of Public Citizen and distributed free to Public Citizen supporters; a complete list of reports and publications by Ralph Nader and other consumer advocates; a complete list of publications available from the Public Citizen Health Research Group.

WHAT CAN I DO?
Internship descriptions:
Interns and volunteers work in all of the current projects listed above. Interns for Congress Watch, for example, supplement the work of the lobbyists through research, grass-roots work of organizing constituents, and clerical duties. Each of the eight separate Public Citizen groups has its own needs and work descriptions for interns.

CAN I GET IN?
Academic requirements: Varies according to the group. But most of the interns should have research and writing skills, a social science background and an interest in consumerism, political science, government and communications.
Age: 18
Length of commitment to internship: Varies up to a year
Number of 1978 interns: Ranges from two in Congress Watch to 60 in Visitors Center

DO I GET PAID, EXPENSES, OR CREDIT?
College credit: Can be arranged and many interns or volunteers receive credit.

HOW DO I GET IN?
Closing date for application: On-going
Interview required: Preferred
When will I know about application: No formal plan

WHERE CAN I GET MORE INFORMATION?
Write: Litigation Group: Florence Dembling, Personnel Director, Public Citizen, 2000 P Street, N.W., Washington, DC 20036
Phone: (202) 785-3702
Congress Watch: David Coleman, Assistant to the Director, 133 C Street, S.E., Washington, DC 20003
Phone: (202) 546-4996
Visitors Center: The Director, 1200 15th Street, N.W., Washington, DC 20005
Phone: (202) 956-9053
Health Research Group: Public Citizen Intern Director, 2000 P Street,

N.W., Washington, DC 20036
    Phone: (202) 872-0320
  Tax Reform Research Group: Public Citizen Intern Director, 133 C
    Street, S.E., Washington, DC 20003
    Phone: (202) 544-1710
  Citizen Action Group: Personnel, Public Citizen, 2000 P Street,
    N.W., Washington, DC 20036
    Phone: (202) 785-3702
Read: Send for complete list of publications and reports from above addresses

ZERO POPULATION GROWTH

Washington, D.C.

WHAT'S IT DO?
  Purpose and goals:
    To end population growth so as to prevent the further deterioration of
    our environment, depletion of our energy and natural resources and dimi-
    nishment of our quality of life.
  Current projects and activities:
    Immigration. To reform U.S. immigration law; halt illegal immigration;
      reduce legal immigration to 150,000 per year.
    Population policy. To have the U.S. adopt a population policy complete
      with goals for reaching zero population growth (zpg) by the year 2000.
    National Reporter. Newspaper informing members and press of ZPG activities
      and of current population issues.
    Media. To educate the press and public about zpg, and population issues.
    Chapter coordination. To assist local efforts and help develop grassroots
      input into our national efforts.
    Fundraising. To obtain new funds and new members.
    Other lobbying activities. For abortion rights, Equal Rights Amendment;
      expanded funding of contraceptive research and services to all who
      desire them; voluntary availability of sterilization services.
    Population education. To instruct teachers nationwide about population
      dynamics and the need for population education in the schools.
  Number of permanent staff: 18   Annual budget: $360,000
  Publications: National Reporter, various brochures on population related
    topics: teenage pregnancy, immigration, only children and abortion.

WHAT CAN I DO?
  Internship descriptions:
    Each of our project directors could easily find work for a full-time,
    semester- or year-long intern in the above projects.

CAN I GET IN?
  Academic requirements: College junior   Age: 20
  Experience: Prefer candidates who have writing and organizational skills
  Special: Writing skills and some knowledge of population issues
  Length of commitment to internship: Semester or year
  Number of 1978 interns: 7
  Number planned for the future: 7 or 8

DO I GET PAID, EXPENSES, OR CREDIT?
  Pay: Some interns are paid a stipend from $1,000 to $3,000 a year.
  College credit: Can be arranged, and many do receive credit.

HOW DO I GET IN?
  Closing date for application: On-going
  Interview required: No
  When will I know about application: One month after application is in

WHERE CAN I GET MORE INFORMATION?
  Write: Sandy Schline, Zero Population Growth, 1346 Connecticut Avenue, N.W.,
    Washington, DC 20036
  Phone: (202) 785-0100
  Read: Population and the American Future, The Limits to Growth by
    D. H. Meadows, et al.; The Population Bomb by Paul R. Erlich and The End
    of Affluence: A Blueprint for Your Future by Erlich.

THE RELIGIOUS-SPONSORED AGENCIES CLUSTER

    Christian Service Corps
    Church of the Brethren
    Friends Committee on National Legislation
    LAOS, Inc.
    Lutheran World Ministries
    Mennonite Voluntary Service
    Neighborhood Ecumenical Witness and Service
    United Church of Christ
    United Presbyterian Church USA Voluntary Service
    Volunteer Corps - The Episcopal Church

CHRISTIAN SERVICE CORPS
Washington, D.C.

WHAT'S IT DO?
  Purpose and goals:
    The Christian Service Corps is the "Peace Corps" of the Church. It is an evangelical organization which aids the Church in obtaining personnel by performing five services: recruiting, selecting, placing, directly assisting in raising the necessary finances, training. Corps members are skilled Christian men and women from 18 to 70 years of age who work for two years within the existing program of the Church. Each volunteer receives a choice of assignments with established mission agencies in the United States or overseas. The CSC believes that Christians should plan their lives in such a way that they provide a two-year period in which they can lay aside other responsibilities and completely give their lives and skill to the work of the Lord. Service and witness on a full-time basis for a two year period should be as common and accepted as going to school.
  Current projects and activities:
    In the United States, Corps members work with established missions which serve Indian reservations, farm labor camps, Appalachia, inner city and student groups (both American and foreign students). Corps members help ministers raise up congregations in areas where there are few churches and not enough money to hire assistant pastors. They also move into an area to organize a congregation under the supervision of a denomination or another congregation.

WHAT CAN I DO?
  Corps descriptions:
    The following are representative skills needed on the mission field, both here and abroad: agriculture, art, business and clerical, communications, construction, counseling and personnel services, education, language, literature, medicine and health, ministry, music, social work, and cooks, repairers, and tailors.

CAN I GET IN?
  Academic requirements: Depends on type of service desired
  Age: 17
  Special: Commitment to the particular Christian faith of the Corps
  Length of commitment to internship: Two years
  Number of previous Corps workers: Over 300
  Number planned for the future: Open

DO I GET PAID, EXPENSES, OR CREDIT?
  Pay: Most get $20 to $30 a month plus room and board.

HOW DO I GET IN?
  Closing date for application: On-going
  Special procedures: Application includes extensive Christian experience and theology sections.
  When will I know about application: About a month after it is completed

WHERE CAN I GET MORE INFORMATION?
  Write: Robert N. Meyers, President, Christian Service Corps, 1509 16th
    Street, N.W., Washington, DC 20036
  Phone: (202) 462-8822

CHURCH OF THE BRETHREN

Elgin, Illinois

WHAT'S IT DO?
  Purpose and goals:
    The World Ministries Commission has as its chief function assisting the
    Church of the Brethren in its corporate participation in God's reconciling
    activity in the world. To do this, it enlists participation in specific
    efforts aimed at peace and justice, joins in partnership to establish and
    strengthen the Christian fellowship for mission and ministry, and parti-
    cipates with churches and other agencies to improve the conditions of
    persons in health, education, and general welfare.
  Current projects and activities:
    At any given time, there are about 130 persons on projects in the USA and
    11 other countries. Volunteers are scattered throughout 20 states and a
    dozen nations. They work in the fields of medicine, teaching, agriculture,
    construction, community development, care of the aging, inner city,
    material aid and disaster relief, child care, youth centers, Christian
    education, maintenance of facilities and grounds, social justice, peace
    education and secretarial tasks.
  Number of permanent staff: 3 in the Volunteer Service Program office
  Annual budget: $200,000

WHAT CAN I DO?
  Volunteer descriptions:
    Here are a few examples of the 134 jobs available in the United States
    with Brethren Volunteer Services.
      Christian Migrant Ministry of Florida needs a volunteer for at least a
        two-year commitment to coordinate, negotiate, and work at reconcilia-
        tion between farm workers, growers and consumers. Some knowledge of
        Spanish and also field experience desirable. It seeks to help place
        the farm worker movement on more creative foundation. Theological and
        college training desirable plus the ability to stand up to growers and
        know how to negotiate.
      Illinois Public Action Council is in need of a volunteer for an 18 to 24
        month commitment to work alongside a trained community organizer in the
        campaign for human development. On the job training. Mature. Politi-
        cal science major helpful. Live in apartment with another person.
        Chicago, Illinois area.
      LOGOS, Inc. in need of volunteer to work at community organization--help
        people in rural black and white communities to see each other as
        persons, each having pride in themselves, a sense of pride in community.
        Demanding. Ability to be assertive and yet loving and caring about
        both blacks and whites. Mature. Live in mobile home. Christian
        philosophy. Dongola, Illinois.

Voice of Calvary Community Center is in need of photographer, skilled in layout, taking pictures for publication and promotional materials for VOC newspaper. Forty hours. Expected to worship with VOC. Jackson, Mississippi.

Volunteers needed at KOINOS House to work with drug addicts and alcoholics who are attempting to shake the habit. Average stay of resident is six to nine months. Work with twelve or more persons. Long hours. Seven days a week. Work and live in same house with residents. Volunteer arrives at own work schedule. Must be mature, skilled in group work and counseling, good listener. Team approach. Individual important. Accept and care about people where they are. Adrian, Michigan.

Clergy and Laity Concerned in need of volunteer to work in office answering phone, letters, meeting people who drop in, mailings, scheduling films and speakers in area, particularly, with human rights task force. Help with conference planning. A dynamic interfaith organization with a ten year history of effective religious-political action for peace and justice. Washington, D.C.

NISBCO needs a volunteer with skills and degree in business and English. Mailing list supervisor of 20,000 names. Mailing list heart of organization. Also handle all financial receipts. Work into administrative assistant. Group living. Washington, D.C.

Volunteer key punch operator for mailing list, updating other mailing lists. Needs to be innovator; 40 hours. Expected to attend church activities. Pennsylvania.

A journalist with interest in editing, copy-editing and layout is sought by Communications Team on a one or two year volunteer assignment. Experience in news and feature writing essential, photographic skills helpful. Involves some traveling. Work primarily with production of Messenger. Elgin, Illinois.

Native American Urban Transition Program is in need of an assistant to caseworker. Tasks are transporting clients to appointments, food distribution, stocking food closet, clothing assistance, contacting job possibilities, securing local housing, furnishing living quarters for clients, assisting in welfare contacts and many other. Clients are American Indians in transition. Live at Transition House, private room. Denver, Colorado.

CAN I GET IN?
  Academic requirements: Not specific but more needs are for skills in social work, community organization, agriculture, medical, science, day care, and geriatrics.
  Age: 18
  Special: A statement of personal faith is required, although there is no particular belief necessary to be admitted to program.
  Number of 1978 volunteers: About 130
  Number planned for the future: Open

DO I GET PAID, EXPENSES, OR CREDIT?
  Pay: Board and room are provided by the project and a first-year volunteer is paid $20 per month as an allowance. Some traveling expenses are paid if required on the project, as well as medical and dental care.

HOW DO I GET IN?
  Closing date for application: Three months before the time one wishes to volunteer
  Interview required: No
  Other procedures: Along with application you must submit a photo, school transcript, medical history, faith statement, and a minimum of four references.
  When will I know about application: As soon as file is completed, which usually takes around a month

WHERE CAN I GET MORE INFORMATION?
  Write: Joanne Nesler Davis, Director, Volunteer Services, World Ministries Commission, Church of the Brethren, 1451 Dundee Avenue, Elgin, IL 60120
  Phone: (312) 742-5100

FRIENDS COMMITTEE ON NATIONAL LEGISLATION

Washington, D.C.

WHAT'S IT DO?
  Purpose and goals:
    The Friends Committee on National Legislation was founded in 1943 to provide a channel through which members of the Society of Friends (Quakers) could try to influence legislation by bringing religious convictions to bear upon legislators. FCNL was the first registered Church lobby. It is now an effective non-government organization relating religious faith to national policy.
  Current projects and activities: cutting military spending; disarmament and economic conversion; food and hunger; assistance to nations and peoples; strengthening world institutions; human rights - United States; American Indians. Other concerns include jobs and welfare, human rights (international), environment and energy, equitable distribution, health care, and area tensions.
  Number of permanent staff: 3 full-time lobbyists, a field worker and an administrator and four support workers plus interns and volunteers
  Annual budget: $285,000   Publication: FCNL Newsletter

WHAT CAN I DO?
  Volunteer internships:
    Volunteers help the staff with drafting and developing strong support for legislation and amendments; arranging testimony before appropriate committees; intensive discussions with members of Congress; leadership in coalitions working on the issues; activating the FCNL network through Action Bulletins; Newsletter articles, staff studies, speaking engagements; writing articles for other publications; taking leadership in arranging group interviews with key members of Congress. Assignments also involve general office help for the total FCNL operation. Consideration will be given to planning research projects needed for college credit that will lie within the fields of FCNL priority emphasis, if desired.

CAN I GET IN?
  Academic requirements: College students

Experience: Character, reliability, and motivation are more important than experience. The ability to work without close supervision and to carry out assignments with a minimum of instruction are desirable qualities. Self-discipline in the use of time is helpful. Candidates with some office skills can render much needed service and may be preferred.
Length of commitment to internship: Semester or year
Number of 1978 interns: 3   Number planned for the future: 3

DO I GET PAID, EXPENSES, OR CREDIT?
  Pay: Volunteer interns must be able to pay all personal expenses.
  College credit: Can be arranged

HOW DO I GET IN?
  Closing date for application: On-going
  Interview required: No, references can substitute for interview.
  When will I know about application: A prompt decision will be made.

WHERE CAN I GET MORE INFORMATION?
  Write: Nick Block, FCNL, 245 Second Street, N.E., Washington, DC 20002
  Phone: (202) 547-4343
  Read: Uphill for Peace, by Raymond Wilson. A history of FCNL from the above address, $7.95.

LAOS, Inc.

Washington, D.C.

WHAT'S IT DO?
  Purpose and goals:
    LAOS is a clearinghouse for volunteers. It finds places of service for the volunteer. "Laos" is the New Testament word for "the whole people of God." It is an ecumenical volunteer agency which enables persons to involve themselves in the struggle to make life whole for all the family of humans. LAOS is a non-profit, ecumenical agency which matches concerned persons with church and other private projects working to improve the quality of life for persons in this country and abroad. Volunteers work for terms varying from one month to several years. Through the sharing of their skills with others, LAOS volunteers have gained an awareness of the kinds of forces which keep persons from realizing their human potential, an appreciation for the values and customs of other cultures, and a new perspective of their own lives in relation to conditions in their home communities. LAOS was established as a channel for lay persons to become more actively involved in the mission of the church by serving those in need through their vocational skills. Mission should be open to lay persons who are serious about putting their faith into action. By fostering a widespread acceptance of the servant life-style among the laity, LAOS seeks to make a significant contribution to the renewal of church and society.
  Current projects and activities:
    Action and reflection workshops on issues of global hunger and urban poverty.
  Number of permanent staff: 7   Annual budget: $50,000
  Publications: Conversation, Concerns and Challenges, a newsletter

WHAT CAN I DO?
  Volunteer descriptions:
    Children's work (recreation, tutoring, houseparenting); community organizing; construction; work with mentally, emotionally handicapped people.

CAN I GET IN?
  Academic requirements: No specific ones   Age: 18
  Length of commitment to volunteer service: Varies
  Number of 1978 volunteers: 102
  Number planned for the future: About the same

HOW DO I GET IN?
  Applying: Send LAOS two applications, two photos, two resumes, and $10 to help cover the cost of letters and phone calls required to find placement for you. Medical, dental personnel are asked to provide photostatic copies of diplomas and licenses.
  Research and Placement: LAOS writes your references, researches possible openings for you, and presents options to you when it hears from agency contacts. When you and the agency agree that the match is a good one, LAOS provides a simple contract for both parties to sign. You send LAOS a letter from your family or other designated person indicating a willingness to assume financial responsibility in the event of an emergency. (This letter is for the protection of the agency with which you are placed.)
  Preparation: You begin study on the area in which you will be working (LAOS will provide many of the reading materials and suggest a bibliography.) You begin language study if needed. LAOS sends you the name and address of the director of the agency accepting you, so that you may be in direct contact. LAOS sends you a travel check list regarding requirements of overseas travel.

WHERE CAN I GET MORE INFORMATION?
  Write: Thomas H. Boone, LAOS, Inc., 4920 Piney Branch Road, N.W., Washington, DC 20011
  Phone: (202) 723-8273
  Read: Newsletter sent upon request

LUTHERAN WORLD MINISTRIES

New York, New York

WHAT'S IT DO?
  Purpose and goals:
    World Brotherhood Exchange is a ministry of the Lutheran churches through the Lutheran World Federation (USA). Its responsibility is to serve overseas Lutheran churches and agencies, some domestic service projects, and to inform Lutherans of opportunities for service. Invitations come through WBE to each volunteer from the overseas church or agency. The responsibility of approving each individual placement rests with the source of the invitation. WBE works in placement with several non-Lutheran agencies and is open to all who wish to join this Christian service.
  Current projects and activities:
    Most are overseas, but some volunteer opportunities are available in social service, community work, health, communications in the United States.

WHAT CAN I DO?
  Volunteer opportunities in the United States include:
    Community worker. To assist in social ministry in Kentucky; room and board; two-year term preferred.
    Communications and office assistant. With Council of the Southern Mountains in Virginia; photography, editing and writing skills; can use single applicant or couple; one year or more.
    Medical people. At rural clinic housed in new facilities in Lowndes County, Alabama; timing negotiable.
    Clerical specialist. For general office work plus some administration at veterans counseling center in Oregon; some Spanish helpful but can be learned; partial room and board, if necessary; three months plus.

CAN I GET IN?
  Academic requirements: None special; the more skilled the volunteer, the more chances for placement.
  Length of commitment to internship: Varies from a few months to two years

DO I GET PAID, EXPENSES, OR CREDIT?
  Expenses: Sometimes the local agency provides board and room
  College credit: Can be arranged on some assignments

HOW DO I GET IN?
  You can expect the placement process to take one month or more and to follow roughly this outline: 1) dossier completed - questionnaire, resume, recommendations, other; 2) specific job possibility brought to your attention, you react, WBE contacts the source of the request for their opinion, then possible negotiation and/or definite invitation; 3) with no specific job possibility firmly in mind, WBE makes general contact with those who may be interested in knowing of your availability; 4) having received a definite invitation for you and your definite affirmative response, the travel arrangements begin.

A word about a resume: 1) All volunteers serve at the express invitations of the church, agency or institution with which they will be working. WBE and USA staff contribute to the process, but it is usually someone else, representing the placement location, who makes the final decision and offers the final invitation to a specific volunteer. 2) That means that WBE must be able to translate you personally to sheets of paper. Therefore, you should provide the most complete picture possible of you and your skills-- information relevant and useful to someone trying to decide whether or not you should spend your money to come and work with them. 3) There are four basic elements to this "picture": the questionnaire, the resume, the recommendations, anything else useful and relevant. 4) In your covering letter to the questionnaire and resume, put in whatever did not seem to fit either of them and what you think WBE may--even on a long shot--like to know.

WHERE CAN I GET MORE INFORMATION?
  Write: Harold T. Hanson, World Brotherhood Exchange Volunteer Service,
    Lutheran World Ministries/LWF, 360 Park Avenue South, New York, NY 10010
  Phone: (212) 532-6350

MENNONITE VOLUNTARY SERVICE

Elkhart, Indiana

WHAT'S IT DO?
  Purpose and goals:
    Mennonite Voluntary Service is an attempt to relate human resources to human needs in the spirit of Jesus. Born out of the quest for a constructive alternative to the military draft, MVS continues beyond the draft to enlist volunteers for a variety of service ministries. Mennonite Voluntary Service seeks to live out the affirmation of the Anabaptist heritage expressed by Hans Leopold in 1528: "If they know of anyone who is in need, whether or not he [or she] is a member of their church, they believe it their duty, out of love to God, to render help and aid."
  Current MVS Community Action Projects:
    Arvada, Colorado. In this suburban Denver community Jeffco Action Center provides emergency assistance such as food and clothing, advocacy for low-income housing and the rights of welfare recipients.
    Denver, Colorado. The West Side is a Chicano neighborhood rich in culture but with real human needs. Volunteers work with housing rehabilitation.
    Hutchinson, Kansas. MVS personnel work as chaplain's staff with prisoners at Kansas State Industrial Reformatory.
    Kansas City, Kansas. Persons work with inter-church and neighborhood organizations serving needs of poor people in a tri-racial community located within a few miles of one of the most affluent suburbs in America.
    Lame Deer, Montana. Volunteers will work on Northern Cheyenne Indian Reservation with Cheyenne Mennonite churches and community organizations in this southeastern Montana region.
    Western Oklahoma. Cheyenne and Arapaho Indian communities need assistance in community building in isolated towns in southwestern Oklahoma. Volunteers work in conjunction with Mennonite Indian congregations and tribal leaders in four rural communities.

Wichita, Kansas. Volunteers are developing a Neighborhood Health Program and assisting in housing repair for low income families throughout the city.

Other projects presently under development include such locations as Tulsa and Oklahoma City, Oklahoma; Lakeview/Chicago and Markham, Illinois; St. Louis, Missouri; Cincinnati, Ohio; and Portland, Oregon.

Number of permanent staff: 64
Annual budget: $113,000 in the Commission on Home Ministries: $579,918
Publications: Many booklets and pamphlets including Voluntary Service Handbook

WHAT CAN I DO?
Voluntary service jobs:
Service. MVS reaches out to people in need in North America as one of the service arms of the Mennonite churches. Rooted in the spirit of Jesus, MVS invites persons from varied religious, racial, and ethnic backgrounds to join together in different kinds of caring ministries.
Personal and unit life. Mennonite Voluntary Service is concerned that individuals grow through their service experience. Volunteers are encouraged to explore new kinds of personal disciplines and group relationships in the modest lifestyle of MVS. Volunteers usually live in units--groups of 3 to 12 people. Within a unit, team members join together in emergency welfare projects, interpersonal sharing, congregational activities, and group recreation. Sometimes volunteers remain in the community to work, live, and worship after the MVS assignment is completed. Some units have matured into vital centers for creative life and action. MVS is committed to work toward more open and modest life-styles and to find ways for this search to be brought into the churches. MVS believes that meaningful group experience, personal confrontation, decision making, and commitment to action are important and vital parts of a serious worshiping community. MVS volunteers are encouraged to be a part of the local congregation's search for new life and ministry.

CAN I GET IN?
Academic requirements: None   Age: 19
Special: A commitment to the Mennonite life style, although 40% of the volunteers have no Mennonite background.
Length of commitment to voluntary service: Two years is recommended but one year is acceptable in some programs.
Number of 1978 volunteers: 173   Number planned for the future: 185

DO I GET PAID, EXPENSES, OR CREDIT?
Pay: $35 a month   Expenses: Board and room
College credit: Can be arranged

HOW DO I GET IN?
The screening process basically takes the following steps. First an applicant completes and returns the Personnel Information Form. MVS then requests references, and after receiving them attempts to arrange an interview with the applicant. If the applicant is at that point acceptable to MVS, assignment explorations begin. After an assignment is confirmed, the applicant is asked to come to MVS headquarters for a 10 day orientation

before proceeding to the service site.
When will I know about application: About 6 to 8 weeks

WHERE CAN I GET MORE INFORMATION?
  Write or phone Mennonite Voluntary Service:
    Velma Loewen, Mennonite Board of Missions, Box 370, Elkhart, IN 46515
      Phone: (312) 294-7523
    MVS Office, 722 Main Street, Box 347, Newton, KS 67114
      Phone: (316) 283-5100
    MVS Office West, 5927 Miller Avenue, Arvada, CO 80004
      Phone: (303) 424-6261
    MVS Office East, 3248 West 163rd Street, Markham, IL 60426
      Phone: (312) 596-6963
  Read: Voluntary Service Handbook

NEIGHBORHOOD ECUMENICAL WITNESS AND SERVICE

Kansas City, Missouri

WHAT'S IT DO?
  Purpose and goals:
    NEWS is a small, inner-city organization with church support which serves a neighborhood of low income white, black, and a sprinkling of ethnic groups. It has a small, flexible staff and its needs and programs change with the needs and concerns of the neighborhood. NEWS is a resource to individual families and to the immediate neighborhood enabling them to cope with the problems of inner city living. Programs are developed to meet expressed needs of the neighborhood.
  Current projects and activities:
    Emergency assistance, tutoring, Neighborhood Newsheet, food co-op, block club development, leadership development; youth activities include art classes, minimally competitive sports and youth clubs.
  Number of permanent staff: 2½   Annual budget: $22,000
  Publications: Neighborhood Newsheet, bi-monthly

WHAT CAN I DO?
  Internship descriptions:
    NEWS would be happy to negotiate with any potential volunteers about a job description matching their skills and interests with its needs. Volunteers would work on the current projects.

CAN I GET IN?
  Academic requirements: No special requirements
  Length of commitment to internship: Semester or year
  Number of 1978 interns: None
  Number planned for the future: Open

DO I GET PAID, EXPENSES, OR CREDIT?
  Expenses: Housing provided for full-time volunteers
  College credit: Can be arranged

HOW DO I GET IN?
  Closing date for application: On-going
  Interview required: No
  When will I know about application: No formal plan

WHERE CAN I GET MORE INFORMATION?
  Write: Ronald T. Roberts, N.E.W.S., 811 Benton Boulevard, Kansas City,
    MO 64124
  Phone: (816) 231-5745

UNITED CHURCH OF CHRIST

ONE YEAR VOLUNTARY SERVICE

New York, New York

WHAT'S IT DO?
  Purpose and goals:
    To recruit, place and support volunteers in programs of social need and
    action, most of which have a Christian basis.
  Current projects and activities:
    More than 50 projects across the USA including the following categories:
    institutions (homes for emotionally disturbed children, homes for aging,
    homes for mentally retarded, and hospitals); community service (including
    inner city activities such as social service centers, neighborhood houses,
    community centers, and inner city churches); community action organizing;
    and special team projects.
  Number of permanent staff: 1   Annual budget: $1,000

WHAT CAN I DO?
  Volunteer descriptions:
    Volunteers work with the staff and other volunteers, both one-year and
    long-term, in the projects listed above.

CAN I GET IN?
  Academic requirements: High school graduate   Age: 17
  Special: Commitment to the project and to Christian principles
  Length of commitment to internship: One year
  Number of 1978 volunteers: 20   Number planned for the future: 30

DO I GET PAID, EXPENSES, OR CREDIT?
  Expenses: Board, room, necessary expenses, and travel home are provided.
  College credit: Can be arranged

HOW DO I GET IN?
  Closing date for application: No formal plan for admission--send a letter
    and resume at any time.

WHERE CAN I GET MORE INFORMATION?
  Write: Carol A. Bade, Training for Mission, United Church Board for Homeland
    Ministries, Room 81, Park Avenue South, New York, NY 10010

UNITED PRESBYTERIAN CHURCH USA VOLUNTARY SERVICE

New York, New York

WHAT'S IT DO?
  Purpose and goals:
    Volunteers in Mission (VIM)--the young adult program provides opportunities in mission-related service for young adults between the ages of 17 and 25. It is designed to meet service needs for persons without specific professional skills but with interest and enthusiasm for the church and a desire to be involved in its work--for young people who want to take a year off between high school and college, who want to find out if the church is for them--in an open-ended style.
  Current projects and activities: The projects reflect the variety of ministries in which the church is engaged, both through congregations and church agencies and through community programs.
  Publications: Voluntary Service Bulletin, annual

WHAT CAN I DO?
  Examples of a few of the VIM Young Adult program descriptions are:
  Nome, Alaska. Aywaan Bering Sea Larger Parish needs youth workers. Music (guitar/piano) helpful as well as love for church as a viable institution. Work with white and Eskimo (Yupik and Inupiat) youth. Program is joint Methodist and Presbyterian. Communal living style with church.
  Las Vegas, New Mexico. First Presbyterian Church needs extended ministry staff person with secretarial skills to help organize church program for persons 3 to 85 years old. Also to work with diverse community including alcoholics, youth, and institutional programs.
  Albuquerque, New Mexico. Menaul School, UPC-related boarding high school, needs year-round assistant librarian, campus hostess to also work with student work program, plumber/electricians/repairers, teachers, houseparents.
  Corvallis, Oregon. United Campus Ministry at Oregon State University needs student assistant working in areas of interpreting campus ministry to students, program planning and cooking for Sunday evening program, public relations to community and campus while living in campus ministry community.
  Mt. Pleasant, Utah. Wasatch Academy, a UPC secondary school, needs two tutors, two dormitory assistants and recreation person in six-week summer session, including trips to nearby national parks. Year-round needs for tutor, houseparent, general maintenance, recreation.

CAN I GET IN?
  Academic requirements: High school graduate   Age: 17 to 25
  Special: Church membership not required but volunteer must accept the disciplines of a Christian community and to share in this aspect of the life and mission of the church.
  Length of commitment of volunteer service: One year

DO I GET PAID, EXPENSES, OR CREDIT?
  Expenses: Board, room, travel, and necessary expenses are provided
  College credit: Can be arranged

HOW DO I GET IN?
  Closing date for application: Apply early
  When will I know about application: Varies with the project; as soon as possible

WHERE CAN I GET MORE INFORMATION?
  Write: J. Wilbur Patterson, Associate for Volunteers in Mission, UPUSA,
    475 Riverside Drive, Room 1126, New York, NY 10027
  Phone: (202) 870-2801
  Read: Voluntary Service Bulletin, available upon request from above address

VOLUNTEER CORPS - THE EPISCOPAL CHURCH

New York, New York

WHAT'S IT DO?
  Purpose and goals:
    The Volunteer Corps matches volunteers with parishes, church-related
    agencies, and some secular programs. It is the only national program for
    voluntary service placement now operating in the Episcopal Church.
  Current projects:
    In 1970 the first volunteer went to Alaska. Since then, the Volunteer
    Corps has placed volunteers around the country. Volunteers include a lab
    technician for a ghetto clinic, a houseparent for a home for abandoned
    children. Plumbers, teachers, counselors have all found ways, for a
    summer, a year, or more, to explore their calling to a life of Christian
    service.
  Number of permanent staff: 1   Annual budget: $10,000
  Publications: Volunteer Corps, a pamphlet

WHAT CAN I DO?
  Volunteers are now counseling youth in an inner-city parish; developing
  community organizations in rural Appalachia; teaching arts and crafts to
  senior citizens; supervising recreation in a parish summer program; working
  with migrant children in a day care center; leading adult Bible study groups;
  serving as a lab technician in an inner-city clinic; caring for neglected
  children in a group home; beginning a Christian coffee house ministry.

CAN I GET IN?
  Academic requirements: None   Age: 18
  Length of commitment to internship: Varies up to two years
  Number of 1978 volunteers: 9   Number planned for the future: Open

DO I GET PAID, EXPENSES, OR CREDIT?
  Expenses: Room and board and necessary expenses are paid.

HOW DO I GET IN?
  Closing date for application: On-going
  Interview required: Preferred
  When will I know about application: No formal plan

WHERE CAN I GET MORE INFORMATION?
  Write: Mary Teresa Rogers, Volunteer Corps, Episcopal Church Center,
    815 Second Avenue, New York, NY 10017
  Phone: (212) 687-1365
  Read: Volunteer Corps, from the above address

THE WOMEN AND MINORITIES CLUSTER

Aswalos House YWCA
Black Women's Community Development Foundation
Joint Center for Political Studies
Kentucky Neighborly Organization of Women
Lutheran Church and Indian People of South Dakota
National Organization for Women
National Women's Education Fund
National Women's Political Caucus
National Youth Alternatives Project
Women's History Research Center
Women's International League for Peace and Freedom

ASWALOS HOUSE YWCA
Dorchester, Massachusetts

WHAT'S IT DO?
  Purpose and goals:
    The aim of Aswalos House is to serve constructively, first, the Roxbury, North Dorchester and Mattapan community in general and second, and more specifically, the women of that community. This community holds within its boundaries, a growing diversity of cultural and ethnic elements, many of whom have their historic ancestral roots in Africa. The Aswalos House program is directed primarily toward the needs and interests of these women. It believes that women can function more effectively when they have a strong positive understanding of themselves, their families, and their communities. Aswalos House holds absolute responsibility to develop a program that endeavors to address itself to the various age, social, cultural, occupational and educational groups within the community. Moreover, because of the destructive effects that European imperialism, capitalism and racism have brought upon all these diverse ethnic and cultural life styles and life functions of the peoples of African and Spanich descent, it is imperative that Aswalos House work to create a program which will offer constructive alternatives to the present consequences to such destruction. In addition, it draws together into responsible membership women and girls of diverse experiences and faiths, that their lives may be open to new understanding and deeper relationships and that together they may join in the struggle for peace and justice, freedom and dignity for all people.

                       Nguzo Saba
        Umoja . . . . Unity
        Kujichagulia . . . . . Self Determination
        Ujima . . . . Collective Work and
                                    Responsibility
        Ujamaa . . . . Cooperative Economics
        Nia . . . . Purpose
        Kuumba . . . . Creativity
        Jmani . . . . Faith

  Current projects and activities:
    Adult program, teen program, children's program, independent living program, tutorial, teen summer project, after-school summer project, drop-in child care, and motivational and career counseling program.
  Annual budget: Varies with the number of special grants we receive

WHAT CAN I DO?
  Internship descriptions:
    1) Three program assistants for the adult evening activities
    2) Three program assistants for after-school tutorial and cultural programs
    3) Three job placement assistants
    4) One environmental education specialist for summer program with teens

CAN I GET IN?
  Academic requirements: Varies with position
  Length of commitment to internship: Semester or year
  Number of 1978 interns: 3   Number planned for future: 5

DO I GET PAID, EXPENSES, OR CREDIT?
  Expenses: Sometimes funded   College credit: Can be arranged

HOW DO I GET IN?
  Closing date for application: On-going   Interview required: Yes
  When will I know about application: After references have been checked

WHERE CAN I GET MORE INFORMATION?
  Write: Patricia Bonner Lyons, Director, Aswalos House, 246 Seaver Street, North Dorchester, MA 02121
  Phone: (617) 442-9645
  Read: Aswalos House, a booklet

BLACK WOMEN'S COMMUNITY DEVELOPMENT FOUNDATION

Washington, D.C.

WHAT'S IT DO?
  Purpose and goals:
    The Black Women's Community Development Foundation (BWCDF) is a non-profit, tax-exempt corporation designed to strengthen the role of black women in the improvement of conditions which have been barriers to the full participation of black people in American life. Since 1968, BWCDF has initiated, participated in, and supported in varying degrees many activities which have had a significant impact on social change.
  Current projects and activities:
    Support organizations that have the potential for contributing significantly to black economic or social advancement. The underwriting of publications which contribute to the understanding of the black heritage. The sponsorship of educational projects which will: 1) promote self-understanding; 2) increase awareness of and knowledge about important national and international issues; 3) help young blacks make wiser vocational choices; 4) provide experiences which will make formal education more relevant and meaningful. The identification of emerging opportunities for the black community; this task involves taking an idea and testing it out, and has been particularly effective with respect to new Federal program areas. BWCDF has periodically held large symposiums and smaller "miniconsultations" in different geographical regions of the country. BWCDF also takes on the planning and initiation of projects of its own. An example of this is the Juvenile Justice Project; located in northeast Washington, the JJP was a community based program whose aim was to de-emphasize the institutionalization of children by creating a small residential facility for female juveniles.
  Number of permanent staff: 5 plus project staff
  Publications: "Together" Black Women, by Inez Smith Reid, (1972); Binding Ties, a monthly newsletter; Mental and Physical Health Problems of Black Women, 1978, available for $9.95 at the agency address.

WHAT CAN I DO?
  Interns assist the staff in all of the projects according to their particular needs and interests.

CAN I GET IN?
  Academic requirements: College student
  Length of commitment to internship: Semester or year
  Number of 1978 interns: 3   Number planned for the future: Open

DO I GET PAID, EXPENSES, OR CREDIT?
  College credit: Can be arranged

HOW DO I GET IN?
  Closing date for application: On-going
  Interview required: Preferred
  When will I know about application: Soon after interview

WHERE CAN I GET MORE INFORMATION?
  Write: Patricia F. Eaton, Executive Director, Black Women's Community
    Development Foundation, 1028 Connecticut Avenue, N.W., Suite 1020,
    Washington, DC 20036
  Phone: (202) 466-6220
  Read: Publications listed above

JOINT CENTER FOR POLITICAL STUDIES

Washington, D.C.

WHAT'S IT DO?
  Purpose and goals:
    The Joint Center is a non-profit, tax-exempt organization which provides,
    on a non-partisan basis, research, public policy analysis, training,
    technical assistance, and information programs for black and other mino-
    rity elected and appointed officials.
  Current projects and activities:
    1) Research on all aspects of black and other minority political partici-
    pation. 2) Technical assistance and consulting assistance for elected
    officials. 3) Clearinghouse of information about minorities in politics.
    4) Educational projects.
  Number of permanent staff: 25   Annual budget: $500,000
  Publications: Focus, a monthly newsletter; The National Roster of Black
    Elected Officials; The Making of a Black Mayor.

WHAT CAN I DO?
  Internship descriptions:
    Internships are in the fields of research, public affairs, and institu-
      tional development:
    Research internship. Interns participate in continuing research on public
      policy issues which affect minority and poor Americans. Current
      research projects deal with small town planning, urban development, drug
      abuse, housing needs of the black elderly, and various aspects of black
      political participation. Interns must be prepared to contribute sub-
      stantially to major research efforts and to participate in JCPS seminars
      and conferences. Students with the following majors are encouraged to
      apply: political science, black studies, urban affairs/planning,
      economics, public affairs/administration, sociology, geography, history,

statistics, education and law.

Public affairs internship. Work with staff specialists in print and broadcast journalism--duties include editing, media relations, public relations, and writing articles on public policy issues and minority political participation. Students with journalism, advertising, and public relations majors are encouraged to apply. Students in other disciplines may apply also, if their long-term interest is in journalistic careers.

Institutional development internship. Work with the director of development. Duties will include research of source data on the philanthropic world, identification of JCPS markets, and assisting in the formulation of development plans. Students with backgrounds in marketing, journalism, or business are preferred.

CAN I GET IN?
  Academic requirements: College students with backgrounds as cited under internship descriptions above.
  Length of commitment to internship: Semester or year
  Number of 1978 interns: 8
  Number planned for the future: Up to 10

DO I GET PAID, EXPENSES, OR CREDIT?
  College credit: Can be arranged, and many interns do receive credit.

HOW DO I GET IN?
  Closing date for application: On-going
  Interview required: Preferred
  When will I know about application: No formal plan

WHERE CAN I GET MORE INFORMATION?
  Write: Intern Coordinator, Louise E. Taylor, Deputy Director of Research, Joint Center for Political Studies, 1426 H Street, N.W., Suite 926, Washington, DC 20005
  Phone: (202) 638-4477
  Read: Focus, available at above address

KENTUCKY NEIGHBORLY ORGANIZATION OF WOMEN

Lexington, Kentucky

WHAT'S IT DO?
  Purpose and goals:
    This program is funded through the College of Agriculture Cooperative Extension Service to provide preschool opportunity for inner city children. Also to involve the parents of the children in the classroom to sustain the child's development.
  Current projects and activities:
    Preschool programs and Child Care Center - 7 a.m. to 6 p.m.
  Number of permanent staff: 1   Annual budget: $68,000

WHAT CAN I DO?
  Positions available are home visitor, teacher, teacher aide.

CAN I GET IN?
  Academic requirements: None, an interest in young children
  Length of commitment to internship: Semester or year
  Number of 1978 interns: 5
  Number planned for the future: About the same

DO I GET PAID, EXPENSES, OR CREDIT?
  College credit: Can be arranged; most have received credit.

HOW DO I GET IN?
  Closing date for application: On-going
  Interview required: No
  When will I know about application: No formal plan

WHERE CAN I GET MORE INFORMATION?
  Write: Jean Sabharwal, Program Coordinator, Carver Community Center, 522 Patterson Street, Lexington, KY 40508
  Phone: (606) 255-4112

LUTHERAN CHURCH AND INDIAN PEOPLE OF SOUTH DAKOTA

Sioux Falls, South Dakota

WHAT'S IT DO?
  Purpose and goals:
    In obedience to the Gospel of Jesus Christ it shall be the purpose of Lutheran Church and Indian People of South Dakota to maximize consistency between God's plan for His creation and the social behavior of Indian and non-Indian people in South Dakota.
    This purpose implies growing communication with Indian people and growing resolve to:
      1) Proclaim the Gospel with total integrity.
      2) Practice mutuality in ministry and sharing among Indian and non-Indian people.
      3) Provide necessary counsel and information to Lutheran Churches.
      4) Promote Lutheran awareness of Indian concerns and current status.
      5) Elicit individual and institutional Lutheran responses to Indian concerns.
      6) Multiply God-pleasing forms of Christian fellowship and community purpose.
    This purpose shall be pursued with respect for the policies and organizations of the Lutheran Church bodies involved and with relevance to the concerns of Indian people. The LUCHIP of SD (Lutheran Church and Indian people of South Dakota) has demonstrated in very practical ways that Lutheran churches nurture Christian people who care about their neighbors--and who witness to a love in Christ that embraces all peoples.
  Current projects and activities:
    Illustrative projects:
      Sioux Falls. In-service training for board and staff of American Indian Services of Sioux Falls. Developmental implementation of a legal assistance program for Indian inmates at the South Dakota Penitentiary. Aid in the securement of Indian population statistical data in Sioux Falls through the Office of the Sioux Falls Indian Education Specialist.
      Mitchell. Development support for an Indian Information and Referral Center.
      Bonesteel. Supplemental assistance to Milk's Camp Industries, a Rosebud Reservation business.
      Waubay. Indian community assistance for Enemy Swim Elderly Home, through purchase of a sewing machine. Facility procurement and usage for Waubay Area Human Relations Association.
      South Dakota. Theological dialogue plans involving Christian and Native American church interests.
      Eagle Butte. Indian Boy Scout troop maintenance and camping equipment.
      Lower Brule. Educational aid for Indian student at Lutheran college, preparing for the pastoral ministry.
      Sisseton. Development assistance for establishment of Sisseton Human Relations Commission.

Custer. Development support for production of a motion picture called "The Grass That Never Breaks" as an educational tool in cross-cultural growth of Indians and non-Indians.

Yankton. Food supply for the CONTACT Referral Center, for human resources emergency pantry project.

Mission. Emergency loan to the Rosebud Association of Indian Ranchers for the purchase of hay necessary for winter survival of a "Project Heifer" herd of cattle.

Number of permanent staff: 2
Annual budget: $40,000

WHAT CAN I DO?

Volunteer descriptions:

Volunteers will work with regular staff on current projects. In addition, the following new activities will be opportunities for the volunteer:

1) Provide an informational piece for congregational distribution encouraging more cross-cultural sharing in the Gospel and greater Christian response to issues of justice involving Indians and non-Indians today in South Dakota.

2) Provide for intercultural workshops in eastern and western South Dakota designed to focus on contemporary issues of justice involving Indians and non-Indians in South Dakota. These workshops shall acquaint participants with the recently published analysis, Justice for American Indians--A Christian Perspective on Federal Indian Policy. The ALC has prepared this publication in order to stimulate thinking, promote discussion, and motivate informed Christian response.

3) Satisfy more specialized staff requirements and other extra budgetary needs in connection with a Lutheran Training Workshop on Racism and Sexism, organized to equip participants for educational tasks in South Dakota Lutheran congregations and in communities through visiting teams. This constitutes another follow-up stage in the continuing education and mobilization of Lutherans for more effective intercultural ministry in local Lutheran congregations. It also enhances the prospect of more Lutheran parishioner efforts in achieving the Indian ministry and mission objectives of LUCHIP of SD.

4) Facilitate more South Dakota Indian participation in National Indian Lutheran Board/Lutheran Church and Indian People conferences. In a church which operates nationally, regionally, and locally, American Indian concerns and involvement require coordination and communication throughout all areas. Conferences help to improve this coordination and communication.

5) Subsidize a Lutheran para-professional or professional volunteer for Indian community service in cooperation with the World Brotherhood Exchange and the Rosebud Indian House of Friendship or other interested Indian community service organizations. Volunteer service arrangements, like this, provide Lutheran response to Indian service needs, on-the-job cross-cultural education and opportunity for the acceptable practice of Christian presence and witness.

CAN I GET IN?
  Academic requirements: College student
  Length of commitment to voluntary service: Varies

DO I GET PAID, EXPENSES, OR CREDIT?
  Expenses: Sometimes are available
  College credit: Can be arranged

HOW DO I GET IN?
  Closing date for application: On-going
  Interview required: Not always
  When will I know about application: No formal plan

WHERE CAN I GET MORE INFORMATION?
  Write: Walter W. Wever, Office of Indian Concerns Consultant, LUCHIP of SD, 600 West 12th Street, Sioux Falls, SD 57104
  Phone: (605) 336-3387
  Read: Selections of assorted information about American Indian people and Lutheran participation in American Indian ministry and mission ($3 and $2 packets upon request from the address above).

NATIONAL ORGANIZATION FOR WOMEN

Washington, D.C.

WHAT'S IT DO?
  Purpose and goals:
    To bring women into the mainstream of American society in full partnership with men.
  Current projects and activities:
    The first priority is the ratification of the Equal Rights Amendment (ERA). The national task forces also work toward additional priorities: reproductive rights (freedom to choose), lesbian civil rights, Title IX compliance, and employment discrimination. There are also continuing task forces on women and the arts, older women, credit, criminal justice, media, minority women, health, education, labor unions, child care, religion, and many more.
  Number of permanent staff: 15   Annual budget: $1,100,000
  Publications: National NOW Times, a monthly newsletter

WHAT CAN I DO?
  Internship description:
    Assist a national officer or national staff member with projects and activities as listed above.

CAN I GET IN?
  Academic requirements: College student
  Length of commitment to internship: Semester
  Special: Committed to working for equality for women
  Number of 1978 interns: 15
  Number planned for the future: About the same

DO I GET PAID, EXPENSES, OR CREDIT?
  College credit: Can be arranged

HOW DO I GET IN?
  Closing date for application: On-going   Interview required: Yes

WHERE CAN I GET MORE INFORMATION?
  Write: Martha Buck, Vice President, National NOW Action Center, 425 13th
    Street, N.W., Suite 1048, Washington, DC 20004
  Phone: (202) 347-2279
  Read: National NOW Times

NATIONAL WOMEN'S EDUCATION FUND

Washington, D.C.

WHAT'S IT DO?
  Purpose and goals:
    The NWEF goal is the political education of women. It seeks to aid women to gain full participation at leadership levels of public life. It works to:
      --Expand the number of women familiar with the political parties and processes.
      --Convey a working knowledge of governmental operations.
      --Teach political skills such as those needed in campaigning, lobbying, or organizing.
      --Research and analyze the problems women face in seeking leadership in government.
      --Increase public awareness of women's political participation.
      --Stimulate women's organizations to conduct political programs.
      --Develop educational tools and guides for use by individual women and by women's groups.
  Current projects and activities:
    Three-day regional campaign techniques institute, where more than 500 women from 19 states have acquired campaign skills. Institutes emphasize practical experience, local orientation, interchange among women from various states and backgrounds, and accessibility through financial aid and low tuition fees.
    Workshops in campaign techniques, political skills, and political motivation designed and conducted for state and national women's organizations.
    Programs which stimulate universities to offer courses in practical politics through continuing education or extension divisions. NWEF assistance includes advice to program coordinators on selection of materials, speakers, resource people, and course formats.
    Consultation to a developing national network of women's colleges which will provide public leadership education programs for both undergraduate and community women.
    Study of Congressional campaign finances comparing male and female candidates to identify funding trends and patterns which differ.
    Compiling statistics and biographical information on women candidates seeking state legislative, statewide, and Congressional office.
  Number of permanent staff: 3   Annual budget: $200,000

WHAT CAN I DO?
An intern's responsibilities are dependent on NWEF's activities at the time of availability, but in general, interns are involved in research, writing, and making conference arrangements.

CAN I GET IN?
Academic requirements: High school graduate   Age: 18
Length of commitment to internship: Semester or year
Number of 1978 interns: 3   Number planned for the future: Open

DO I GET PAID, EXPENSES, OR CREDIT?
College credit: Can be arranged

HOW DO I GET IN?
Closing date for application: On-going
Interview required: Preferred
When will I know about application: No formal plan

WHERE CAN I GET MORE INFORMATION?
Write: Betsy Wright, Director, National Women's Education Fund, 1532 16th Street, N.W., Washington, DC 20036
Phone: (202) 462-8606

NATIONAL WOMEN'S POLITICAL CAUCUS

Washington, D.C.

WHAT'S IT DO?
Purpose and goals:
The National Women's Political Caucus, a multi-partisan organization, was formed in July 1971, in Washington, D.C., to awaken, organize, and assert the vast political power represented by women--53% of the voting population. NWPC channels its efforts to educate and inform both women and men that equality of political participation means a richer quality of life for all Americans. The Caucus asserts the political power of women by increasing the number of women candidates, cabinet officers and party activists.
Current projects and activities:
Win With Women programs to provide the extra campaign expertise women candidates need. WWW helps Congressional candidates and women running for state legislatures in key states which have not yet ratified the Equal Rights Amendment. The program brings together outstanding women candidates and political consultants who can help them raise funds, organize their campaigns, recruit volunteers, survey public opinion and develop effective campaign materials. Throughout the campaign year, NWPC urges state and national parties, labor unions and other special interest groups to support and give financial contributions to women candidates. Monitors both parties' affirmative action efforts, works for inclusion of a "woman's plank" in party platforms, and helps women become delegates to Presidential conventions. Lobbies for pro-choice. State work on ratification push for the ERA.
Number of permanent staff: 3   Annual budget: $200,000
Publications: Newsletter, press releases and campaign pamphlets

WHAT CAN I DO?
  Internship descriptions:
    Interns are assigned to specific tasks or staff members depending on their interests, experience, and priorities. NWPC projects in which interns have been involved have included an intensive candidate research study, Democratic and Republican delegate selection, party reform, ERA, legislative issues, fundraising, and membership development. These areas offer interns an exposure to the fundamentals of political organizing, legislative research, lobbying and how national organizations function. In addition to substantive assignments, interns assist staff members in the on-going management of the office and perform clerical tasks.

CAN I GET IN?
  Academic requirements: Selected on the basis of interest, ability, past involvement and commitment to women in the political process.
  Special: Minimal typing skills are required
  Length of commitment to internship: Semester or year
  Number of 1978 interns: 8   Number planned for the future: Open

DO I GET PAID, EXPENSES, OR CREDIT?
  College credit: Can be arranged; many interns do receive college credit.

HOW DO I GET IN?
  Closing date for application: On-going
  Interview required: Preferred
  Other procedures: Letters of application should include a resume of relevant academic background or other experience and indicate areas of special interests.
  When will I know about application: Within a month after application is completed

WHERE CAN I GET MORE INFORMATION?
  Write: Sylvia M. Ware, Internship Coordinator, National Women's Political Caucus, 1411 K Street, N.W., Suite 1110, Washington, DC 20005
  Phone: (202) 347-4456
  Read: NWPC newsletter, available upon request

NATIONAL YOUTH ALTERNATIVES PROJECT
Washington, D.C.

WHAT'S IT DO?
  Purpose and goals:
    The National Youth Alternatives Project (NYAP) is an advocate for youth and youth service programs nationwide, serving as a national resource center and clearinghouse for youth workers. Helping meet the needs of local programs since 1973, NYAP was founded on the premise that all youth have the right to human service programs which are accessible and acceptable to them, and that youth have the right to participate in developing, operating, and evaluating such services.
  Current projects and activities:
    The provision of training and technical assistance to youth services staff; network and coalition building among youth programs; research on the problems of youth; development of innovative program models; teaching evaluation skills to existing programs; and publication and distribution of manuals, directories, and other specialized youth work information. In addition NYAP monitors and lobbys Congress and Federal agencies for youth alternatives.
  Number of permanent staff: 15   Annual budget: $500,000
  Publications: Youth Alternatives, a monthly newsletter; Stalking the Large Green Grant, Adolescent Life Stress as a Predictor of Alcohol Abuse and/or Runaway Behavior; The Grass Roots Fundraising Book; The National Directory of Runaway Programs.

WHAT CAN I DO?
  Internship descriptions:
    Interns help the staff with the projects described above according to their talent, experience and interest.

CAN I GET IN?
  Academic requirements: High school graduate   Age: 17
  Length of commitment to internship: Semester or year
  Number of 1978 interns: 4   Number planned for the future: 4

DO I GET PAID, EXPENSES, OR CREDIT?
  Expenses: If it relates to expenditures on the internship

HOW DO I GET IN?
  Closing date for application: On-going   Interview required: Yes
  When will I know about application: Soon after interview

WHERE CAN I GET MORE INFORMATION?
  Write: Tom McCarthy, Assistant Directory, National Youth Alternatives Project, 1346 Connecticut Avenue, N.E., Washington, DC 20036
  Phone: (202) 785-0764
  Read: The Children's Rights Movement, edited by Beatrice Gross, pages 375-576; also publications listed above and Youth Alternatives, the newsletter.

WOMEN'S HISTORY RESEARCH CENTER

Berkeley, California

WHAT'S IT DO?
  Purpose and goals:
    From 1968 to 1974 the Women's History Research Center, in Berkeley,
    California, collected and organized over a million documents relating to
    the role of women in our society. Its major collections--the largest and
    most comprehensive such compilations anywhere--are published on microfilm.
    Its purpose now is to encourage use of these microfilm collections.
  Current projects:
    Three major collections on microfilm:
      --Herstory contains complete issues of women's serials
      --Women & Health/Mental Health and Women & Law microfilms include
          articles gathered from women's publications, mass and alternative
          press, professional journals, and unpublished pamphlets and manu-
          scripts, from all over the world.
  Number of permanent staff: 4 or 5   Annual budget: $50,000
  Publications: Female Artists Past and Present; Films by and/or about Women,
    a directory; and the microfilms mentioned above.

WHAT CAN I DO?
  Internship descriptions:
    Interns would work on the production, publicizing, and distributing of its
    materials. There are several printed publications, mostly directory/
    bibliographies, for sale by mail order. Much of the work involves
    correspondence with individuals, libraries, teachers, academicians, the
    press, and various institutions internationally. Therefore assistance is
    needed with all the clerical work, of which there is a tremendous backlog.
    WHRC has very little working space--two small rooms in a church basement,
    and many of the staff work out of their homes. It is important, then,
    that you are able to work in relative isolation without other WHRC workers,
    rather than in a business atmosphere, and still be able to get your work
    done. WHRC staff are expected to do cooperative jobs, such as answering
    the phones, running errands (going to the post office, xeroxing, picking
    things up at the store, etc.), going to conferences to represent WHRC and
    distribute literature. All WHRC staff are equal, whether paid or volun-
    teer, and that means that your ideas and contributions to the organization
    are needed to help run it more efficiently. You can work full- or part-
    time; at least 10 hours a week is preferred because of the huge effort it
    takes to coordinate dozens of people and lug supplies all over town. If
    you have a typewriter, bring it along to use, and all kinds of supplies
    for yourself and others. Try to secure a place to stay before you come
    to Berkeley. Bring your friends, lovers, cats, dogs, or whatever for
    emotional support. This is very important to maintain your sanity because
    people's work time is almost all they have to give WHRC, and their other
    obligations to school, jobs, and family prevent frequent get-togethers of
    the staffers. Have some means of financial support, whether it be savings,
    a sabbatical, or a part-time job elsewhere. The cost of living in
    Berkeley is high. If you are a student, you can arrange with your academic
    advisor to receive credit for working here as part of a field studies or
    intern program.

CAN I GET IN?
  Academic requirements: No restrictions
  Experience: Some office experience preferred
  Length of commitment to internship: Semester or year
  Number of 1978 interns: 3 or 4
  Number planned for the future: Same

DO I GET PAID, EXPENSES, OR CREDIT?
  College credit: Can be arranged

HOW DO I GET IN?
  Closing date for application: On-going
  Interview required: No
  Other procedures: Write a letter stating your skills, interests, and time you are available.
  When will I know about application: One month after application is in

WHERE CAN I GET MORE INFORMATION?
  Write: Shelagh Nugent, Office Coordinator, Women's History Research Center, 2325 Oak Street, Berkeley, CA 94708
  Phone: (415) 548-1770
  Read: Female Artists Past and Present, and brochures from address above

WOMEN'S INTERNATIONAL LEAGUE FOR PEACE AND FREEDOM

Washington, D.C. and Philadelphia, Pennsylvania

WHAT'S IT DO?
  Purpose and goals:
    The League was founded in 1915 during World War I, with Jane Addams as its first president. Throughout its history its purpose has been to work for the achievement by peaceful means of those political, economic, social, and psychological conditions throughout the world which can assure peace, freedom, and justice for all. Peace is more than the absence of war or the maintenance of order through force. Peace requires the dedication to nonviolent means for the resolution of conflict and the building of institutions for world development and world community. WILPF believes that to achieve freedom and justice in our own country and peaceful relations with other countries we must build a non-exploitative society.
  Current projects and goals:
    WILPF works in their projects to change the economic and social causes of oppression through a nonviolent revolution in priorities that would end: the arms race, militarism, government repression, U.S. interference abroad, sexism, racism. It is working to specifically transfer funds of the Federal budget from military to human needs areas.
  Number of permanent staff: 3 in Washington, more in Philadelphia
  Publications: WILPF Legislative Bulletin, Action Alert, newsletters

WHAT CAN I DO?
  An intern would have primary responsibility for one issue area. Possible topics include: human rights (U.S. aid to dictators), arms sales and foreign aid, nuclear proliferation and disarmament, intelligence and civil

liberties, employment and other economics legislation, and other issues of particular interest to women. An intern's responsibility would involve all facets of whatever topic he or she chooses, i.e. research, attending meetings, keeping informed of latest developments, writing material for use in our office and for distribution to members, and sharing clerical work. WILPF helps the intern get started and then provides guidance and assistance as necessary. WILPF would expect an intern to feel comfortable visiting Congressional offices, and to have a political perspective complementary to that reflected in its literature.

CAN I GET IN?
  Academic requirements: College student
  Length of commitment to internship: Semester or year
  Number of 1978 interns: 2
  Number planned for the future: 2 or 3 in each office

DO I GET PAID, EXPENSES, OR CREDIT?
  College credit: Can be arranged

HOW DO I GET IN?
  Closing date for application: On-going
  Interview required: Yes
  Other procedures: For a year long internship, an applicant should submit a resume to the Washington office, along with a project proposal, outlining what topic(s) the intern would like to work on, what form the project would take, and why the intern is particularly interested in that topic. WILPF will review the applications and then contact the student; a personal interview in Washington would be necessary before an intern could be hired.
  When will I know about application: No formal plan

WHERE CAN I GET MORE INFORMATION?
  Write: Internship Program, WILPF Legislative Office, 120 Maryland Avenue, N.E., Washington, DC 20002. Phone: (202) 546-8644
  or Internship Program, WILPF, 1213 Race Street, Philadelphia, PA 19107 Phone: (215) 563-7110
  Read: <u>Legislative Bulletin</u>, available at the above addresses

STOPOUT FOR MONEY

<u>Stopout! Working Ways to Learn</u> is designed for students who want a work experience in place of a classroom experience. Some of you, however, will be stopping out of college to work not because you want to, but because you have to. You need the work because you need the money.

What your parents can do for you compared to what they had planned to do may have drastically changed because of inflation and the sky-rocketing costs of college. Your parents have been in good jobs, making good money and they always assumed that they could easily afford to send all of their kids to college. Their first child goes off to college and it's OK. It's the second and third that does them in, all in college at the same time, needing take-home cash to pay from $3,000 to $5,000 a year times three. The money just isn't there--regardless of how high the income sounds and what the home is worth. These are families in a high income bracket making from $25,000 to $50,000 a year! These are the families who live in $100,000 homes, drive two or three cars and work in high prestige, middle management or professional jobs.

It's really hard on you because you didn't see it coming. Your parents didn't either. You and your parents are getting less financial help for college than anyone else in the country becasue--on paper--your family looks good. Like they can afford to send you to college.

Besides all of that, you don't get any sympathy from your friends or your cousins who have a little less, because there are all kinds of financial plans and government guaranteed loans for families making under $25,000 a year.

What are your choices as you stopout of college to make money? All the other students leaving school for the same reasons have about the same skills as you do. In these times of high unemployment your options diminish.

One place to check is with the military (for many kinds of paid educational plans). Or check out spending a year in a transferable liberal arts program at your community college--at an average cost of $387 a year, compared to $2790 at a public college or $4568 at a private college.

Other students learn a skill so that they can earn their way through college as an X-ray technician, licensed practical nurse, emergency medical technologist (80 hours of training), elementary carpenter, or basic printer. These skills can often be learned at low cost through public education in an adult education program, or at your regional technical high school. Or look in the <u>Yellow Pages</u> for private short-term schools teaching saleable skills in bartending, cooking or hair cutting.

It's tough for a student to earn enough money to live on plus to save for the next year of college. You have to really plan your time and living expenses carefully so that your time at making money does count and you actually come up with money saved for school.

The particular job you find has to pay. The big question is, where can you find a job?

Most people find a job through their friends. Or from friends of their family. As you look into everything you can think of including newspaper ads, free state employment agencies, your college employment counselor, and the Civil Service Office (listed under "Government" in the <u>Yellow Pages</u>), check your relatives and your parents' friends too. For more specifics on finding a job and getting skilled, read "How Can I Find a Job?" in <u>The Work Book</u> by J. S. Mitchell, Bantam, 1978. This book describes skilled jobs and in addition gives you the necessary steps to find a job.

It usually helps to know that you aren't alone. Thousands of college students from similar families as yours are having the same financial problems. The colleges will increasingly have to think of more financial programs to help you to stay in college.

Before you actually leave school to work for money, contact your financial officer who is almost as interested as you are in keeping you in school. She or he will have the latest information on student financial aid, jobs, loans and suggestions for you to make money.

If you do stopout to work for money, try to remember that everything you do counts toward what you eventually become. There isn't any job that will be a waste of time. Use that time to learn about the world of work and things you like and things you don't like. Turn the experience around so that when you stopin again for your degree, like most stopouts, you will have gained a better idea of where you want to be.

ALPHABETICAL INDEX (Page numbers cited)

ACTION: Volunteers in Service to America   88
Alaska Bureau of Land Management   90
Alternatives Unlimited   38
American Cancer Society, Massachusetts Division   134
American Enterprise Institute for Public Policy Research   39
Andrew W. Johnson Alcohol Detoxification Center   135
Appalachian Regional Hospitals   136
Appalshop   18
Association for World Education   40
Association of Community Organizations for Reform NOW   148
Aswalos House YWCA   192
Atlanta Urban Corps   91

Black Women's Community Development Foundation   193
Blue Grass Association for Mental Retardation   41
Boston City Council   93
Boston Community Schools Program   42
Boston Coordinating Council on Drug Abuse   137
Boston Film/Video Foundation   19
Boston Museum of Science   20
Boston Visual Artists Union   21
Bureau of Rehabilitation   149

California Coastal Commission   94
California Department of Alcoholic Beverage Control   95
California Department of Corrections   96
California Department of Education   97
California Department of Finance   98
California Department of Fish and Game   99
California Department of Food and Agriculture   101
California Department of Forestry   102
California Department of Health   103
California Department of Housing and Community Development   104
California Department of Motor Vehicles   105
California Department of Parks and Recreation   106
California Department of the Youth Authority   107
California Employment Development Department   109
California Highway Patrol   110
California Postsecondary Education Commission   111
California Public Utilities Commission   112
California State Library   113
California State Office of Substance Abuse   114
California State Water Resources Control Board   115
Cambridge YWCA   44
Center for Defense Information   151
Center for National Security Studies   152
Central Kentucky Community Action Council   140
Cheff Center for the Handicapped   45
Chesapeake Bay Center for Environmental Studies   70
Christian Service Corps   178

Church of the Brethren   179
Citizens for Participation in Political Action   154
Citizens Organization for a Sane World   155
Coalition of Concerned Medical Professionals   141
Coalition of Independent College and University Students   46
College Republican National Committee   47
Colonial Cablevision   31
Common Cause   156
Community for Creative Nonviolence   159
Community Services Program   48
Connecticut General Assembly Legislative Intern Program   116
Connecticut Public Television   32
Consumer Federation of America   160
Council for Retarded Citizens   49

Dayton Board of Education   50
Decordova Museum   23
Defenders of Wildlife   72
Direct Relief Foundation   142

Environmental Action Foundation   73
Environmental Learning Center   76

French Library   51
Friends Committee on National Legislation   181
Friends of the Earth   77

Girls Club of Lynn   52

Health/PAC   144

Institute for Local Self-Reliance   161
Institute for Responsive Education   53
International Program for Human Resource Development   24

Joint Center for Political Studies   194
J. U. Kevil Mental Retardation-Mental Health Center   54

Kentucky Bureau of Corrections   117
Kentucky Community Educating Office   56
Kentucky Neighborly Organization of Women   196
Kentucky Office of Public Defender   118
Kentucky School for the Deaf   57

LAOS, Inc.   182
Los Angeles City Volunteer Corps   120
Louisville YWCA   58
Lutheran Church and Indian People of South Dakota   197
Lutheran World Ministries   184

Massachusetts Department of Corrections   121
Massachusetts Department of Food and Agriculture   123
Massachusetts Department of Mental Health Neighborhood Day School   124
Massachusetts House of Representatives - Representative James E. Smith   125

Mennonite Voluntary Service   185
Metropolitan Washington Council of Governments   126
Minneapolis Institute of Arts   25
Muhlenberg County Opportunity Center   59
Museum of African Art   26

National Abortion Rights Action League   163
National Committee Against Repressive Legislation   164
National Labor Federation   165
National Organization for the Reform of Marijuana Laws   167
National Organization for Women   199
National Parks and Conservation Association   78
National Self-Help Resource Center   169
National Student Lobby   60
National Taxpayers Union   170
National Wildlife Federation   79
National Wildlife Federation Raptor Information Center   82
National Women's Education Fund   200
National Women's Political Caucus   201
National Youth Alternatives Project   203
Nature Conservancy   83
Neighborhood Ecumenical Witness and Service   187
New Jersey Shakespeare Festival   29
New York City Urban Corps   128
North American Student Cooperative Organization   62
Northwest College and University Association for Science   63

Occupational Health Project   145
Oxfam-America   171

Political Discovery   66
Port Jefferson Record Newspapers   33
Public Citizen   172

Rachel Carson Trust for the Living Environment   84
Radio Station WKCM   34
Rhode Island Intern Consortium   130

St. Paul's School   64
Student Conservation Program   85

United Church of Christ   188
United Presbyterian Church USA Voluntary Service   189
United States National Student Association   67

Volunteer Corps - The Episcopal Church   190

Washington Monthly   35
WFRV-TV News Intern   36
White House Fellowships   131
Women's History Research Center   204
Women's International League for Peace and Freedom   205

Zero Population Growth   175

GEOGRAPHICAL INDEX (Page numbers cited)

ALASKA
    Alaska Bureau of Land Management   90

ARKANSAS
    Association of Community Organizations for Reform NOW   148

CALIFORNIA
    California Coastal Commission   94
    California Department of Alcoholic Beverage Control   95
    California Department of Corrections   96
    California Department of Education   97
    California Department of Finance   98
    California Department of Fish and Game   99
    California Department of Food and Agriculture   101
    California Department of Forestry   102
    California Department of Health   103
    California Department of Housing and Community Development   104
    California Department of Motor Vehicles   105
    California Department of Parks and Recreation   106
    California Department of the Youth Authority   107
    California Employment Development Department   109
    California Highway Patrol   110
    California Postsecondary Education Commission   111
    California Public Utilities Commission   112
    California State Library   113
    California State Office of Substance Abuse   114
    California State Water Resources Control Board   115
    Direct Relief Foundation   142
    Los Angeles City Volunteer Corps   120
    Women's History Research Center   204

CONNECTICUT
    Association for World Education   40
    Connecticut General Assembly Legislative Intern Program   116
    Connecticut Public Television   32

DISTRICT OF COLUMBIA
    ACTION: Volunteers in Service to America   88
    American Enterprise Institute for Public Policy Research   39
    Black Women's Community Development Foundation   193
    Bureau of Rehabilitation   149
    Center for Defense Information   151
    Center for National Security Studies   152
    Christian Service Corps   178
    Citizens Organization for a Sane World   155
    Coalition of Independent College and University Students   46
    College Republican National Committee   47
    Common Cause   156
    Community for Creative Nonviolence   159
    Consumer Federation of America   160
    Defenders of Wildlife   72
    Environmental Action Foundation   73
    Friends Committee on National Legislation   181
    Friends of the Earth   77
    Institute for Local Self-Reliance   161
    Joint Center for Political Studies   194
    LAOS, Inc.   182

    Metropolitan Washington Council of Governments   126
    Museum of African Art   26
    National Abortion Rights Action League   163
    National Committee Against Repressive Legislation   164
    National Organization for the Reform of Marijuana Laws   167
    National Organization for Women   199
    National Parks and Conservation Association   78
    National Self-Help Resource Center   169
    National Student Lobby   60
    National Taxpayers Union   170
    National Wildlife Federation   79
    National Wildlife Federation Raptor Information Center   82
    National Women's Education Fund   200
    National Women's Political Caucus   201
    National Youth Alternatives Project   201
    Public Citizen   172
    Rachel Carson Trust for the Living Environment   84
    United States National Student Association   67
    Washington Monthly   35
    White House Fellowships   131
    Zero Population Growth   175
GEORGIA
    Atlanta Urban Corps   91
ILLINOIS
    Church of the Brethren   179
INDIANA
    Mennonite Voluntary Service   185
KENTUCKY
    Appalachian Regional Hospitals   136
    Appalshop   18
    Blue Grass Association for Mental Retardation   41
    Central Kentucky Community Action Council   140
    Community Services Program   48
    Council for Retarded Citizens   49
    J. U. Kevil Mental Retardation-Mental Health Center   54
    Kentucky Bureau of Corrections   117
    Kentucky Community Educating Office   56
    Kentucky Neighborly Organization of Women   196
    Kentucky Office of Public Defender   118
    Kentucky School for the Deaf   57
    Louisville YWCA   58
    Muhlenberg County Opportunity Center   59
    Radio Station WKCM   34
MARYLAND
    Chesapeake Bay Center for Environmental Studies   70
    International Program for Human Resource Development   24
MASSACHUSETTS
    Alternatives Unlimited   38
    American Cancer Society, Massachusetts Division   134
    Andrew W. Johnson Alcohol Detoxification Center   135
    Aswalos House YWCA   192
    Boston City Council   93
    Boston Community Schools Program   42
    Boston Coordinating Council on Drug Abuse   137
    Boston Film/Video Foundation   19
    Boston Museum of Science   20

Boston Visual Artists Union   21
Cambridge YWCA   44
Citizens for Participation in Political Action   154
Colonial Cablevision   31
Decordova Museum   23
French Library   51
Girls Club of Lynn   52
Institute for Responsive Education   53
Massachusetts Department of Corrections   121
Massachusetts Department of Food and Agriculture   123
Massachusetts Department of Mental Health Neighborhood Day School   124
Massachusetts House of Representatives - Representative James E. Smith   125
Oxfam-America   171
Political Discovery   66

MICHIGAN
Cheff Center for the Handicapped   45
North American Student Cooperative Organization   62

MINNESOTA
Environmental Learning Center   76
Minneapolis Institute of Arts   25

MISSOURI
Neighborhood Ecumenical Witness and Service   187

NEW HAMPSHIRE
St. Paul's School   64
Student Conservation Program   85

NEW JERSEY
New Jersey Shakespeare Festival   29

NEW YORK
Association for World Education   40
Coalition of Concerned Medical Professionals   141
Health/PAC   144
Lutheran World Ministries   184
National Labor Federation   165
New York City Urban Corps   128
Occupational Health Project   145
Port Jefferson Record Newspapers   33
United Church of Christ   188
United Presbyterian Church USA Voluntary Service   189
Volunteer Corps - The Episcopal Church   190

OHIO
Dayton Board of Education   50

PENNSYLVANIA
Women's International League for Peace and Freedom   205

RHODE ISLAND
Rhode Island Intern Consortium   130

SOUTH DAKOTA
Lutheran Church and Indian People of South Dakota   197

VIRGINIA
Nature Conservancy   83

WISCONSIN
WFRV-TV News Intern   36

WASHINGTON
Northwest College and University Association for Science   63